Space Power Integration
Perspectives from Space Weapons Officers

Edited by

KENDALL K. BROWN
Lieutenant Colonel, USAFR, PhD

Air University Press
Maxwell Air Force Base, Alabama

December 2006

Disclaimer

Opinions, conclusions, and recommendations expressed or implied within are solely those of the authors and do not necessarily represent the views of Air University, the United States Air Force, the Department of Defense, or any other US government agency. Cleared for public release: distribution unlimited.

Air University Press
131 West Shumacher Avenue
Maxwell AFB AL 36112-6615

Published by Books Express Publishing
Copyright © Books Express, 2011
ISBN 978-1-78039-973-7

Books Express publications are available from all good retail and online booksellers. For publishing proposals and direct ordering please contact us at: info@books-express.com

Contents

CONTENTS

Illustrations

Tables

About
the Editor

Lt Col Kendall K. Brown, USAFR, PhD, is a technical analyst at the Airpower Research Institute, College of Aerospace Doctrine, Research and Education (CADRE), Air University (AU), Maxwell Air Force Base, Alabama. He is an Air Force Reserve individual mobilization augmentee (IMA) and conducts research to support CADRE and AU in the area of advanced space system technologies and serves to bridge the gap between technologists and the operational war fighter.

He has over 20 years' experience within the Air Force, National Aeronautics and Space Administration (NASA), private companies, and academia in the research, design, development, and testing of facilities, liquid-rocket engines, and launch-vehicle development. He served on active duty at Fairchild AFB, Washington, and as a reservist at McChord AFB, Washington; Arnold AFB, Tennessee; Eglin AFB, Florida; and currently, Maxwell AFB, Alabama.

Dr. Brown is a registered professional engineer in the state of Alabama and is employed by NASA's Marshall Space Flight Center in Huntsville, Alabama, as a liquid-rocket-engine system engineer. He holds a BS in mechanical engineering from Oklahoma State University, an MS in aeronautics and astronautics from the University of Washington, and a PhD in mechanical engineering from the University of Alabama in Huntsville. Colonel Brown's professional military education includes the Squadron Officer School and the Air Command and Staff College, both located at Maxwell AFB.

Acknowledgments

This book is the culmination of Gen Lance Lord's, former commander of Air Force Space Command, vision to initiate a vigorous discussion about how to best integrate space to support the war fighter. Part of General Lord's vision was for the Space Weapons Officer Air and Space Integration Conference to become a regular event where space weapons officers with experiences from recent operations could gather to discuss those events and propose new and perhaps radical ideas to improve the way space supports the war fighter. In the spirit of the Air Corps Tactical School, the best of these ideas could then be tested during war games and exercises. On behalf of the authors who participated in the conference and their support to this book, I extend our appreciation to General Lord for the opportunity to be part of such a unique event.

The Space Weapons Officer Air and Space Integration Conference in 2005 was a joint event between Air Force Space Command and Air Education and Training Command. The conference could not have been held without the hard work of numerous people at Space Command and Air University, including Brig Gen John Hyten, Col Dwayne Lamb, numerous members from the Space Warfare Center, the 595th Operations Support Squadron, Col Al Sexton, USAF, retired, Mr. Brent Marley, and the Maxwell AFB protocol.

Credit for this work belongs to the space weapons officers who participated in the conference and contributed their perspectives. And last, but certainly not least, the editor wants to recognize the outstanding support of the editorial staff at Air University Press, Dr. Philip Adkins, Mrs. Sherry Terrell, and Mrs. Vivian O'Neal. Their creation of an integrated book from nine distinctly separate research papers was a more complex effort than manuscripts written by a single author.

Introduction

Lt Col Kendall K. Brown, USAFR, PhD

In March 2005 the first Space Weapons Officer Air and Space Integration Conference was held at Maxwell Air Force Base, Alabama, as a joint effort between Air Force Space Command (AFSPC) and Air Education and Training Command. As then-AFSPC commander Gen Lance Lord stated in the invitation to the cadre of space weapons officers (SWO):[1] "We want to hear from the Space Weapons Officers on the best way to integrate space capabilities at the operational level of warfare. What do they think is the best way to do business? Differing views are okay. Articulate pros/cons and support with past experiences—what's worked, what hasn't." General Lord envisioned a regular event where SWOs would gather in the spirit of the Air Corps Tactical School to discuss, argue, and generate new ideas that could then be tested in war games and exercises for incorporation in doctrine, organization, strategy, tactics, and procedures.

General Lord set the stage for the conference with his introductory remarks:

> We've got to get ready for what's going to happen next in the medium of space. When Space starts in a big way, and it will, we have to have the conventional war fighters who have the capabilities, who know the rules of engagement, who are familiar with the laws of armed conflict, who know how to work in this medium and are able to shape and influence and make the right kind of decisions and direct the operational application of space capabilities.

The authors of each chapter presented their ideas directly to General Lord and over a dozen general officers from around the Air Force. The entire cadre of space-officer graduates of the Air Force Weapons School at Nellis AFB, Nevada, was invited, and more than 60 attended. The SWOs presented their ideas not only to senior leadership but also to their colleagues and peers. In the Air University tradition of nonattribution, most of the ideas presented generated lively debate. In particular, a recurring theme of "normalizing" the presentation of space forces to the theater commander was greeted with approval from most SWOs, although some of the senior officers in attendance were not quite as enthusiastic.

The chapters in *Space Power Integration* address issues across a spectrum of air- and space-integration topics at the operational level of war. Several studies argue that current space doctrine regarding organization and command relationships needs to be revised, with recommendations ranging from subtle modifications to paradigm-changing constructs. It is important to note that a major revision to Air Force Doctrine Document (AFDD) 2-2, *Space Operations*, was in process at the time of the conference and during the preparation of this book. As such, many of the fundamental arguments about organizing space forces to best support the theater joint force commander may have been addressed within doctrine. Doctrine does not and cannot provide extensive implementation guidance and direction; therefore, *Space Power Integration* provides some perspectives from space operators who have had direct responsibilities for integrating air and space power at the operational level of war.

Space Power Integration begins with a chapter providing a space-power framework and a recommendation for how the space-coordinating authority should enable unity of effort for diverse information services from space. The next chapter builds upon that background by discussing the importance of counterspace operations and how they are needed to support counterterrorism. Background information in the early chapters helps the nonspace operator put the remaining chapters in better context. The following six chapters discuss various perspectives on problems due to the current command and control (C2) of deployed space forces' organizational models. Some overlap of ideas is present, and no attempt was made to remove this overlap during the development of *Space Power Integration*. Rather, this overlap serves to identify areas of consensus. Conversely, the areas of conflicting observations and recommendations highlight the difficulty of reaching a common understanding on such a complicated subject. The final study was the last presentation of the conference, and rather than focus on the organizational charts and C2 relationships that should or should not be in the doctrine, the author takes a very personal perspective on what problems he has experienced, what he believes are the fundamental root causes, and specific recommendations to address those issues.

Discussions that occurred during the conference could not have taken place in the past because SWOs did not have the operational experience of integrating air and space at the operational level of war. SWOs have learned many lessons and are proposing we use those lessons to improve future operations. These discussions also point out how the Air Force is moving more and more towards a seamless integration of air and space capabilities versus the technically based centralization of space capabilities in the not-so-distant past.

As Gen Gregory Martin, former commander of Air Force Materiel Command, commented during his remarks:

> We do space, the United States Air Force does space, the others use it. We have the preponderance of space warriors and space equipment. It is these advances in technology and personnel that have provided the Air Force the communication, navigation, and imaging capabilities that provide the United States a critical asymmetric advantage. Operation Iraqi Freedom was the first major engagement where these capabilities were so thoroughly integrated in support of the theater commander, through the combined force air and space commander and the air and space operations center. As future adversaries increase their space capabilities, the United States must meet the challenge by improving the efficiency of integrating our space capabilities across the entire spectrum of operations.

That is the challenge for the future, providing effective and efficient integration of air and space capabilities in support of the commanders' objectives. For this level of integration in the theater to become a reality, deployed space forces will be called upon to more actively participate in the commanders' planning and operations. Hopefully, the discussions in *Space Power Integration* will help spur the discussion and debate to arrive upon the doctrine and organizational models needed to provide that support. Planning for the second Space Weapons Officer Air and Space Integration Conference, to be held in spring 2007, has begun and will provide the forum for these discussions to continue.

Note

1. Space weapons officer (SWO) is an unofficial title for career space officers who have graduated from the US Air Force Weapons School. By having a common knowledge basis with their airpower brethren, SWOs have worked in theater operations centers during multiple recent operations to more fully integrate space capabilities into operational planning.

Chapter 1

Space Coordinating Authority

Information Services from Space

Maj Tyler M. Evans, USAF

Too often, combatant commanders are not as involved in space as they need to be—in our current and projected way of war, this paradigm needs to change. Warfighters need to remain personally and persistently engaged.

—Lt Gen Norton A. Schwartz
Director for Operations, the Joint Staff

In recognizing the importance of space to military operations, joint doctrine recommends a single authority to coordinate joint-theater space operations and integrate space capabilities.[1] The space coordinating authority (SCA) facilitates unity of effort as operations often utilize civil, commercial, national, and military space capabilities. This research report provides a space-power framework and recommends how the SCA should enable unity of effort for diverse information services from space.

The 2004 *National Military Strategy* (*NMS*) prescribes three objectives for armed forces: (1) protect the United States, (2) prevent conflict and surprise attack, and (3) prevail against adversaries.[2] The joint force commander (JFC) seeks full-spectrum dominance to achieve these objectives. The ability to control any situation or defeat any adversary across the range of military operations increasingly exploits advantages of space. In seizing and relying upon space, commanders must grasp a relevant sense and intuitive meaning of the nebulous term *space*. Notions of "articulating space to the war-fighter" or "space at the operational level of war" conflict with providing consequential thought to planning and executing military operations.

As a rather new concept, employment of the SCA occurred for the first time when the combined forces commander designated the combined force air component commander (CFACC) as the

1

SCA in Operation Iraqi Freedom (OIF).[3] The Air Force has es-
poused the concept by training, exercising, embedding, and deploying space operators to coordinate operations and integrate
capabilities. The latest evolution of the SCA is the director of
space forces (DIRSPACEFOR). Originally called the senior space
officer (SSO), the DIRSPACEFOR is an Air Force construct that
provides a senior space advisor who coordinates, integrates,
and staffs activities for tailored space support.

Military operations use space predominately to aid and accelerate observations, decisions, and actions across the entire spectrum of conflict. Space-based capabilities are foundational to
the information domain, providing communications; warning;
intelligence, surveillance, and reconnaissance (ISR); positioning,
navigation, and timing (PNT); environmental; and weather data.
These information services, from space, enable war fighters to
improve operations through space-integrated applications of
combat power. This integration of supporting space services,
combined with space superiority, acts as a force multiplier for
military commanders.

This chapter conveys an Airman's perspective for operations
in joint and coalition environments. Intended readers include
the JFC, associated joint staffs, component commanders, and
the designated SCA. Any reference to the JFC implies this
broader audience. Readers should realize that the SCA concepts are new and still evolving. Since all doctrine written on
the SCA has yet to withstand a historical test of time, the likelihood of the SCA becoming an enduring bedrock of joint operations is unknown. Future events and decisions could easily
antiquate any recommendations contained herein. With little
written on the SCA, the author attempts to capture and propose pertinent thoughts on the subject. Although not specifically addressed, readers can gather applicable information on
the DIRSPACEFOR position from the SCA discussion.

This treatise begins by revealing space boundaries, definitions, and seams to provide a basis for exploring space capabilities and space power. A survey of space frameworks and cate-
gorizations follows to articulate a recommended space-power
framework for the SCA. A document review and comparison
provides a noteworthy summary of SCA concepts. Finally, a
functional-management versus medium-management discus-

sion ensues, illuminating how to utilize the spectrum of coordination and control with existing process mechanisms. This includes recommending changes to the responsibilities of the SCA in doctrine.

Boundaries, Definitions, and Seams

A common space perspective is required for any SCA discussion with the JFC. This begins with the most basic question: What is space? Doctrine defines *space* as "a medium like the land, sea, and air within which military activities shall be conducted to achieve US national security objectives."[4] The boundary of the space medium does not expose an exact and legalistic delimitation between sovereign airspace and nonsovereign outer space. Since the launch of *Sputnik I*, the first artificial satellite, on 4 October 1957, a de facto definition has developed that any object in orbit under the physical principles of astrodynamics is in space. Complementing this practical approach, an altitude of about 100 kilometers above sea level is generally recognized as the lower limit of space.[5] In the current context of military operations, there is no upper limit to the space medium. For example, the civil *Advanced Composition Explorer* (*ACE*) satellite provides advance warning of solar storms, which can disrupt military communications, from a vantage point of roughly one million miles from Earth.

Operations involving orbiting satellite systems best describe military activities in space. Satellite systems are generically composed of three segments:

1. The satellites or spacecraft in space constitute the space segment.
2. The ground segment consists of users, operators, and associated terminals normally located in air, land, or sea mediums.
3. The space-ground link, connecting the space and ground segments via electromagnetic or radio-frequency communications, is the third segment.

Common infrastructure supporting satellite systems includes launch ranges, tracking systems, and communication networks.

Some may view surface-to-surface ballistic missiles, to include intercontinental ballistic missiles, as military space activities due to short transitory flight through the space medium and scientific similarities to launching satellite systems. However, they should be excluded due to lack of lasting space activity or influence.

Space capabilities form the foundation for space power. The first primary source of military space-power thought is the 1946 Project RAND report titled *Preliminary Design of an Experimental World-Circling Spaceship.*[6] Here, noted radar expert Louis N. Ridenour theorized using satellites to bomb targets, guide missiles, assess bomb damage, forecast weather, relay communications, and scientifically study the planet and solar system.[7] This study eventually led to the first military-satellite-conceived weapon system, WS 117L, and the advanced reconnaissance system (ARS), in 1954.[8] The ARS was the forerunner to today's Defense Support Program (DSP) and national electro-optical imagery intelligence (IMINT) satellites.

The JFC should concentrate on space power and not individual space capabilities in planning and executing operations. Doctrine defines *space power* as the total strength of a nation's capabilities to conduct and influence activities to, in, through, and from space to achieve objectives.[9] This definition devolves into two parts: capabilities to conduct space activities and capabilities to influence space activities. The latter is actually a prerequisite to the former.

Space-capable nations and actors have historically pursued diplomatic cooperation in space rather than outright confrontation. However, the uncertain world found after 11 September 2001 (9/11) precludes the belief of unchallenged freedom of action in a peaceful space medium. Terrorists and adversaries will attempt to defeat asymmetric space capabilities. The *NMS* recognizes this by describing three key aspects of the security environment facing combatant commanders (CCDR): (1) a wider range of adversaries, (2) a more complex and distributed battlespace, and (3) technology diffusion and access to drive concepts and capabilities in future operations.[10] The JFC will seek to control space pursuant to the *NMS* objectives of protect, prevent, and prevail.

With the freedom that comes from control of space, forces are then able to conduct space activities. Space power has traditionally been unchallenged, allowing space capabilities to develop into a robust set of enabling information services and utilities. The JFC utilizes a wide arsenal of space capabilities to aid air, land, maritime, and special operations forces. Capabilities are a part of weapon systems, creating space-integrated applications of combat power. Here it is impossible to unravel and separate space power from other combat functions. For example, positioning and communications space services are a part of combat search and rescue (CSAR), permitting personnel recovery operations to locate and save lost elements. Table 1.1 lists space capabilities and integrated applications available to joint forces. Representative civil, commercial, and foreign systems are included for completeness, but the table does not exhaustively list all operational capabilities. Futuristic and unrealized space capabilities are not listed or considered applicable, as their likelihood of fulfillment cannot be assured.[11] Uncertain future acquisitions are not useful for current operations to the JFC.

Table 1.1. Current space capabilities and space-integrated applications

Agency	Purpose	Space System
US Department of Defense (DOD)	PNT Information	Global Positioning System (GPS)
	Weather Information	Defense Meteorological Satellite Program (DMSP)
	Surveillance Information	DSP Satellites Space-Based Infrared System (SBIRS)
	Communications	Defense Satellite Communications System (DSCS) Military Strategic and Tactical Relay (MILSTAR) Satellite Global Broadcast Service Ultrahigh Frequency Follow-on (UFO) Satellites Polar Satellite Communications
	Counterspace	Space Situation Awareness (SSA) Systems Defensive Counterspace (DCS) Systems Offensive Counterspace (OCS) Systems
	Space-Integrated Applications of Combat Power	CSAR Theater Missile Defense (TMD) Blue Force Situation Awareness

5

Table 1.1. (continued)

Agency	Purpose	Space System
US National Intelligence	Reconnaissance Information	IMINT Overhead Signals Intelligence (SIGINT) Overhead Measurement and Signature Intelligence
US Civil	Weather Information	National Oceanic and Atmospheric Administration (NOAA) Geostationary Operational Environmental Satellites NOAA Polar Operational Environmental Satellites
	Remote Sensing Information	National Aeronautics and Space Administration (NASA) Landsat
Commercial	Remote Sensing Information	DigitalGlobe QuickBird Satellite ORBIMAGE OrbView Satellites Space Imaging IKONOS Satellite
	Communications	Intelsat Communications Satellites Inmarsat Communications Satellites Eutelsat Communications Satellites
Allied	Communications	North Atlantic Treaty Organization Communications Satellites
Foreign	PNT Information	Russian Global Navigation Satellite System
	Weather Information	European Meteosats
	Remote Sensing Information	Indian Remote Sensing Satellite System French SPOT Satellite System
	Reconnaissance	Russian SIGINT
	Communications	British Skynet Communications Satellites

In applying space power, the JFC should comprehend that total strength stems from assorted sources of space capabilities. It is easy to fixate on the DOD and national satellite systems. However, the military campaign should consider all space capabilities from military services, national and civil agencies, commercial companies, allied and coalition partners, multinational and consortium organizations, and independent foreign countries to conduct and influence space operations. The *NMS* describes a complex battlespace spanning the common global arena of international space and anticipates "unique demands on military organizations and interagency partners, requiring more detailed coordination and synchronization of activities both overseas and at home."[12] Varied sources of space power create a potential seam or disconnection for the JFC to appreciate in leading military operations.

A second seam to be aware of is the imprecise boundary between global and theater space operations. Many space capabilities operate globally and are able to service nearly the entire Earth's surface. For example, constellations of geosynchronous communication satellites provide persistent worldwide coverage all day long, and low-Earth-orbiting reconnaissance satellites can survey areas around the world multiple times per day. Contrary to this global nature of space, some satellite systems are configurable to serve only a specific theater or area of interest. The command and control (C2) of military space capabilities reveals potential friction between global and theater space operations. The Unified Command Plan (UCP) designates US Strategic Command (USSTRATCOM) as the functional combatant command (COCOM) for military space operations. However, the principle of unity of command directs all forces to operate under a single commander. Military space power is a balance between USSTRATCOM's global responsibilities and geographic COCOMs.

Doctrine describes this relationship by suggesting that there are global space capabilities producing global effects, global space capabilities delivering theater-only effects, theater space capabilities yielding global effects, and theater space capabilities supplying theater-only effects. Doctrine then recommends an appropriate command relationship based upon this global versus theater determination.[13] A potential friction point lies in the interpretation of where global space operations stop and theater space activities begin. A manifestation of this occurs when the space power in one geographic area affects multiple military operations. One possible starting point for the boundary between global and theater space power is the UCP assignment of regions to geographic CCDRs. However, with multiple operations occurring in a geographic CCDR area of responsibility (AOR), the boundary could be drawn at the area of operations (AO), joint operations area (JOA), theater of operations

7

(TO), or operational area (OA) level.[14] The JFC should use care in creating battlespace boundaries as networked space systems could easily extend past normal geographic definitions.

A third link to space power exists between the levels of war. The application of space power has differing emphasis at the strategic, operational, and tactical levels of war. In the 1950s and 1960s the Cold War forced early space power towards the strategic level of war. Space-based reconnaissance became strategically paramount after the downing of Francis Gary Powers and his U-2 aircraft by the Soviet Union on 1 May 1960.[15] First launched in 1970, the DSP alerted the president and national security leadership of detected intercontinental and sea-launched ballistic missiles heading towards the United States. Even today, space-based reconnaissance and communication capabilities remain integral to high-priority strategic users. This has forced some low-density space capabilities to follow the principle of centralized control and execution, rather than the airpower tenet of centralized control and decentralized execution.

At the tactical level of war, space capabilities are increasingly more integrated. For example, after debuting in the 1991 Gulf War, the GPS became the primary radio-navigation system source of PNT information for the DOD. Congress has mandated that all new or modified aircraft, ships, armored vehicles, or indirect-fire weapon systems come equipped with a GPS receiver after 30 September 2005.[16] Tactical forces often compete with strategic users for space capabilities. Ultrahigh frequency satellite communications (SATCOM) bandwidth is oversubscribed and in high demand with mobile users. The JFC and component commanders at the operational level of war are sandwiched between strategic and tactical space power. With space requirements of their own, operational commanders must potentially balance, lobby, and orchestrate space power across the three levels of war.

The final space-power seam the JFC may contend with is the spectrum of conflict. From stability and support operations and military operations other than war through major theater war, space power will bring to bear advantages to joint and coalition forces. The spectrum of conflict for military operations stretches in increasing intensity from stable peace to unstable peace, crisis, and war. Space power will be utilized as conflict escalation progresses from peacetime operations to preventative diplomacy, crisis operations, and peacemaking. This continues as de-escalation progresses from peace enforcement to peacekeeping, post-conflict peace building, and back to peacetime diplomacy.

Most information services from space will be employed across the entire spectrum of conflict. Forces will need communications, warning, ISR, PNT, environmental, and weather data during all phases of operations. Of course, the quantity of data may not be equal for all phases. Before forces deploy and hostilities occur, large quantities of space-based surveillance and reconnaissance may be needed to perform intelligence preparation of the battlespace and predictive battlespace awareness. After forces engage the enemy, SATCOM and the GPS could be the most critical space capabilities for the JFC. In campaign planning, the JFC will anticipate the demand for specific space information services across the phases and spectrum of conflict. The JFC should realize that the tempo and emphasis of space power will change as military operations progress.

In understanding the medium of space and application of space power, the JFC can begin to frame an appreciation of the complexity and usefulness of space and associated capabilities. Space capabilities woven into air, land, maritime, and special operations forces enable swift achievement of assigned objectives and tasks. Information services from space are instrumental to and cannot be separate from military operations. However, there are four potential seams in this war-fighting cloth: (1) the various sources of space power, (2) boundaries between global and theater space power, (3) different levels of war, and (4) space employment across the spectrum of conflict. These seams create potential friction points that the JFC should expect to account for and prevent from degrading operations in achieving the assigned military objectives.

Frameworks and Categorizations

We've got in excess of 50 satellites that we're working as part of my quiver in air and space applications. The satellites have been just unbelievably capable . . . in

9

> *being able to support conventional ground forces, the naval forces, special operations, and the air forces.*
>
> —Lt Gen T. Michael Moseley
> CFACC for OIF

The complexity and diversity of space power encourage the JFC to have a framework or intellectual way to organize the application of space power. Otherwise, the fog and friction from seams in space power combined with competing priorities will inhibit operational economy and balance, thus reducing combat effectiveness. A starting point for intellectual organization is to divide space power into categories. The question becomes, What are the best categories in which to divide space power? A logical choice would be to look at the roles, missions, and functions associated with space power as it applies to the JFC. Roles relate to purpose, missions to tasks, and functions to responsibilities.[17] Since roles are broad and normally associated with military services rather than with war-fighting forces, only missions and functions are appropriate starting points.

The national space policy directs that the DOD maintain the capability to execute mission areas of space support, force application, space control, and force enhancement.[18] This mission framework formed the structure of space power in joint doctrine, but not all mission areas are relatable to the JFC in the context of joint-force operations. *Space support* is defined as "combat service support operations to deploy and sustain military and intelligence systems in space."[19] This includes launch, maintenance, and termination of satellite systems. While analogous to the basic air operations of taking off, flying, and landing an airplane, space support of satellite systems tends to be very deliberate, infrastructure-intensive activities conducted from the continental United States (CONUS). Unlike most military weapon systems, space support is, for the most part, detached and unrelated to JFC objectives and joint-force operations.

Space power is currently unable to force an adversary to capitulate. Joint doctrine defines s*pace force application* as "combat operations in, through, and from space to influence the course and outcome of conflict."[20] There are no force-application capabilities in space. At some point in the future, indirect or direct firepower in space may be decisive against enemy centers of gravity (COG). However, until that time, the JFC should not be concerned with force application from space.

As stated before, capabilities to influence space activities are half of space-power formation. The terms *space control*, *counterspace*, and *space superiority* describe military actions to influence space. Joint doctrine defines *space control* as "combat, combat support, and combat service support operations to ensure freedom of action in space for the United States and its allies and, when directed, deny an adversary freedom of action in space."[21] Space control should be viewed as the way, mission, or purposeful task to influence space. Space control has a doctrinal divide in the tasks of surveillance, prevention, protection, and negation. The Air Force component to USSTRATCOM conducts space surveillance operations to build and maintain situational awareness of space for all US departments, agencies, and interests. Prevention and protection are defensive actions conducted to ensure friendly space operations with desired exclusivity from adversary efforts. Negation involves offensive actions to disrupt, deny, degrade, destroy, and deceive enemy space capabilities through kinetic or nonkinetic means by joint forces to achieve national security objectives.

Next, *counterspace* is "those offensive and defensive operations conducted by air, land, sea, space, special operations, and information forces with the objective of gaining and maintaining control of activities conducted in or through the space environment."[22] Counterspace is the means, function, or responsibility for resources and capabilities to influence space. Counterspace is doctrinally divided into SSA, DCS, and OCS. There is a direct task-to-action relationship between surveillance to SSA, prevention and protection to DCS, and negation to OCS. Also noteworthy to the JFC, SSA is a global function, OCS is a theater function, and DCS is a combined theater and global function.

Finally, *space superiority* is "the degree of dominance in space of one force over another that permits the conduct of operations by the former and its related land, sea, air, space, and special operations forces at a given time and place without prohibitive interference by the opposing force."[23] It is the desired effect (or ends) of influencing the space medium. Concentrating on this, the JFC normally sets an objective of gaining and maintaining space superiority.

The last space mission area is *space force enhancement*, defined as the "combat support operations to improve the effectiveness of military forces as well as support other intelligence, civil, and commercial users."[24] This includes ISR, warning, communications, PNT, and environmental monitoring. Space force enhancement is better defined as space-based, decision-quality information or data used in military operations plus space-based systems that collect, process, store, transmit, display, disseminate, and act on information. Therefore, a more descriptive term for space force enhancement to the JFC is *information services from space*. This is the other half of space power, the capability to conduct space activities.

Once space superiority is established, information services from space assist and accelerate observations, decisions, and actions across the entire spectrum of conflict. By controlling space, space power rewards the JFC with greater freedom of action for joint forces. The colossal contribution of space power to military operations is its constant ability to speed up the decision-making cycle. Two process models, the "OODA loop" and the "kill chain," illustrate this point.

Col John R. Boyd realized that behavior is a continuous and interactive cycle of observe, orient, decide, and act (OODA). As applied to military operations at all levels of war and across the entire spectrum of conflict, information from persistent space-based systems overshadows the observation phase of the loop. The JFC and joint forces exploit space-originating ISR information to gain critical awareness of the battlespace and the adversary. Using their cognitive ability to orient and reason, commanders and forces are able to turn observations into decisions and actions. Space-integrated command, control, and communications capabilities aid these decisions and actions, allowing the JFC to respond quicker than the enemy in the battlespace. Feedback, combined with an interactive environment, then drives new observations for iterative continuation of the loop. Destructive manipulation of the opponent ensues as the friendly OODA engine outpaces the foe's ability to seize the initiative.

The ability to find, fix, track, target, engage, and assess (F2T2EA) is commonly referred to as a kill chain. These steps mark the process to "kill" something in combat at the operational and tactical levels of war. The process starts with finding and fixing an object to identify it as worthy of attacking. Next, forces will track and target the object to zero in before pulling the trigger to fire. Finally, assessment closes the cycle to determine success and sets up the next attack. Integrated space information services augment each step in the kill chain. Space-based ISR supplies flexible and versatile eyes and ears to the chain. The GPS provides common referencing across all steps and greater precision during engagement, limiting collateral damage. SATCOM helps bind the steps together between dispersed tactical forces and centralized operational C2. The JFC profits from information services from space, increasing the ability to execute the kill chain.

A contrary framework comes from Air Force doctrine. It is relevant to consider an Air Force perspective, as the Air Force is the executive agent for space. Additionally, the air component commander or commander, Air Force forces (COMAFFOR) is the leading candidate to execute the SCA on behalf of the JFC. The Air Force normally has the preponderance and expertise of space-power C2 in joint operations. The Air Force doctrinally divides air and space power into 17 key operational functions. Air Force doctrine describes these functions as "the actual operations constructs Airmen use to apply air and space power to achieve objectives."[25] These functions are:

- Strategic Attack
- Counterair
- Counterspace
- Counterland
- Countersea
- Information Operations
- Combat Support
- Command & Control
- Airlift
- Air Refueling
- Spacelift
- Special Operations
- Intelligence
- Surveillance & Reconnnaissance
- Combat Search & Rescue
- Navigation & Positioning
- Weather Services

Obviously, some of the functions like air refueling are airpower unique and do not apply to space. Certain functions are directly mapped to space mission areas, while others intermingle between multiple mission areas. Spacelift is a function of space support, and force enhancement contains space-based weather services. Tougher to separate is C2, which is integral to all mission areas. The benefit of Air Force operational functions is finer granularity and visibility of specific effects from space power. Effects-based operations (EBO) propel the JFC-led campaign. The JFC directs operations, utilizing space power against adversary systems, which create specific effects. These effects directly contribute to campaign objectives and result in the desired end state. By grouping the relevant operational functions into the two components of space power—space superiority and information services from space—the JFC has a tangible and usable space-power framework to employ in military operations.

Space superiority, from space control and the capability to influence space activities, exploits the operational functions of counterspace, information operations, special operations, combat support, C2, and ISR. It is important to recognize the potential overlap between counterspace, information operations, and special operations as space operations conduct influence, psychological, and electronic warfare operations against the enemy. The JFC needs C2 and combat support communications to carry out effective counterspace operations to gain and maintain space superiority. Also important to counterspace, ISR is the primary mechanism for SSA.

Information services from space, or the capabilities to conduct space activities, furnish combat support, C2, ISR, CSAR, navigation and positioning, and weather services. One focal linkage is SATCOM to combat support. Space-integrated applications of combat power intertwine space information services. For example, space-enabled CSAR performs speedy recovery of isolated personnel by using space-based ISR, SATCOM, and the GPS. Global space utilities enable joint forces to fight with agility. Operations in joint environments leverage space-derived information to be more efficient with better synergy, simultaneity, depth, and anticipation. Greater operational reach and approach are possible with space information services. These space services allow the JFC to capitalize on the facets of operational art found in all military operations.

Therefore, the recommended space-power framework for the JFC is to divide space power into space superiority and information services from space. This simplified approach allows the JFC to appreciate, appropriately, the contributions to military operations that result from space power. *Space superiority* best describes the effect of controlling the space medium, while *information services from space* accurately portrays the current functional benefits of space to joint forces. This framework, when combined with the boundaries and seams of space, compels the JFC to designate an SCA to achieve unified action in the battlespace. However, a still larger problem regarding the SCA is that current documentation on the SCA is potentially ambiguous and unrealistic, leading to confusion rather than simplicity for the JFC in utilizing space power.

References to Space Coordinating Authority

[Desert Storm] was a watershed event in military space applications because, for the first time, space systems were both integral to the conduct of terrestrial conflict and crucial to the outcome of the war.

—Lt Gen Thomas S. Moorman Jr.
Commander, Air Force Space Command

Because of the continual evolution of space integration in warfare, there is no single document encapsulating the roles, responsibilities, and employment of the SCA. The genesis of the SCA can be traced to the Gulf War of 1991. Operational and tactical theater forces used, for the first time in a major conflict, strategic space capabilities designed for the Cold War. Previously, communications, weather, and reconnaissance satellites predominately served strategic users in Washington during the Vietnam War. In 1991 the GPS and DSP along with communications, weather, and reconnaissance satellites provided instrumental information directly to the JFC and joint forces.

From the Gulf War two major space-integration efforts emerged. First, emphasis was placed on technological improvements to focus space capabilities towards tactical- and operational-level users. Major weapon systems were modified or designed to receive and integrate information from space. For example, the

GPS became the timing and navigation standard for all military systems. Second, space personnel deployed and embedded into theater organizations to aid in planning and executing operations. This grew from a limited number of deployable forward space support teams in 1994 to several hundred permanently assigned space personnel by 2000. Reinforced by sustained operations in Southwest Asia enforcing United Nations (UN) resolutions against Iraq and major combat operations in Europe with Operation Allied Force (OAF) in 1999, doctrinal thought anticipated military operations needing SCA.

In analyzing the major doctrine documents and references to SCA, the following terms should be viewed as synonymous: *space coordinating authority, coordinating authority for space, coordinating authority for space operations, coordinating authority for joint theater space operations*, and *space authority*. They are synonymous with a common definition of a consultation relationship for space power within a geographic or regional COCOM. The purpose of SCA is to achieve unity of effort for space power across the spectrum of conflict. It is not a command authority and does not apply beyond theater operations to functional or global COCOMs. A point to ponder is whether the United States Transportation Command (USTRANSCOM) would ever need SCA for intertheater lift operations. SCA does not achieve unity of command. USSTRATCOM is the functional COCOM with command authority for military space operations. The terms *global space coordinating authority* (GSCA) and *joint space coordinating authority* (JSCA) refer to consultation relationships for USSTRATCOM in working with other space-power agencies.[26]

Even though early drafts of Joint Publication (JP) 3-14, *Joint Doctrine for Space Operations*, contained SCA language, the first doctrine published with the SCA language was Air Force Doctrine Document (AFDD) 2-2, *Space Operations*, in November 2001. AFDD 2-2 recommends that the joint task force (JTF) commander appoint a coordinating authority for space operations to represent appropriate space requirements. With the possibility of interference between various space operations, redundant space efforts, and conflicting space support requests, the JTF commander should assign the joint force air component commander (JFACC) the responsibility of the SCA. AFDD 2-2 also proposes that the JTF commander assign the role of supported commander for joint space operations to the JFACC. AFDD 2-2 lists seven responsibilities of the SCA:

- Deconflict/prioritize military space requirements for the JTF
- Recommend appropriate command relationships for space to the JFC
- Help facilitate space target nomination
- Maintain space situational awareness
- Request space inputs from JTF, joint staff (J-staff), and components during planning
- Ensure optimum interoperability of space assets with coalition forces
- Recommend JTF military space requirement priorities to JFC.[27]

JP 3-14, published in August 2002, validated the existence of the SCA in AFDD 2-2 by stating that a supported JFC normally designates a single authority to coordinate joint-theater space operations and integrate space capabilities. Using the term *space authority*, JP 3-14 prescribed the following responsibilities:

- Coordinate space operations, and integrate space capabilities
- Primary responsibility for in-theater joint space-operations planning
- Coordinate with the component space-support teams and/or embedded space operators
- Gather space requirements throughout the joint force
- Provide to the JFC a prioritized list of recommended space requirements based on the joint-force objectives.[28]

Common to JP 3-14 and AFDD 2-2 are the SCA responsibilities to collect, prioritize, and provide space requirements to the JFC. Additionally, both documents stipulate coordinated military operations through integration of space capabilities or interoperability of space assets. Captured in JP 3-14, responsibility of joint space-operations planning as normal planning functions

17

is the AFDD 2-2 responsibilities of space target nomination and command relationship recommendations. The only real difference is the AFDD 2-2 responsibility to maintain space situational awareness, which JP 3-14 does not include.

Another important distinction between AFDD 2-2 and JP 3-14 is that JP 3-14 does not specify the JFACC as the recommended SCA. JP 3-14 allows the JFC to either retain the SCA or designate a component commander. Using criteria of mission, nature and duration of operations, preponderance of space-force capabilities, and C2 capabilities, the JFC would typically designate the JFACC, joint force land component commander, or joint force maritime component commander as the SCA. The special operations component commander could be an option for smaller task force operations.

Furthering the argument that the JFACC is the most logical choice for SCA, the Air Force published two more documents articulating the point. The *Air and Space Commander's Handbook for the JFACC*, published in January 2003, recommends in the JFACC checklist to advocate as the SCA in-theater during crisis-action planning.[29] Of note, the designation of the SCA in OIF to the CFACC occurred on 18 March 2003, only days before combat operations commenced and well after the operational plan was finalized. Secondly, AFDD 1, *Air Force Basic Doctrine* lists the SCA as a JFACC function.[30]

USSTRATCOM recognized the SCA from a global perspective by publishing Strategic Command Directive (SD) 505-3, *Space Support to Joint Force Commander or Designated Space Coordinating Authority*, in February 2004. It established responsibilities, guidelines, and procedures for USSTRATCOM organizations and personnel to work with the SCA in-theater. Even though it only references JP 3-14, the list of SCA responsibilities in SD 505-3 contains a combination of responsibilities found in JP 3-14 and AFDD 2-2. Specifically, it describes the SCA responsibility of space-target nomination.[31]

In August 2004, the Air Force published AFDD 2-2.1, *Counterspace Operations*. It reiterates the SCA responsibilities of AFDD 2-2 and recommends the DIRSPACEFOR as the senior space advisor to the COMAFFOR or COMAFFOR/JFACC.[32] Documents and publications dated after August 2004 are slowly propagating the SCA concept. These include Air Force policy and operational tactics, techniques, and procedures (TTP) documents. Additionally, material is also referencing the DIRSPACEFOR position. Noteworthy is a concept of operations for the combined air operations center (CAOC) in Qatar.

Space Coordinating Authority Responsibilities

While the designation of a Space Coordinating Authority was a success [in OIF], we need to . . . codify those roles and responsibilities into our doctrine.

—Dr. James G. Roche
Secretary of the Air Force

There is a spectrum, range, or depth to the term *coordination.* Coordination can vary from simple deconfliction to prioritization, synchronization, collaboration, synergy, integration, interoperability, or complex interdependence. Obviously, the SCA will utilize different levels of coordination based upon the situation and JFC guidance. To grasp the SCA language in AFDD 2-2, it is important to understand the definitional differences between coordinating authority and supported commander. The term *command* is central to all military action. It is authority over subordinates that a commander lawfully exercises. The level of command authority is divided into four types of command relationships: (1) COCOM, (2) operational control (OPCON), (3) tactical control (TACON), and (4) support.[33] The first three command relationships pertain to forces assigned or attached to a commander. Lastly, support is a command authority between commanders. A supported commander is the commander having primary responsibility for all aspects of a task. The supported commander receives assistance from another commander's forces or capabilities and is responsible for ensuring that the supporting commander understands the assistance required.[34]

On the other hand, coordinating authority is a commander or individual assigned the responsibility for coordinating specific functions or activities. It is beyond the four types of command relationships. The commander or individual has authority to require consultation between agencies involved but does

19

not have the authority to compel agreement. In the event of disagreement, the matter is referred to the appointing authority. Coordinating authority is a consultation relationship between commanders, not an authority by which command may be exercised.[35] While command authority and relationships are important to the planning and execution of military operations, this last section of recommendations will focus on SCA that is not tied to force assignment. For the foreseeable future, no single geographic or regional JFC will have consolidated control of space power and as such must rely on the SCA to achieve unity of effort.

There are two recommendations from analyzing the responsibilities in AFDD 2-2. First, maintaining space situational awareness was updated to maintaining SSA as part of AFDD 2-2.1 in 2004. There is a subtle difference between space *situational* awareness found in AFDD 2-2 and space *situation* awareness found in AFDD 2-2.1 that may not be generally recognized. Space situational awareness is a knowledge condition or situational awareness of space, while SSA [space situation awareness] is having actual knowledge or awareness of the space situation. The latter is more relevant to the JFC than the former because of the need to integrate the space situation into joint-force operations. Space target nomination and maintaining SSA fall into the framework of space superiority or medium influence. Space target nomination is an OCS planning activity normally done by the JFACC within the joint air operations center (JAOC). As mentioned before, the Air Force component of USSTRATCOM predominately performs SSA globally for all geographic CCDRs. A better SCA responsibility would be to integrate the USSTRATCOM-generated SSA with the theater-common operating picture for more complete awareness of the battlespace. Not included as part of the SCA is any coordination of DCS activities. Protection of theater space operations is the JFC's responsibility and most likely a task for the JFACC to accomplish. As the supported commander for joint space operations, the JFACC needs to coordinate DCS with all sources of space power. The SCA should coordinate DCS for all theater space operations. Second, ensuring optimum interoperability of space assets with coalition forces is possibly beyond the resources of the JFC. For example, some NATO and British communications satellites were designed to be interoperable with US SATCOM terminals, allowing greater flexibility. However, without significant planning and budgetary programming, the ability to modify foreign-made weapon systems to be interoperable with US satellite technology could be significantly challenging for the JFC. Additionally, security considerations could prevent interoperability with certain coalition partners. Ensuring a collaboration of space capabilities in coalition operations should replace the interoperability SCA responsibility. This is a more realistic SCA responsibility.

The final point regarding the SCA is that information services from space emphasizes the SCA as coordinating the functional aspect of space power, while space superiority emphasizes the SCA as controlling the medium aspect of space power. Information services from space needs unity of effort because of the various sources of space power. Space superiority requires unity of command as a military principle of war. The JFC should use a stronger authority than the SCA to compel agreement with space superiority. Lack of deliberate command authority over counterspace capabilities could jeopardize the JFC's ability to influence space operations and freedom of action in space.

Conclusion

In prosecuting the Global War on Terrorism, we have traded the traditional necessity for massed forces by using space capabilities for precision, speed, and the ability to quickly maneuver on the battlefield.

—Gen Lance W. Lord
Commander, Air Force Space Command

The JFC should understand that space power is crucial to achieving strategic guidance. Attaining the national military strategy objectives of protect, prevent, and prevail requires joint forces to exploit the medium of space. The JFC should use a simplified intellectual framework of two space-power categories to ease the planning, coordination, integration, and execution of theater space operations. Space superiority comes from influencing space activities with counterspace capabilities. Information services from space are space-based capabilities providing communications, warning, ISR, PNT, environment, and weather data to strategic, operational, and tactical users across the entire spectrum of conflict. These space information services woven together enable space-integrated applications of combat power.

In directing space power, the JFC should understand the boundaries and seams inherent to space. The JFC should designate the JFACC as the SCA to coordinate joint-theater space operations and integrate space capabilities. As the senior space advisor to the COMAFFOR/JFACC, the DIRSPACEFOR should facilitate and lubricate potential friction points or seams in space power, while joint forces engage adversaries in combating terrorism. As an asymmetric advantage of US strength, space power enables full-spectrum dominance.

Notes

1. JP 3-14, *Joint Doctrine for Space Operations*, 9 August 2002, III-1.

2. Gen Richard B. Meyers, *National Military Strategy of the United States of America* (Washington, DC: Department of Defense, May 2004), 2.

3. Maj Mark T. Main, "An Examination of Space Coordinating Authority and Command Relationships for Space Forces" (unpublished paper, Fourteenth Air Force, 2003), 1.

4. JP 1-02, *Department of Defense Dictionary of Military and Associated Terms* (As amended through 31 August 2005), 12 April 2001.

5. Glenn A. Reynolds and Robert P. Merges, *Outer Space: Problems of Law and Policy* (Boulder, CO: Westview Press, 1989), 12; and Carl Q. Christol, *The Modern International Law of Outer Space* (Elmsford, NY: Pergamon Press, 1982), 435–546.

6. David N. Spires, *Beyond Horizons: A Half Century of Air Force Space Leadership* (Maxwell AFB, AL: Air University Press, 1998), 14–16.

7. Project RAND, *Preliminary Design of an Experimental World-Circling Spaceship*, RAND Report SM-11827 (Santa Monica, CA: Douglas Aircraft Company, 2 May 1946), 9–16.

8. Spires, *Beyond Horizons*, 35–47.

9. JP 1-02, *DOD Dictionary*.

10. Meyers, *National Military Strategy*, 4–6.

11. Spacelift and space transportation capabilities are not listed in table 1.1. While these capabilities provide assured access to space, they are space-support missions that launch and replenish space systems. Military, civil, commercial, and foreign spacelift capabilities are available to deploy and replace satellites. Several countries also have manned spaceflight capabilities,

such as the US Space Transportation System, or space shuttle. The JFC should characterize spacelift, space transportation, and satellite-control capabilities as supportive to maintaining the capabilities listed in table 1.1.

12. Meyers, *National Military Strategy*, 5.

13. AFDD 2-2.1, *Counterspace Operations*, 2 August 2004, 15–17.

14. The point is not to recommend a specific geographic term to use, but rather to highlight the ambiguity and confusion these terms can cause in a space-power situation. Here are some of the JP 1-02 definitions for bounding geographic area. *Area of responsibility* is the geographical area associated with a COCOM within which a CCDR has authority to plan and conduct operations. *Area of operations* is an OA defined by the JFC for land and naval forces. An AO does not typically encompass the entire OA of the JFC, but should be large enough for component commanders to accomplish their missions and protect their forces. *JOA* is an area of land, sea, and airspace, defined by a geographic CCDR or subordinate unified commander, in which a JFC (normally a JTF commander) conducts military operations to accomplish a specific mission. A JOA is particularly useful when operations are limited in scope and geographic area or when operations are to be conducted on the boundaries between theaters. *TO* is a subarea within a theater of war defined by the geographic CCDR required to conduct or support specific combat operations. Different theaters of operations within the same theater of war will normally be geographically separate and focused on different enemy forces. A TO is usually of significant size, allowing for operations over extended periods of time. *OA* is an overarching term encompassing more descriptive terms for geographic areas in which military operations are conducted.

15. Spires, *Beyond Horizons*, 84.

16. Chairman of the Joint Chiefs of Staff Instruction (CJCSI) 6130.01C, *2003 CJCS Master Positioning, Navigation, and Timing Plan*, 31 March 2003, A-2.

17. JP 0-2, *Unified Action Armed Forces* (*UNAAF*), 10 July 2001, I-6.

18. DOD Directive (DODD) 3100.10, *Space Policy*, 9 July 1999, 7.

19. JP 1-02, *DOD Dictionary*.

20. Ibid.

21. Ibid.

22. AFDD 2-2.1, *Counterspace Operations*, 51.

23. JP 1-02, *DOD Dictionary*.

24. Ibid.

25. AFDD 1, *Air Force Basic Doctrine*, 17 November 2003, 38–40.

26. Lt Col Brian E. Fredriksson, "Space Power in Joint Operations: Evolving Concepts," *Air and Space Power Journal* 18, no. 2 (Summer 2004): 93–94. USSTRATCOM order, FRAGO 04 to OPORD05-02 Ch 1, assigned GSCA to Commander, Air Force Space Command/COMAFFOR on 3 February 2005. Maj Lina Cashin, USSTRATCOM/J515, proposed *JSCA* as an alternative term to *GSCA* on 17 February 2005 in conversation with author. (FRAGO [fragmentary order] is a partial change to an operations order [OPORD].)

27. AFDD 2-2, *Space Operations*, 27 November 2001, 23–34.

28. JP 3-14, *Joint Doctrine for Space Operations*, III-3.

29. Air Force Doctrine Center Handbook (AFDCH) 10-01, *Air and Space Commander's Handbook for the JFACC*, 16 January 2003, 6.

30. AFDD 1, *Air Force Basic Doctrine*, 66.

31. Strategic Command Directive (SD) 505-3, *Space Support to Joint Force Commander or Designated Space Coordinating Authority*, 6 February 2004.

32. AFDD 2-2.1, *Counterspace Operations*, 12–15.

33. JP 0-2, *UNAAF*, III-1.

34. JP 1-02, *DOD Dictionary*.

35. JP 0-2, *UNAAF*, III-12.

Chapter 2

Oriented Toward Superiority

Counterspace Operations and
the Counterterrorism Fight

Lt Col Michael J. Lutton, USAF

A process of reaching across many perspectives; pull-
ing each and every one apart (analysis), all the while
intuitively looking for those parts of the disassembled
perspectives which naturally interconnect with one an-
other to form a higher order, more general elaboration
(synthesis) of what is taking place. As a result, the pro-
cess not only creates the "Discourse" but it also repre-
sents the key to evolve the tactics, strategies, goals,
unifying themes, etc., that permit us to actively shape
and adapt to the unfolding world we are a part of, live-
in, and feed-upon.

—Col John R. Boyd

To say that the world we live in became more complex on
9/11 is a gross understatement and a misstatement of fact. The
incredibly perilous situation existing prior to 9/11 simply had
not been recognized in the United States, or so many thought.
In fact, as history now reveals, the events of 9/11 appear to be
a dramatic and tragic series of terrorist actions that many, if not
all, in the United States were ill prepared to counter—the seeds
sown nearly a decade prior. The United States failed to alter its
methods of addressing terrorism on a global scale or terrorism
aimed at the United States before 9/11. The events of 9/11
forced our nation to change. Figure 2.1 shows significant terrorist activity from 1991 to 2003.[1]

National Strategy for Combating Terrorism was not published
until 2003—shortly before the invasion of Iraq. As an expression of President Bush's strategic intent for counterterrorism
(CT), the *National Strategy for Combating Terrorism* clearly outlines our national effort to prevent future terrorist actions at

25

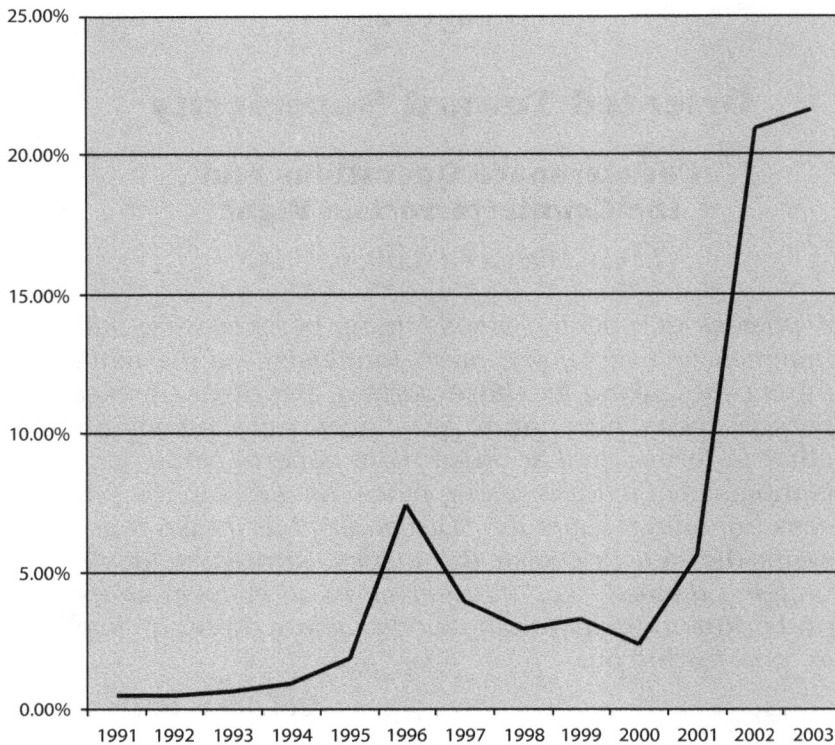

Figure 2.1. Percent of significant terrorist attacks, 1991–2003. (*Adapted from* US State Department, Office of the Coordinator for Counterterrorism, "Annual Reports," http://www.state.gov/www/global/terrorism/annual_reports .html.)

home and abroad. The challenge is in its execution—to view the national strategy as a road map to end terrorism is premature and results at best in a partial success. It serves as a fundamental call for reorientation in our approach to CT operations.

Colonel Boyd's unpublished work, "A Discourse on Winning and Losing," achieves what few authors ever accomplish. He provides the reader with a skill set for approaching the many challenges we face in today's world. Colonel Boyd's famous OODA loop symbolizes the skill set used for the continual process of analysis and synthesis—a means to reorient. Throughout this chapter, Colonel Boyd's process is utilized as a means to analyze and synthesize—in short, to orient toward superiority in space operations.

Given the nature of terrorist networks today and the focus of the *National Strategy for Combating Terrorism* to provide "direct and continuous action against terrorist groups," it is necessary to broaden the discussion of CT options and consider counterspace operations as an element in the fight against transnational terrorism.[2] Figure 2.2 shows the various links of terrorist networks.

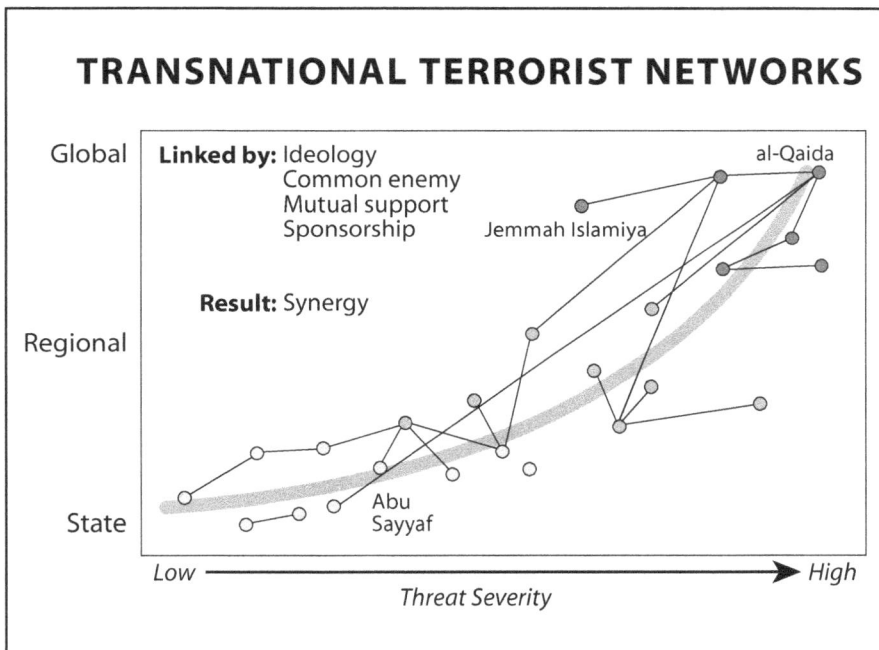

Figure 2.2. Transnational terrorist networks. (*Reprinted from* Pres. George W. Bush, *National Strategy for Combating Terrorism, February 2003* [Washington, DC: White House (Office of the Press Secretary), 14 February 2003], 9.)

While counterspace operations are not a "go-it-alone" option with respect to CT, the author contends that counterspace operations must be considered as a new option in our nation's arsenal. For without effective counterspace operations, the

United States concedes the use and capability of the medium of space and all its benefits—once the sole domain of superpowers—to terrorist networks. This is a mistake our nation can ill afford to make as we seek to accomplish the goals set forth in our national strategy.

To advance the discussion, this chapter analyzes three essential areas for the effective employment of counterspace operations in combating terrorism: (1) the significance of the medium to the CT fight, (2) articulating and assessing counterspace effects, and (3) the value of consistent and realistic training. The goal is a synthesized solution for future support to CT that enables military forces to establish superiority.

The Significance of the Medium to the Counterterrorism Fight

The Greeks, lying encamped on the mountains, could watch every movement of the Persians on the plain below, while they were enabled completely to mask their own. Militiades also had, from his position, the power of giving battle whenever he pleased, or of delaying it at his discretion, unless Datis were to attempt the perilous operation of storming the heights.

> —*The Fifteen Decisive Battles of the World: From Marathon to Waterloo*
> Sir Edward Shepherd Creasy, 1851

As warfare evolves, the ability to exploit and dominate the mediums of warfare (air, land, sea, and space) becomes a critical factor in a military's success or failure on the battlefield as well as a nation's success or failure in realizing its political objectives—objectives that likely drove the nation to war. The requirement to establish superiority in a medium of warfare is driven by many factors—enemy capability, military objectives, end state, and so forth. Table 2.1 examines the definitions of superiority across mediums.[3] Yet the fundamental precept for a state of superiority in a medium of warfare is offensive as well as defensive.[4]

Table 2.1. Definitions of superiority across mediums

Medium	Definition of Superiority
Land (fire superiority)	The degree of dominance in the fires of one force over another that permits that force to conduct maneuver at a given time and place without prohibitive interference by the enemy.
Sea (maritime)	That degree of dominance of one force over another that permits the conduct of maritime operations by the former and its related land, sea, and air forces at a given time and place without prohibitive interference by the opposing force.
Air	That degree of dominance in the air battle of one force over another that permits the conduct of operations by the former and its related land, sea, and air forces at a given time and place without prohibitive interference by the opposing force.
Space	The degree of dominance in space of one force over another that permits the conduct of operations by the former and its related land, sea, air, space, and special operations forces at a given time and place without prohibitive interference by the opposing force.

Adapted from US Army Field Manual (FM) 3-90, *Tactics*, 4 Jul 2001; and JP 1-02, *DOD Dictionary of Military and Associated Terms*, 12 April 2001.

Offensive superiority in a medium enables an efficiency of military action that increases the likelihood of military success. Defensive superiority, on the other hand, sustains the military capability employed in or through a medium and the use of the medium itself. For example, all mediums of warfare hold strategic lines of communication as critical to sustaining military operations and seek to defend these strategic lines of communication whether they are on land, at sea, in the air, or in and through space. Without defense of these strategic lines of communication, a military engaged in combat becomes more susceptible to defeat and more likely to fail.

As viewed through the lens of CT operations, military planners must utilize the mediums of warfare as interdependent gears in a machine. Historically, interdependence of mediums challenged military thinking and employment. The US military, without a doubt one of the most skilled and proficient in the world, recently embraced interdependent operations as a preferred method for military employment. With CT, however, the concept of interdependent employment of all mediums of warfare must guide military planners. In Stephen Sloan's *Beating*

International Terrorism, he cites the challenge of current military doctrine as it confronts terrorism: "'Environmental doctrine . . . is a compilation of beliefs about employment of military forces within a particular operating medium.' Since modern terrorism is very much a product of technology, we cannot overstate the importance of environmental doctrine in developing a capacity for terrorism preemption. Such a doctrine is 'significantly influenced by factors such as geography and technology.'"[5]

To most military planners, the interdependent employment of the three classical mediums of warfare (land, sea, and air) in CT operations goes without question. Quite often, however, the addition of the space medium as a coequal among the classical mediums of warfare in the interdependent employment of CT operations often seems unnecessary. Reorientation toward the terrorist threat today paints a different picture.

In *Mastering the Ultimate High Ground*, Benjamin Lambeth notes that "the United States is now unprecedentedly invested in and dependent on on-orbit capabilities, both military and commercial."[6] Quite objectively, recent military operations in Afghanistan and Iraq were not possible without the use of the space medium. Furthermore, our nation's national and international economic lifeblood are dependent on the use of the space medium. If denied, our ability to project power—economically, diplomatically, and militarily—throughout the world would be severely degraded. Therefore, access to the space medium and all its inherent benefits—perspective, persistence, speed, and situation awareness—becomes decisive in any outcome. Yet, most military planners see the space medium and our use of it as unchallenged.

Apparently, state sponsors of terrorism view access to space as a medium worth challenging. In August 2003, *Daily Insight* posted a story outlining Iran's recent attempt to challenge our use of the space medium. In the article titled "Iran and Cuba Zap U.S. Satellites," the author outlined Iran's effort to disrupt US satellite communications from Cuba. Specifically, the author notes:

> State sponsors of terrorism not only threaten U.S. interests on land, at sea and in the air, but now they have teamed up to attack U.S. assets in space. By successfully jamming a U.S. communications satellite over the Atlantic Ocean, the regimes of Cuba and

> Iran challenged U.S. dominance of space and the assumptions of free access to satellite communication that makes undisputed U.S. military power possible.[7]

The current *NMS* clearly makes the case for the space medium to take its place alongside the classical mediums of warfare. The *NMS* demands interdependence of all mediums of warfare as a prerequisite for achieving its priorities. Furthermore, the current *NMS* identifies winning the war on terrorism while protecting the United States as the first priority for success—access to and superiority in the space medium in a CT fight become more apparent as national military priorities reorient.

With a reorientation of national military priorities, an examination of terrorist networks and their use of the space medium becomes even more pressing. As stated in the *National Strategy for Combating Terrorism*, the terrorist networks facing our nation today are diverse, interconnected, and global. "The al-Qaida network is a multinational enterprise with operations in more than 60 countries" and "its [al-Qaida] global activities are coordinated through the use of personal couriers and communications technologies emblematic of our era—cellular and satellite phones, encrypted e-mail, internet chat rooms, videotape, and CD-ROMs."[8] In essence, terrorist networks, that have long been a part of our world, now reorient their practices to take advantage of modern globalization as well as modern technology. Consequently, terrorist networks, once confined to a region, begin to expand influence and action to a global stage utilizing many communication capabilities including those offered through the medium of space.

Indeed, globalization and technology increase the reach of terrorist networks while allowing them to remain well coordinated across the globe. In *The Pentagon's New Map*, Dr. Thomas Barnett submits, "The real asymmetrical challenge we will face will come from globalization's disenfranchised, or the losers largely left behind in the states most disconnected from globalization's advance."[9] While transnational terrorist networks may be many things, they are far from being disconnected. It is important to realize that Dr. Barnett is discussing an economic disconnectedness experienced by many nations found in the "gap"—not a technological disconnectedness. With respect to CT, the true challenge of globalization lies in the result of economic disconnectedness—nation-states vulnerable to parasitic transnational terrorist networks.

Modern technology, facilitated by space-based communications, establishes a ready-made communications architecture for transnational terrorist networks. Transnational terrorist organizations are enabled by "modern technology . . . to plan and operate worldwide as never before. With advanced telecommunications they can coordinate their actions among dispersed cells."[10] With an understanding of transnational terrorist networks' utilization of the space medium, the relevance of the space medium becomes ever clearer.

Yet, the use of the space medium, while critical to transnational terrorist networks, is not an absolute prerequisite for the conduct of terrorist actions. John Arquilla and David Ronfeldt provide excellent counsel on the relevance of technology and its impact to transnational terrorist networks. "New technologies, however, enabling for organizational networking, are not absolutely necessary for a netwar actor. Older technologies, like human couriers, and mixes of old and new systems may do the job in some situations."[11] Arquilla and Ronfeldt's counsel makes the space medium no less important in CT operations.

Their counsel serves to underscore a primary concept in warfare expressed by Colonel Boyd. "Idea: Simultaneously compress own time and stretch-out adversary time to generate a favorable mismatch in time and ability to shape and adapt to change. Goal: Collapse adversary's system into confusion and disorder by causing him to over and under react to activity that appears simultaneously menacing as well as ambiguous, chaotic, or misleading."[12] As discussed later in this chapter, military planners must recognize and take advantage of the mismatch in operating tempo and use the mismatch to combat terrorist networks.

Being oriented toward a transnational terrorist network's use of the space medium is incomplete orientation. It is critical to comprehend the type of warfare we expect terrorist networks to wage, given the use of the medium of space. With a greater insight into the type of warfare we expect terrorist networks to conduct, reorientation in order to counter terrorist networks becomes more complete.

The word *netwar*, described by Arquilla and Ronfeldt as the type of warfare expected of transnational terrorist networks, is somewhat misleading. The temptation to brand netwar as dependent on the technology of the twenty-first century intoxicates most and appeals to our strengths as a nation. However, netwar depends primarily on organizational networking and utilizes the current explosion in technology as a quasi-circulatory system to extend organizational networking.[13] Arquilla and Ronfeldt caution the reader about overestimating the importance of technology in netwar—"netwar may be waged in high-, low-, or no-tech fashion."[14]

However, netwar on a global scale requires some element of technology to effectively conduct operations in a sustained manner and maintain the integrity of the transnational terrorist network. In fact, Arquilla, Ronfeldt, and Michele Zanini all acknowledge the importance of transnational terrorist networks and their relationship to technology. "Terrorist groups are taking advantage of information technology to coordinate activities of dispersed members."[15] Additionally, these networks utilize technology to "better organize and coordinate dispersed activities."[16]

Once constrained by local or regional reach, netwar and the integration of advancing information technologies enable transnational terrorist networks to develop relationships, plan activities, and conduct operations. In "Networking of Terror in the Information Age," Zanini and Sean Edwards outline the impact of these new technologies on netwar—new communication and computing technologies allow the establishment of networks in three critical ways: "First, new technologies have greatly reduced transmission time. . . . Second, new technologies have significantly reduced the cost of communication, allowing information-intensive organizational designs such as networks to become more viable. . . . Third, new technologies have substantially increased the scope and complexity of the information that can be shared."[17]

The conclusion appears obvious but must be underscored— netwar operates across all mediums of warfare. Netwar does not discriminate based on preconceived insular notions of warfare. Netwar adapts and exploits the unique advantages of all mediums and at times challenges the use of those mediums by adversaries that threaten network survivability. Consequently, when considering offensive and defensive actions to counter these networks, planners must reorient to an adversary very much unlike conventional enemies. Accordingly, planners must begin to develop effects-based counterspace strategies that effectively establish the defensive in all four mediums of warfare while simultaneously taking the offensive in all four mediums of warfare.

Articulating and Assessing Counterspace Effects

Counterterrorism efforts should target the information flows of netwar groups . . . policymakers should consider going beyond the passive monitoring of information flows and toward the active disruption of such communications . . . over time the integrity and relevance of the network itself will be compromised.

—"Networking of Terror in the Information Age"
Michele Zanini and Sean J. A. Edwards

The *National Strategy for Combating Terrorism* provides sufficient guidance for military planners to consider "going beyond the passive monitoring of information flows."[18] In fact, the strategy outlines a multidimensional plan of attack with two over-arching effects: "reduce scope and reduce capability."[19] Geographic reach defines scope and its three subcategories: global, regional, and state. On the other hand, the severity of threat the terrorist organization possesses defines capability. Figure 2.3 outlines the three stages of attacking terrorism and the expected outcomes.

However, the inherent efficiency and adaptability found in transnational terrorist networks complicate execution of the national strategy. Without an initial understanding of the challenge of EBO in a CT fight, articulating desired effects and measuring an outcome become challenging at best. Terrorist networks pose many challenges to planners, but two seem to rise above others—efficiency of terrorist networks vis-à-vis military organizations and an ability to rapidly adapt to new technologies.

OPERATIONALIZING THE STRATEGY

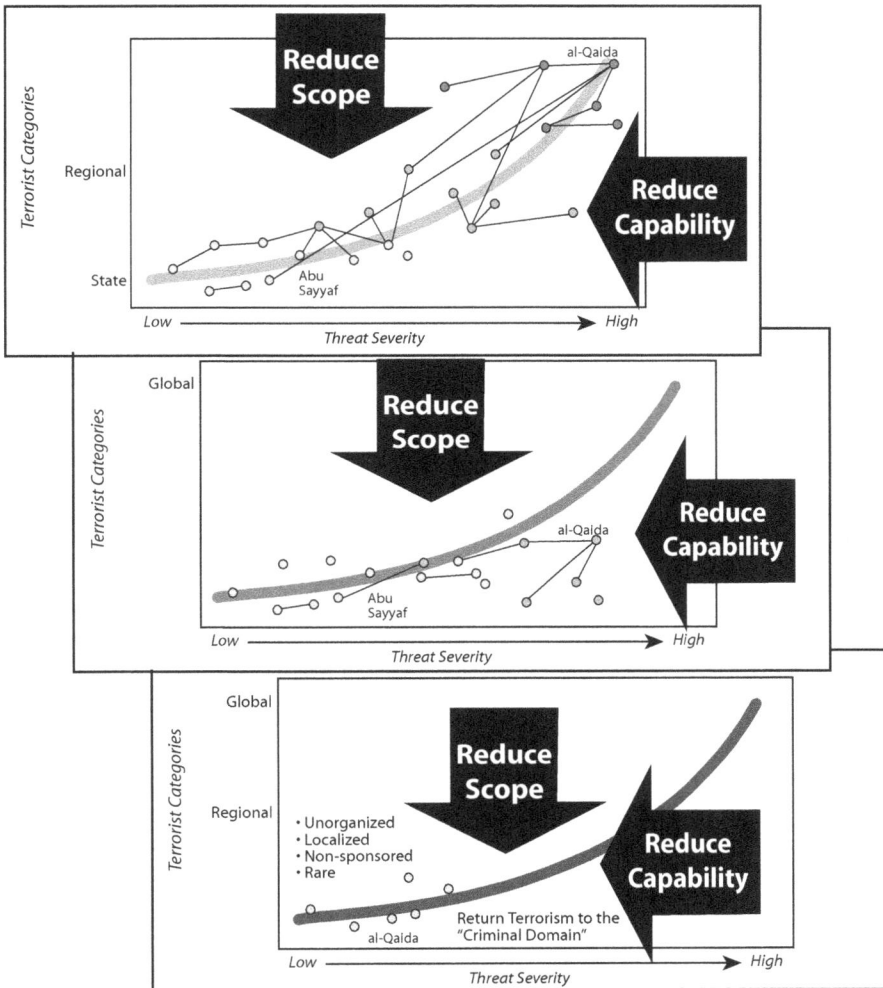

Figure 2.3. Operationalizing the strategy. (*Reprinted from* Pres. George W. Bush, *National Strategy for Combating Terrorism, February 2003* [Washington, DC: White House (Office of the Press Secretary), 14 February 2003], 13.)

Terrorist networks enjoy an advantage in efficiency for many reasons. Yet, the primary reason for efficiency lies in the competition between a nonbureaucratic organization, like a transnational terrorist network, and a modern military organization that is highly bureaucratic.[20] In fact, scholars recognize the unique attributes of a networked organization in transnational terrorist groups.[21] Specifically, the attributes of networked organizations consist of "relatively flat hierarchies, decentralization and delegation of decision-making authority, and loose lateral ties among dispersed groups and individuals."[22] Due to the efficiency, a transnational terrorist network enjoys an advantage in terms of time—time to plan, time to organize, time to adapt, and time to reorient—an advantage not to be taken lightly. As Alfred Thayer Mahan noted, "Time is a supreme factor in war."[23]

Transnational terrorist networks couple efficiency with adaptability. Adaptability becomes particularly critical for the networks' survival. Clearly, military organizations fighting terrorist networks often enjoy an advantage in monetary and physical resources. Consequently, transnational terrorist networks must adapt to the environment to deliver global effects. Much has been made of the wealth of certain terrorist organizations and their support architecture. However, Zanini and Edwards highlight a primary reason for adaptability: "Terrorist groups are likely to channel their scarce organizational resources to acquire those [information technology] skills that have the greatest leverage for the least amount of cost and effort."[24]

Soon after 9/11, the world understood the extent of a transnational terrorist network's ability to adapt. While most global armies require an advanced C2 center to conduct operations, the world found out that the Internet Café served as a surrogate C2 center—the quintessential example of terrorist adaptability. Consequently, adaptability occurs not only in the acquisition of information technologies but also in the employment of nonstandard war-fighting means like civil or commercial organizations, institutions, and resources required to maintain a global reach necessary for a transnational terrorist network to survive.

With these challenges as a backdrop, military planners must be capable of effectively articulating effects, specifically counterspace effects, designed to meet the nation's CT strategy—reduced scope and reduced capability. Work by RAND provides organization to the various thoughts on EBO. Figure 2.4 outlines the "simple taxonomy" used by RAND to express the scope of EBO.

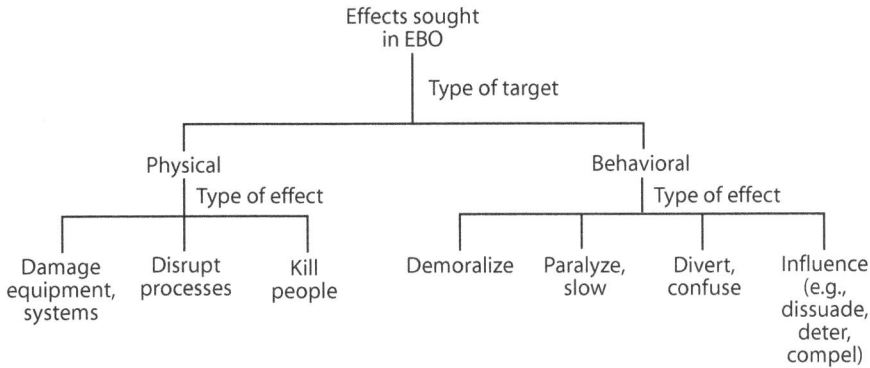

Figure 2.4. RAND's taxonomy of effects. (*Reprinted from* Paul K. Davis, *Effects-Based Operations: A Grand Challenge for the Analytical Community* [Santa Monica, CA: RAND, 2003], 17, http://www.rand.org/pubs/monograph _reports/MR1477/MR1477.ch2.pdf.)

Effects, according to RAND's taxonomy, are divided into physical and behavioral. Based on current USAF doctrine, counterspace effects are physical and behavioral in nature. For example, AFDD 2-2.1, *Counterspace Operations*, highlights the physical and behavioral effects inherent in counterspace operations. See table 2.2 for offensive effects and table 2.3 for defensive effects.

Table 2.2. Offensive counterspace effects

	OCS Physical	OCS Behavioral
	Destruction	Deception
	Degradation	
	Disruption	
	Denial	

Adapted from AFDD 2-2.1, *Counterspace Operations*, 2 August 2004, 31.

Table 2.3. Defensive counterspace effects

	DCS Physical	DCS Behavioral
	Defend	Deter
	Recover	

Adapted from AFDD 2-2.1, *Counterspace Operations*, 2 August 2004, 25.

An effect, either offensive or defensive, must center on the outcome of the intended action. "Effects consist of a full range of outcomes, events, or consequences that result from a specific action."[25] Proper articulation of counterspace effects is a critical first step in supporting a military strategy of CT designed to meet the overall national strategy. Whether physical or behavioral, effects occur in warfare as either direct or indirect. A direct effect results from the action, such as destruction, with "no intervening effect or mechanism between act or outcome."[26] On the other hand, an indirect effect, such as degradation, results "often from the cumulative or cascading result of many combined direct effects."[27] As noted in *Thinking Effects*, indirect effects often contain a temporal element and are "typically more difficult to recognize than direct effects."[28]

Effects, therefore, serve as the means by which military forces reduce the scope and the capability of transnational terrorist networks. Consequently, the expression of offensive and DCS effects must focus on physical as well as behavioral effects. Additionally, proper expression of a desired effect serves not as an end point in strategy but as a starting point for effects, which are fundamentally intended results. To be accomplished, intended results must be measured. Therefore, complete counterspace strategy must be comprised of a desired effect as well as a measure to determine if the effect is achieved. The challenge in counterspace EBO is not in expressing effects but in delivering on effects, which means an ability to assess effects—physical or behavioral and direct or indirect.

Fundamentally, the challenge of assessing counterspace effects results from several issues facing modern military operations. First, the focus of counterspace effects, in our case transnational terrorist networks, is challenging to model and analyze. Second, the military readily adapts to the current evolution in information technology; however, the military remains less informed on the accompanying evolution in information theory, which serves to illuminate the process of assessing stated effects.

The information theories serve two purposes for military planners: first, theories provide a reasoned set of principles necessary for a better understanding of information systems used by transnational terrorist networks; and second, these principles serve to inform assessment of effects and why effects are achieved or not achieved. Finally, due to the transnational nature of terrorist networks, assessment naturally occurs across CCDR boundaries. Consequently, military planners must consider various options involving detailed coordination in determining the proper methods to conduct counterspace assessment.

RAND's analysis of the current situation of modeling and analysis highlights several deficiencies in current military planning capabilities. As illustrated in figure 2.5, the current state of modeling and analysis is focused almost exclusively on military forces in a head-on-head conflict.[29] The RAND article concludes that the dashed "portions of the assessment indicate where the model and analysis tend to be quite thin."[30] Even though the lines are not dashed, the most extreme border of the chart indicates an ideal situation not currently available to military planners.[31]

Several reasons impede military planners from reaching an ideal state of modeling and analysis; however, the concept of unpredictability and adaptability surfaces.[32] Quite simply, the reason for unpredictability is a function of the involvement "of antagonists in war," and these antagonists "are human beings who are regularly making assessments and decisions and taking actions. The 'systems' that one is trying to affect is dynamic, and many of its changes are observable—if at all—only indirectly and after delays."[33]

While challenges exist in modeling and analysis, the expression of counterspace effects remains a requirement for effective military planning in CT operations. With a known limitation in modeling and analysis, a planning and execution challenge confronts military planners with an assessment dilemma—how to determine desired effects. Planners must realize that in assessment "one can always choose a coarser or finer metric."[34]

The art of assessment in counterspace operations lies in determining the metric for assessment—a determination influenced by available assessment capabilities. Furthermore, planners must realize that complete assessment of an effect is often late to need. One hundred percent accuracy in assessment, while ideal, is often unrealistic. "There is a limit on the accuracy of any prediction of a given system, set by the characteris-

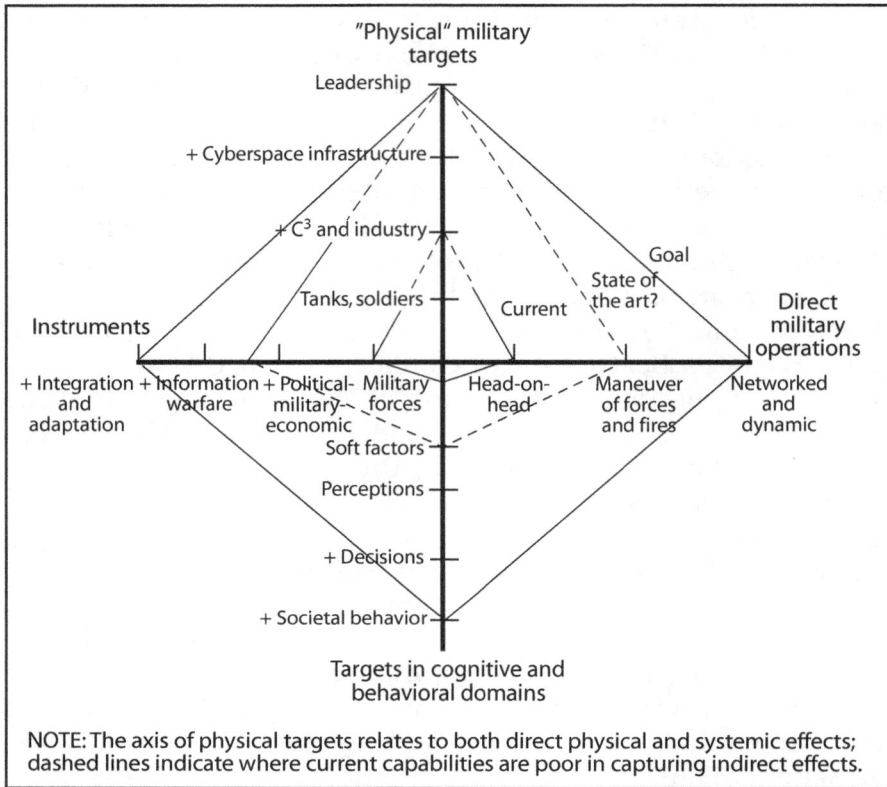

NOTE: The axis of physical targets relates to both direct physical and systemic effects; dashed lines indicate where current capabilities are poor in capturing indirect effects.

Figure 2.5. Characterizing the baseline, state of the art, and goal. (*Reprinted from* Paul K. Davis, *Effects-Based Operations: A Grand Challenge for the Analytical Community* [Santa Monica, CA: RAND, 2003], 9, http://www .rand.org/pubs/monograph_reports/MR1477/MR1477.ch2.pdf.)

tics of the system itself (limited precision measurement, sensitive dependence on initial conditions, etc.)."[35]

While various information theories influence assessment, military planners considering counterspace effects must be aware of the concept of complex adaptive systems (CAS). Examination of CAS serves a vital role in the discussion of assessing counterspace effects. Jurgen Jost highlights the unique nature of CAS: "A complex adaptive system is situated in an environment. The environment is always more complex than the system itself, and therefore, it can never be completely predictable" and "only regularities are useful for the system."[36] Jost notes that regularities serve a vital purpose for a system. "A system will itself be defined by regularities that it constructs from its input and that are maintained through and expressed by internal processes."[37]

Consequently, military planners seeking counterspace effects must not merely focus assessment capabilities on the system targeted for effect but on the environment that interacts with the system as well. By focusing simply on the system targeted for effect, a portion of the assessment equation is conspicuously absent. Thus, military planners usually assure themselves of falling short of meeting the desired effect because the assessment strategy is incomplete or improperly oriented prior to, during, or after execution. Reorientation of assessment, to include the targeted system as well as the terrorist network's use of it, is a prerequisite for military success.

The Targeted System

As stated, reorientation toward the targeted system becomes essential for counterspace EBO. In the case of terrorist networks this involves several elements: organizational structure, COG identification, and an understanding of the action to effect the objective kill chain.

Transnational terrorist network organizational structure informs planners and provides a means of identifying essential elements necessary for the network to function. To better understand terrorist network organizational structure, Robert Keidel provides a model for organizational analysis. In the model, Keidel highlights three organizational design trade-offs that outline essential elements of an organization and how it functions: control, cooperation, and autonomy.[38] With a better understanding of these organizational trade-offs, proper application of counterspace operations through EBO is more likely. Figure 2.6 shows these trade-offs. As an example, Jerrold Post notes that "Al Qaeda was reorganized in 1998 to enable the organization to more effectively manage its assets and pursue its goals."[39] "Strategic and tactical direction comes from Al Qaida's Consultation Council (Majis al-Shura) consisting of five

41

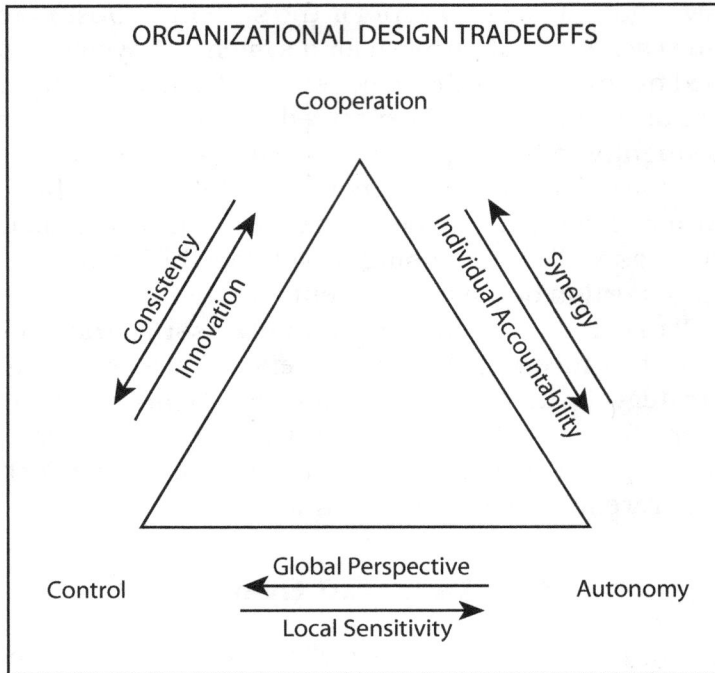

ORGANIZATIONAL DESIGN TRADEOFFS

Cooperation

Consistency
Innovation

Individual Accountability
Synergy

Control

Global Perspective
Local Sensitivity

Autonomy

Figure 2.6. Organizational design trade-offs. (*Reprinted from* Robert W. Keidel, *Seeing Organizational Patterns: A New Theory and Language of Organizational Design* [San Francisco: Berrett-Kockler Publishing, 1995], 6.)

committees (Military, Business, Communications, Islamic Studies and Media)."[40]

Using Keidel's "trade-off" model, al-Qaeda is able to maintain global perspective due in part to its ability to maintain control over the organizations. The control, as Keidel notes, provides the organization with greater ability to maintain a global perspective on operations.[41]

Cooperation appears to be the hallmark of al-Qaeda. Post summarizes al-Qaeda's organization as "a loose umbrella organization of semi-autonomous terrorist groups."[42] Consequently, al-Qaeda appears to have traded consistency in terrorist operations for innovation. In short, al-Qaeda forms loose confederations among terrorist organizations to promote its agenda.

Finally, al-Qaeda appears to provide "guidance, coordination, and financial and logistical facilitation" to supporting terrorist networks.[43] As a result, it appears that al-Qaeda appreciates the synergy of the loose confederations while still maintaining a certain degree of control over their actions, thus limiting autonomy. The result influences targeting—a centrally controlled network seeking cooperation among a loose and ever-changing confederation of terrorist organizations. The net effect is a global perspective leveraging innovation and synergy through diverse association with other terrorist networks.

With a better understanding of the network's organization, planners are able to conduct COG analysis more effectively. Dr. Joe Strange's model provides excellent insight into a transnational terrorist network utilizing COG analysis.

Table 2.4. Dr. Strange's COG model

Dr. Strange's Model	Example
Centers of gravity	Leadership
Critical capability	Remaining informed and communicating with others
Critical requirement	Resources and means to receive intelligence as well as the resources and means to communicate with others
Critical vulnerability	Components of critical requirements which are deficient or vulnerable to neutralization, interdiction, or attack in a manner achieving decisive results

Adapted from Joseph Strange, *Centers of Gravity and Critical Vulnerabilities: Building of the Clausewitzian Foundation So that We Can All Speak the Same Language* (Quantico, VA: Marine Corps University Foundation, 1996), ix.

As shown earlier, offensive counterspace operations (table 2.2) deliver destruction, degradation, disruption, denial, and deception effects, while defensive counterspace operations (table 2.3) deliver defend, recover, and deter effects. Given these effects and the analysis of transnational terrorist network organizations, successful EBO-achieving objectives such as reduction in scope and reduction in capability become more realistic.

For example, utilizing the analysis of EBO in *Thinking Effects*, several options become apparent. Figure 2.7 displays the variety of actions that must occur in order to support the desired effects. Actions and desired effects are connected by causal links. Causal links are critical for targeting and assessment. According to the authors, causal links serve to "explain why the proposed actions are expected to work."[44]

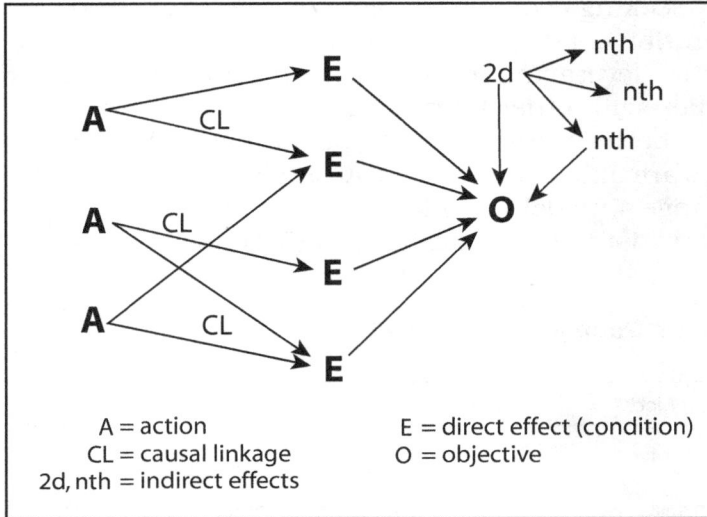

Figure 2.7. Relational model of effects-based operations. (*Adapted from* Edward C. Mann III, Gary Endersby, and Thomas R. Searle, *Thinking Effects: Effects-Based Methodology for Joint Operations* [Maxwell AFB, AL: Air University Press, 2002], 52.)

Consequently, assessment prior to counterspace operations must focus on identification and confirmation of causal links. While not conclusive, Mann's causal links appear to be closely related to Dr. Strange's critical vulnerabilities.

Indirect effects present a challenge to planners. Indirect effects naturally present a temporal challenge to accomplishing an objective that is outside the control of the initiator of the action. For example, Barry Watts discusses the temporal aspect and the challenges faced in Operation Desert Storm. "Resolution of the uncertainty depended on subsequent Iraqi actions, it exemplifies the essential temporal dispersion of fundamental knowledge about military effectiveness."[45] Warfare, as has been stated many times, is a contest between two parties. Planners should expect nothing less in EBO. Consequently, the true measure of effectiveness, in some cases, might rely on adversary action or inaction over time.

Organizational learning provides a way ahead. Specifically, organizations focus on the elements of organizational learning—"gaining experience, building competence, and avoiding the repetition of mistakes, problems, and errors that waste resources."[46] Therefore, as operators are able to train in a more realistic manner, their experience and competence increase. While obvious, the second-order benefits of such training are not as apparent—an increase in explicit and tacit knowledge.[47]

According to Watts, explicit and tacit knowledge serve to remove a certain element of friction in warfare—friction associated with assessment of effects.[48] Explicit knowledge, as defined by Watts, consists of "meaningful information that is available for entry into databases and information systems."[49] Over time and through experience, explicit knowledge of terrorist networks grows. Consequently, COG analysis becomes more objective and accurate as explicit knowledge increases.

However, tacit knowledge, as defined by Watts, refers to "implicit information and processing capabilities that humans carry around inside them by virtue [of] . . . cumulative individual experience."[50] Therefore, gaining experience through consistent and realistic training of counterspace operations in support of CT increases explicit knowledge as well as tacit knowledge. Consequently, a corresponding increase in success of EBO directed at the objectives of reducing the scope and capability of terrorist networks should follow.

Information theory and its relationship to transnational terrorist networks are equally important in the statement and the assessment of counterspace effects. While redundancy is an element of information systems used by transnational terrorist networks, its concept needs to be placed in the proper context. Redundancy enables a network system to operate after a planned or unplanned change in network system status. Information theory, however, reminds military planners that unlike a "failure of a gene is often buffered by the rest of the system. This is not the case for electronic circuits, and to a similar extent, by software networks. Failure of any component typically en[d]s in system's failure, no matter how much [sic] linked is the given unit."[51]

Consequently, information theory illuminates a possible vulnerability in the network systems utilized by terrorists. While adaptability is commonplace among transnational terrorist networks, adaptability of network systems is constrained by design. Accordingly, the implications for assessment appear somewhat clearer. The initial assessment of network systems, critical to maintaining and expanding the scope of transnational terrorist networks, illuminates the level of adaptability afforded to terrorist networks.

In their discussion of information theory, Ricard Sole and Sergei Valverde also identify "three relevant characteristics" that also serve to illuminate a discussion of counterspace effects assessment—"randomness, heterogeneity, and modularity."[52] Table 2.5 shows these characteristics.

Table 2.5. Relevant characteristics of networks

Axes of network	Definition
Randomness	Amount of chance involved in the process of network building
Heterogeneity	Measurement of diversity with respect to the link distribution found in the network
Modularity	Measure of network modularity or standard structural components of the information network

Adapted from Ricard V. Sole and Sergei Valverde, *Information Theory of Complex Networks: On Evolution and Architectural Constraints*, SFI Working Paper 03-11-061 (Santa Fe, NM: Santa Fe Institute, 2003), 2, 4, http://www.santafe.edu/research/publications/workingpapers/03-11-061.pdf.

As network characteristics, Sole and Valverde's randomness, heterogeneity, and modularity begin to define characteristics of information networks used by terrorists. By defining the characteristics of information networks, military planners are more apt to realize potential weaknesses in a planned assessment strategy. For example, assessing an information network as having a high degree of heterogeneity informs planners of the need for additional assessment resources to measure counterspace effects designed to influence the network.

Furthermore, modularity begins to explore the concept of repeatable counterspace effects across information networks. For example, a highly modular information network implies a certain degree of uniformity. Counterspace effects capable of influencing a highly modular network are likely to have similar effects even if the same information network were utilized by a different terrorist network. Consequently, the ability to assess modular networks should become more informed over time and with experience.

Assessment requires the processing of data to gain information on the outcome of an intended counterspace effect. According to Cosma Shalizi, information theory is limited in that data processing inequality suggests that we "can't get more information out of data by processing it than was in there to begin with."[53] However, multiple streams of assessment feeds can be processed to deliver a product greater than the sum of an individual assessment feed. The lesson to military planners assessing counterspace effects is quite simple: do not be one-dimensional in assessment. Multidimensional assessment yields a more complete result and is more capable of determining if a desired effect occurred.

The challenges found in assessing counterspace effects appear to outweigh the challenges of articulating counterspace effects; however, assessment must inform the articulation of effect and not serve to constrain. Arquilla and Ronfeldt summarize the challenge succinctly by stating, "A generation of new assessment methodologies is needed."[54] When considering counterspace effects and counterterrorism operations, two issues seem to rise to the top: parallel warfare requires parallel assessment, and there is a need to pronounce the silent *A* of assessment in (A)F2T2EA.

In order to reduce the scope and the capability of terrorist networks, military planners must consider parallel warfare to achieve devastating effects on every facet of a terrorist network's structure. However, parallel warfare implies an ability to conduct parallel assessment. Yet, the state of parallel assessment necessary to complement parallel warfare remains unclear at best, and likely, fully untested at worst.

One avenue requiring consideration lies in the mutual support current military forces provide each other.[55] By leveraging other forces' capabilities to support counterspace effects assessment, parallel assessment to support parallel warfare becomes more achievable. For example, land force assessment capability could support counterspace effects assessment. By tying seemingly unrelated capabilities together, parallel assessment begins to take form. Through parallel assessment, military planners increase the success of assessment because "if the strategist/analyst/sensor is not present to observe and record an effect, its value as an input to future plans is nil."[56]

F2T2EA is the mantra of the United States Air Force's attack operations. Yet, little discussion centers on the process of assessment needed to focus F2T2EA. Clearly, its construct has a place in CT operations; however, in order for the F2T2EA chain to be effective in CT operations, assessment must focus on F2T2EA. As outlined above, assessment is essential to realizing effects. Without proper assessment, it is unlikely forces are effectively oriented to find or fix most targets requiring engagement. Consequently, assessment is a precondition for effective F2T2EA.

Like the F2T2EA process, Colonel Boyd's OODA loop model serves as an effective method for coping with the challenges of articulating and assessing counterspace effects. His model supports many aspects of the decision cycle critical to counterspace operations in support of CT. However, the model serves a critical role primarily as a mode for analysis and synthesis because "without analysis and synthesis, across a variety of domains or across a variety of competing independent channels of information, we cannot evolve new repertoires to deal with unfamiliar phenomena and unforeseen change."[57]

The model, as Robert Coram suggests, is Colonel Boyd's most famous legacy, yet likely the least understood.[58] Most likely, all military personnel discussed Boyd's OODA loop model during their professional military education. Unfortunately, little discussion centered on key aspects of prosecuting the model. The model and its execution were likely discussed in serial fashion. Speed, most instructors taught, was the central theme of the model. The speed in executing the model assured victory over an adversary. To understand these concepts and nothing else, students are left at best with a partial understanding of the model and its utility to military operations. Most often, students are not instructed utilizing the model in figure 2.8.

Dr. Grant T. Hammond conducted countless hours of interviews with Colonel Boyd and captured the essence of Boyd's contribution to current military thought in *The Mind of War:*

John Boyd and American Security. Dr. Hammond's work captures a nuance lost on most military personnel instructed on the OODA loop: orientation informs observation. Dr. Hammond writes, "Note how orientation, what Boyd has always called the big O, shapes observation, shapes decision, shapes action, and in turn is shaped by the feedback and other phenomena coming into our sensing or observation window of the world."[59]

In terms applicable to counterspace effects and CT operations, military planners must be properly oriented in order to decide on what counterspace effects to accomplish; on what actions to take in order to achieve the desired counterspace effects; and finally, in a position to observe and assess the counterspace effects. Without proper orientation, counterspace effects are likely to achieve substandard results.

Orientation also serves another vital purpose. It determines the tempo at which Boyd's OODA loop is prosecuted. The tempo may vary—quicker execution of the OODA loop is often better, but not always. In "The Cult of the Quick," Dr. Thomas Hugh captures the military's fascination with speed and the challenges posed in continually executing rapidly. "Obsession with speed denies the fundamental truth that in strategy, everything is contextual, and circumstance is paramount. It transforms doctrine into dogma."[60]

The element of time, as Dr. Hugh notes, is "distinct from speed, [and] is of course an essential element of war. One keen observer believes it 'will rule tactically and operationally' and is 'undoubtedly the least forgiving of error among strategy's dimensions.'"[61] Orientation dictates the tempo of counterspace operations in support of CT and serves the strategist well. As former commandant of the US Marine Corps Gen Charles Krulak commented on the application of the OODA loop, "Boyd's OODA loop taught officers how to use 'time as an ally.'"[62]

The OODA loop serves military planners well when considering the appropriate counterspace effects and assessment strategies in CT operations. Proper orientation guides effects and assessment. It enables planners to use time as an ally, an ally that serves to inform planners on the appropriate time to accelerate or decelerate tempo. By utilizing Boyd's model, planners better understand the terrorist network and its capabilities and limitations. With understanding, offensive and defensive

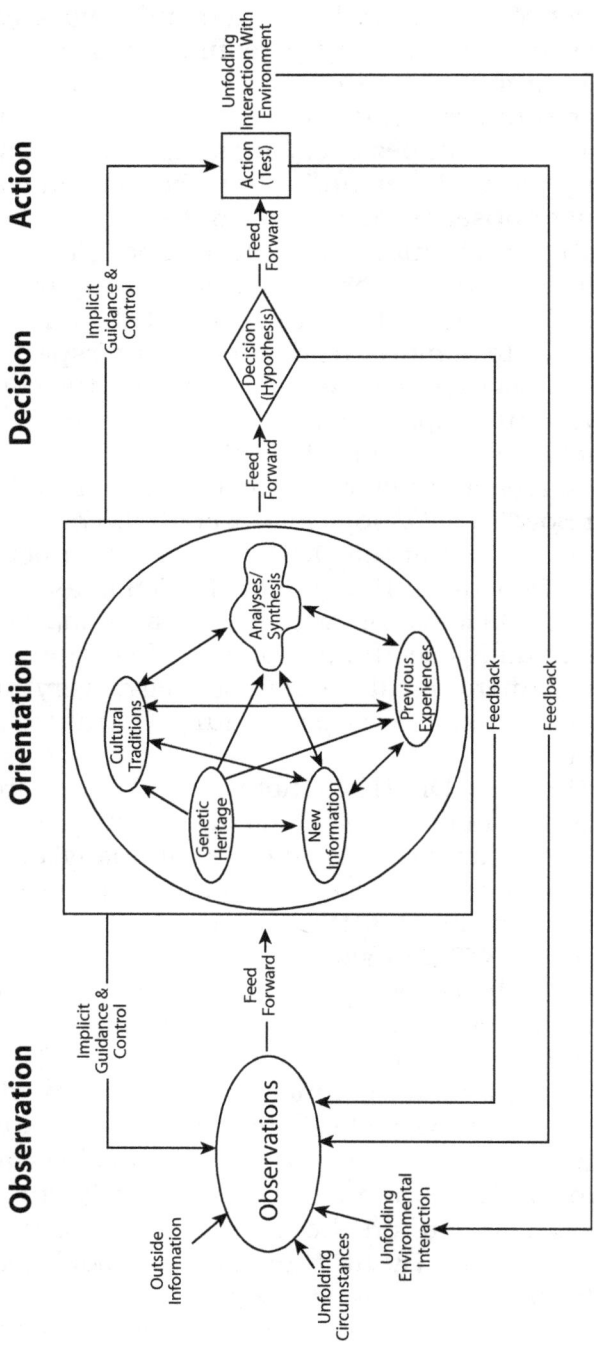

Figure 2.8. Boyd's final sketch of the OODA loop. *(Reprinted from* Grant T. Hammond, *The Mind of War: John Boyd and American Security* [Washington, DC: Smithsonian Books, 2001], 190.)

operations and the associated tempo of these operations are more effectively integrated with greater effect and success. Yet, to achieve superiority in the medium of space and deliver as well as assess effects, military forces must conduct consistent and realistic training.

Consistent and Realistic Training in Counterspace Operations

For [the Romans] do not begin to use their weapons first in time of war, nor do they then put their hands first into motion, having been idle in times of peace; but as if their weapons were part of themselves, they never have any truce from warlike exercises . . . nor would he be mistaken that would call their exercises unbloody battles, and their battles bloody exercises.

—Flavius Josephus

Superiority in a medium, as well as the ability to deliver and assess effects, relies almost solely on consistent and realistic training. For without consistent and realistic training, organizational learning decays over time.[63] According to Anthony DiBella and Edwin News, three essential elements comprise the foundation of organizational learning: gaining experience, building competence, and avoiding the repetition of mistakes, problems, and errors that waste resources.[64] In the history of modern air warfare, one military organization based future combat operations on consistent and realistic training—USAF fighter combat capability—after Vietnam. By examining the rise of USAF fighter combat training, a road map for consistent and realistic counterspace operations becomes more apparent.

The exact point in time for what some call a training revolution in USAF fighter capability is debatable. However, the driving force behind the institutionalization of organizational learning that led to an increase in USAF fighter capability remains, without question, Gen Wilbur L. "Bill" Creech. The cornerstone of organizational learning for fighters mirrored the textbook definition. First, fighter training required a realistic threat—the

Aggressors. Second, fighters needed the ability to objectively assess performance—the debrief assisted by modern technology. Finally, tactics, techniques, and procedures required an exercise environment—Red Flag.[65]

At nearly the same time these concepts were coming online, instructors at the USAF Fighter Weapons School advanced the concept of the building-block approach.[66] According to C. R. Anderegg, the essence of the building-block approach is that "the final objective must drive every aspect of the training program"—an approach to instruction that still exists at the USAF Weapons School.[67] As Anderegg notes, the development of the building-block approach in the mid-1970s and its articulation in the *USAF Fighter Weapons Review* changed fighter training— "the Winter '76 and Spring '77 issues [of the *USAF Fighter Weapons Review*] . . . represented a turning point in the fighter community."[68]

However, General Creech wanted improvements over existing Tactical Air Force (TAF) training. In the mid-1970s, General Creech remained concerned over TAF proficiency in night combat operations and the TAF's ability to gain and maintain air superiority at night. "Reflecting Creech's long-held opinion that the Air Force lacked a credible capability to fight at night, RED FLAG exercises began to incorporate night operations at least twice per year shortly after Creech assumed command."[69] At a TAF war-fighter conference, General Creech institutionalized the training road map for the TAF:

> 1. We are going to dramatically change our approach, simply because it's wrong. We're now going to make defense roll-back and taking the SAMS [surface-to-air missile sites] out our first order of business.
>
> 2. We'll train at low altitude, sure, but we'll also emphasize training at high altitude with the munitions that work.
>
> 3. We'll go on a full court press to develop and field the systems and munitions that fit our new tactics.
>
> 4. We'll also launch a major effort to educate tactical people throughout the Air Force on this major shift and the reasoning that lies behind it.[70]

General Creech also adopted the building-block approach to exercises as well when he "insisted that not every mission at

RED FLAG be flown as if it were 'the first mission, on the first second, on the first day of the war.'"[71]

Furthermore, General Creech changed the method of Red Flag training in two dramatic ways. First, he emphasized the role of assessment and learning from experience. According to Lt Col James Slife, commanders of units participating in Red Flag were "placed in charge of participants' training experience with no formal benefit of others' experience. . . . We saw the same mistakes over and over."[72] General Creech drove change so others learned from previous experience. Second, in order to gain experience and build competency, the concept of "kill removal" was adopted at Red Flag. Aircraft assessed as "dead" were removed from the fight and returned to base. Consequently, aircrews experienced a more realistic training environment in which to hone their combat skills.

Assessment served as a cornerstone of the USAF fighter training program. Instrumental in building a realistic training environment capable of assessing training, the TAF spent more than "$600 million on range improvements and instrumentation. . . . Realism of the threats on the Nellis ranges increased substantially."[73] During this period and as it remains today, the necessity of assessment in training is captured best by the quote "if it ain't on film, it ain't."[74]

Under General Creech's leadership, the TAF set the standard for USAF fighter training, a standard that remains with Air Combat Command (ACC) today. The extent of the revolution in USAF fighter training was not lost during a January 2001 report of the Defense Science Board (DSB) titled *Training Superiority and Training Surprise.* The DSB concluded that "the superb performance of our military in the 1990s was not just a result of technological superiority but equally of training superiority" founded on "new combat training approaches invented 30 years ago, . . . instrumented ranges and combat training centers."[75]

Consequently, superiority in a medium and the effects as well as the ability to assess effects becomes a function of training superiority as well as technological superiority. For superiority through counterspace effects and assessment to occur in CT operations, the foundational elements of organizational learning must be present, "gaining experience, building competence, and avoiding the repetition of mistakes, problems, and errors that waste resources."[76]

The need is apparent. Space superiority and the associated counterspace effects are critical supporting elements of the *National Strategy for Combating Terrorism*. For the USAF, doctrine arrived as early as November 2001. Counterspace doctrine expanded significantly in August 2004 with the publication of AFDD 2-2.1. The challenge now is to understand the organizational learning impact: gaining experience, building competency, and avoiding a repetition of mistakes.

The USAF gains experience through a variety of means. However, exercising in peacetime with combat forces that one expects to fight in combat usually produces the best combat results. Exercises serve a vital role in gaining experience and "serve to orient and reorient."[77] Exercises at all levels achieve many results; however, exercises provide a valuable service for the training audience that builds experience and ensures "better decisions about the future."[78]

Since the publication of AFDD 2-2 in 2001, counterspace experience in support of special operations forces (SOF) and the mission area of CT seems to be lacking for many reasons. The need for exercising is apparent to Headquarters Air Force Special Operations Command (AFSOC) and Air Force Space Command (AFSPC); however, the commands appear limited in their ability to introduce counterspace operations into a counterterrorism exercise. In a recent interview, AFSOC space operations division personnel noted the following challenges:

> Counterspace is a new capability that AFSOC needs to see integrated into exercises to begin training before we go to the fight. . . . Integration occurs as an afterthought and orders of battle are not updated; often [there are] no established master scenario events lists tailored to special operations forces, operations support; and we have not exercised integrating directly with counterspace subject matter experts.[79]

When discussing the issue with AFSPC exercise planners, the planners noted, "No one [in the division] is aware of any time we've denied support to Special Forces, but we also don't have a record of when they requested it."[80] While initially disturbing, Headquarters AFSPC exercise planners provided a possible reason. "We may indirectly support SOCEUR while directly supporting [US]EUCOM [United States European Command]. A good example is [US]EUCOM's SHARP FOCUS '05 exercise, which includes SOCOM's FLINTLOCK '05," and "SOCPAC decided to integrate directly into TERMINAL FURY '05 instead of building a separate exercise."[81]

In order to gain experience, consistent and realistic training must become a priority at AFSOC and AFSPC. The benefits are clear, a consistent and realistic training environment and regimen where counterspace operations integrate with SOF to achieve desired effects. With a realistic environment and consistent training regimen, military forces reorient toward superiority and are more likely to achieve our national strategy for combating terrorism.

With limited exercise exposure in a CT training environment, the ability to build competency in supporting CT operations becomes quite challenging. Building and retaining competency are also challenged by a nonoptimal career "flow" for a counterspace mission designed to deliver superiority in a different medium. Comparing weight of effort in space manning to the objective of space superiority, current Air Force Personnel Center (AFPC) numbers indicate that "23 percent of company grade space operations positions" deal with space superiority support to CT, "19 percent" support space superiority in general terms, and missile operations account for "58 percent of crew positions."[82]

With 58 percent of crew positions in a career field not related to space superiority, the challenge to retain competency in counterspace operations becomes difficult to imagine because most new accessions receive initial assignment to missile operations for four years. Consequently, reassignment to a career field dealing with space superiority becomes difficult in a second tour, and the skill set accompanying reassignment is limited at best. To compound matters, AFPC encourages "interflow between space and missile mission areas."[83] Thus, the pool of experienced operators in the career fields contributing to space superiority is reduced.

In the DSB's *Training Superiority and Training Surprise* report, the board outlined the impact of limited realistic training and indirectly discussed the impact of limited proficiency in combat skills. The DSB noted that training superiority is a function of military performance and investment in training.

The board also advanced the concept of a "hierarchy of learning curves." Effective training designed to achieve training superiority requires continual advancement up the hierarchy of learning until units achieve "high fidelity training with opposing forces historically found at our national training centers." At these centers, the DSB noted that "a culture of frank, critical feedback involving OPFOR" had occurred.[84] To compound matters, the board also noted, "What is learned is often forgotten."[85] The board concluded that "after training, if complex skills are not constantly exercised, proficiency decays substantially in times as short as a few months."[86] With the substandard career flow, counterspace skills developed to support CT operations begin to "decay over time."[87] As a result, organizational learning with respect to counterspace support to CT becomes inhibited because the current architecture in place is not properly oriented toward space superiority.

Today, AFSPC and Air Education and Training Command (AETC) invest a significant amount of resources in developing competency. In order to take the next step and orient toward superiority, AFSPC and AETC must consider the "borrowing a page from the building-block" approach. "The final objective must drive every aspect of the training program."[88]

Our final objective is space superiority. Consequently, AFSPC must examine the current career flow for space operators and adjust initial and follow-on training to compensate for shortfalls in training not focused on superiority in space. Furthermore, wing recurring training must focus on the primary mission of the unit; however, additional training in areas of space superiority must be developed to retain competency learned in initial qualification training. Finally, AFSPC must integrate elements of existing Joint Special Operations University training into the existing space professional training program. By doing so, the command establishes a vital educational link necessary to comprehend the various aspects of special operations.

Finally, organizational learning requires a process to avoid repetition of mistakes. As noted earlier, the data points for exercises involving counterspace operations in support of CT are insufficient to draw conclusions. However, in a recent survey of air operations groups (AOG), the survey in table 2.6 illustrates possible challenges ahead.

Table 2.6. Air operations group survey

Question	Response
Are you satisfied with the debrief process for space following your major exercises?	Debrief experience varies across air operations groups. The spectrum includes weak at best to typically not a portion of the overall air operations center debrief.
What are the qualifications for assessors assessing space operations during your major exercises?	Assessors typically lack a space background. Consequently, assessors provide limited feedback.

Created by Maj Michael J. Lutton, USAF, survey of 607th, 609th, 612th, and 32nd Air Operations Groups, 1 February 2005.

Note: All survey responses were approved by the AOG commanders.

Counterspace support to CT must learn from current AOG experience. To facilitate avoiding repetition of mistakes, subject-matter experts trained as assessors must fulfill the roles of exercise assessors. With experience in the assessor positions, debriefing counterspace support to CT exercises serves the debrief process where lessons learned are captured. With lessons learned, improvement over time should occur.

With improvement in these key organizational learning areas, counterspace operations become more effective at supporting CT operations and directly supporting elements of the *National Strategy for Combating Terrorism*—reduction in scope and reduction in capability. The challenge, however, lies in reorienting toward superiority with respect to counterspace operations and its support to CT. Based on testimony in April 2004, former coordinator for CT Amb. J. Cofer Black testified, "I should stress that while we have made substantial progress toward eradicating the threat posed by al-Qaida, we are on a long, tough road, and we cannot afford to falter."[89]

Conclusion

Following the September 11 attacks, we have forcefully applied the Bush doctrine: any person or government that supports, protects, or harbors terrorists is complicit in the murder of the innocent, and will be held to account. We have done so through our National Strategy to Combat Terrorism, which creates the policy frame-work for coordinated actions to prevent terrorist attacks against the United States, its citizens, its interests, and its friends around the world and, ultimately, to create an international environment inhospitable to terrorists and all those who support them.

—Ambassador-at-large J. Cofer Black
Coordinator for Counterterrorism

As noted earlier, Colonel Boyd achieves what very few authors ever accomplish. He provides the reader with a skill set for approaching the many challenges of the world we live in. Colonel Boyd's famous OODA loop symbolizes the skill set used for the continual process of analysis and synthesis—a means to reorient.

As implied in the *National Strategy for Combating Terrorism,* superiority across all mediums is required to reduce the scope and capability of terrorist networks. In order to achieve space superiority, forces must be capable of delivering and assessing counterspace effects. Training, as history instructs, is vital to superiority in any medium. Additionally, organizations learn when they consistently and realistically train.

The greatest challenge lies in reorienting toward consistent and realistic training for counterspace operations in support of CT. Much work has been done across the USAF by organizations such as AFSPC, Space Warfare Center (SWC), and Air and Space Warfare Center (AWFC). However, reorientation, as Colonel Boyd instructs, remains a continual process—a process critical to success in the world we live in.

In order to orient toward superiority, several areas require additional work. First, the exercise gap must be bridged. Without bridging the gap, experience remains at best incomplete. Furthermore, AFSPC and SWC have taken significant steps to build counterspace operations competency. However, the current career "flow" for space and missile operators inhibits the command's ability to fully realize its contributions to counterspace operations and space superiority. A building-block approach focused on the objective of superiority in space must drive a fundamental review of space operations training. Finally, effective assessment through trained exercise assessors, along with integrated debriefs, remains a prerequisite in avoiding repeating mistakes of the past. Furthermore, the debrief procedure serves as a means of illuminating the need to reorient.

As stated earlier, counterspace operations are not a go-it-alone solution. Coupled with steps outlined to reorient the current focus, effective employment of counterspace effects, supported by assessment, leads to support of CT operations. Balanced with continual organizational learning, superiority in the space medium becomes a reality in CT operations. Without effective superiority in the space medium, our nation concedes the use and capability of the medium of space and all its benefits—once the sole domain of superpowers—to terrorist networks. This is a mistake our nation can ill afford to make as we seek to accomplish the goals set forth in our national strategy.

Notes

1. The Department of State Web site provides the information contained in figure 2.1. It indicates the increase in the percent of "significant" terrorist attacks over the last decade. The total number of terrorist attacks, however, varies year by year. For example, the highest mark of overall terrorist activities in the last 12 years occurred in 1991, with 565 terrorist attacks worldwide. The low occurred in 2002 with 205 attacks occurring. Consequently, while total numbers of attacks do not follow a trend line, significant terrorist attacks have increased over time—"an international incident is judged significant if it results in loss of life or serious injury to persons, major property damage (more than $10,000), and/or is an act or attempt that could reasonably be expected to create the conditions noted." US Department of State, *Chronology of Significant International Terrorist Incidents, 2003* (Revised 22 June 2004), Appendix A, 1, http://www.state.gov/documents/organization/33890.pdf.

2. Pres. George W. Bush, *National Strategy for Combating Terrorism, February 2003* (Washington, DC: White House [Office of the Press Secretary], 14 February 2003), 2, http://www.whitehouse.gov/news/releases/2003/02/20030214-7.html.

3. Examination of the definitions of *superiority* highlights several concepts. First, there is an interrelationship between space superiority and successful execution of warfare in the other three mediums, to include special operations. Consequently, by joint definition, a degree of space superiority, like land, sea, and air, is required for joint operations conducted by forces operating in those mediums. Second, the joint definitions of *maritime* and *air superiority* exclude space forces as forces requiring some degree of maritime or air superiority to conduct operations. For example, a degree of air superiority might be required to destroy an enemy capability inhibiting space operations.

Furthermore, a degree of maritime superiority might be required to defend critical elements necessary for space operations to continue. Consequently, the current joint definitions of maritime and air superiority do not fully recognize the interdependence of the mediums and require further evaluation.

4. Lt Col Gregory M. Billman, "The 'Space' of Aerospace Power: Why and How" (master's thesis, University of Pittsburgh, May 2000), 185.

5. Stephen Sloan, *Beating International Terrorism: An Action Strategy for Preemption and Punishment* (Maxwell AFB, AL: Air University Press, April 2000), 22–23; and Lt Col Dennis M. Drew, "Of Trees and Leaves: A New View of Doctrine," *Air University Review* 33, no. 2 (January–February 1982): 43.

6. Benjamin S. Lambeth, *Mastering the Ultimate High Ground: Next Steps in the Military Use of Space*, RAND Report MR-1649-AF (Santa Monica, CA: RAND, 2003), 99.

7. J. Michael Waller, "Iran and Cuba Zap U.S. Satellites," *Insight on the News* (Washington Times Corporation) 19, no. 18 (19 August–1 September 2003): 35.

8. President Bush, *National Strategy*, 2.

9. Thomas P. M. Barnett, *The Pentagon's New Map: War and Peace in the Twenty-First Century* (New York: G. P. Putnam's Sons, 2004), 93.

10. President Bush, *National Strategy*, 10.

11. John Arquilla and David Ronfeldt, "The Advent of Netwar (Revisited)," in *Networks and Netwars: The Future of Terror, Crime, and Militancy*, eds. John Arquilla and David Ronfeldt (Santa Monica, CA: RAND, 2001), 11, http://www.rand.org/pubs/monograph_reports/MR1382/MR1382.ch1.pdf.

12. John R. Boyd, "A Discourse on Winning and Losing," photocopies of briefing slides (Maxwell AFB, AL: Air University Library, August 1987), slide 7. For Boyd's complete "Discourse on Winning and Losing," see "Boyd and Military Strategy," in *Defense and the National Interest*, http://www.d-n-i.net/second_level/boyd_military.htm.

13. Michele Zanini and Sean J. A. Edwards, "The Networking of Terror in the Information Age," in *Networks and Netwars*, 29, http://www.rand.org/publications/mr/mr1382.

14. Arquilla and Ronfeldt, "Advent of Netwar," 11.

15. John Arquilla, David Ronfeldt, and Michele Zanini, "Networks, Netwar, and Information Age Terrorism," in *Strategic Appraisal: The Changing Role of Information in Warfare*, eds. Zalmay Khalilzad, John P. White, and Andrew W. Marshall (Santa Monica, CA: RAND, 1999), 91, http://www.rand.org/publications/MR/MR1016/index.html.

16. Zanini and Edwards, "Networking of Terror," 30.

17. Ibid., 35–36.

18. Ibid., 53.

19. President Bush, *National Strategy*, 13.

20. Arquilla, Ronfeldt, and Zanini, *Information Age Terrorism*, 89–90.

21. Ibid., 80.

22. Ibid.

23. Alfred Thayer Mahan, *The Influence of Sea Power upon History, 1660–1783* (Boston, MA: Little, Brown and Co., 1918), 48.

24. Zanini and Edwards, "Networking of Terror," 50.

25. Edward C. Mann III, Gary Endersby, and Thomas R. Searle, *Thinking Effects: Effects-Based Methodology for Joint Operations* (Maxwell AFB, AL: Air University Press, 2002), 31.

26. Ibid.

27. Ibid.

28. Ibid., 32–33.

29. Paul K. Davis, *Effects-Based Operations: A Grand Challenge for the Analytical Community* (Santa Monica, CA: RAND, 2003), 9, http://www.rand.org/pubs/monograph_reports/MR1477.

30. Ibid.

31. Ibid.

32. Ibid., 26.

33. Ibid.

34. Robert W. Keidel, *Seeing Organizational Patterns: A New Theory and Language of Organizational Design* (San Francisco, CA: Berrett-Kockler Publishing, 1995), 108.

35. Cosma Rohilla Shalizi, *Methods and Techniques of Complex Systems Science: An Overview* (Ann Arbor, MI: Center for the Study of Complex Systems, University of Michigan, 9 July 2003), 34, http://arxiv.org/abs/nlin.AO/0307015.

36. Jurgen Jost, *External and Internal Complexity of Complex Adaptive Systems* (Sante Fe, NM: Sante Fe Institute, 16 December 2003), 1, http://www.santafe.edu/research/publications/workingpapers/03-12-070.pdf.

37. Ibid.

38. Keidel, *Seeing Organizational Patterns*, 6.

39. Jerrold M. Post, MD, *Killing in the Name of God: Osama bin Laden and al Qaeda*, Future Warfare Studies, no. 18 (Maxwell AFB, AL: USAF Counterproliferation Center, November 2002), 15.

40. Ibid.

41. Keidel, *Seeing Organizational Patterns*, 7.

42. Post, *Killing in the Name of God*, 14.

43. Ibid.

44. Mann, Endersby, and Searle, *Thinking Effects*, 51.

45. Barry D. Watts, *Clausewitzian Friction and Future War* (Washington, DC: Institute for National Strategic Studies, National Defense University, 2004), 76.

46. Anthony J. DiBella and Edwin C. News, *How Organizations Learn: An Integrated Strategy for Building Learning Capability* (San Francisco, CA: Jossey Bass Publishers, 1998), 27.

47. Watts, *Clausewitzian Friction and Future War*, 47.

48. Ibid.

49. Ibid.

50. Ibid.

51. Ricard V. Sole and Sergei Valverde, *Information Theory of Complex Networks: On Evolution and Architectural Constraints* (Santa Fe, NM: Santa Fe Insti-

tute, 2003), 1–2, http://www.santafe.edu/research/publications/working papers/03 -11-061.pdf.

52. Ibid., 4.

53. Shalizi, *Complex Systems Science*, 34.

54. John Arquilla and David Ronfeldt, "Information, Power, and Grand Strategy: In Athena's Camp—Section 1," in *In Athena's Camp: Preparing for Conflict in the Information Age*, eds. John Arquilla and David Ronfeldt (Santa Monica, CA: RAND, 1997), 160, http://www.rand.org/publications/MR/MR880/index.html.

55. Maj Kevin B. Glenn, "The Challenge of Assessing Effects-Based Operations in Air Warfare," *Air and Space Power Chronicles*, 24 April 2002, 5, http://www.airpower.maxwell.af.mil/airchronicles/bookrev/glenn.html.

56. Ibid.

57. Grant T. Hammond, *The Mind of War: John Boyd and American Security* (Washington, DC: Smithsonian Institution Press, 2001), 189.

58. Robert Coram, *Boyd: The Fighter Pilot Who Changed the Art of War* (New York: Back Bay Books, 2002), 334.

59. Hammond, *Mind of War*, 191.

60. Dr. Thomas Hughes, "The Cult of the Quick," *Aerospace Power Journal* 15, no. 4 (Winter 2001): 66.

61. Ibid., 58.

62. Ibid., 67.

63. DOD, *Report of the Defense Science Board Task Force on Training Superiority and Training Surprise* (Washington, DC: Office of the Undersecretary of Defense for Acquisition, Technology, and Logistics, January 2001), 4.

64. DiBella and News, *How Organizations Learn*, 27.

65. C. R. Anderegg, *Sierra Hotel: Flying Air Force Fighters in the Decade after Vietnam* (Washington, DC: Air Force History and Museums Program, 2001), 183.

66. Ibid., 54.

67. Ibid.

68. Ibid.

69. Lt Col James C. Slife, *Creech Blue: General Bill Creech and the Reformation of the Tactical Air Forces, 1978–1984* (Maxwell AFB, AL: Air University Press, 2004), 51.

70. Ibid., 30.

71. Ibid., 29.

72. Ibid.

73. Ibid., 52.

74. Anderegg, *Sierra Hotel*, 103.

75. DOD, *Report of the DSB*, 7.

76. DiBella and News, *How Organizations Learn*, 27.

77. Peter Schwartz, *The Art of the Long View* (New York: Doubleday Currency, 1991), 39.

78. Ibid., 9.

79. Maj Robin Daugherty (HQ AFSOC/DON), interview by the author, 8 February 2005.

80. Maj Brian Livergood (HQ AFSPC/XOTX), interview by the author, 27 January 2005.

81. Ibid.

82. The information was taken from *13S Career Path*, figure 1, http:// gum.afpc.randolph.af.mil/cgi-bin/askafpc.cfg/php/enduser/fattach_get .php?p_sid=NzCfk29i&p_tbl=9&p_id=2356&p_created=1140024665&p_olh =0 (accessed 2 June 2006).

83. Ibid.

84. DOD, *Report of the DSB*, 4.

85. Ibid.

86. Ibid.

87. Ibid.

88. Anderegg, *Sierra Hotel*, 54.

89. Ambassador-at-large J. Cofer Black, coordinator for counterterrorism, Department of State, testimony before the House International Relations Committee, Subcommittee on International Terrorism, Washington, DC, 1 April 2004, http://www.state.gov/s/ct/rls/rm/2004/31018.htm.

Chapter 3

It Isn't Space, It's Warfare!

Joint Warfighting Space and the Command and Control of Deployable Space Forces

Maj Mark A. Schuler, USAF

The Air Force has made great strides in integrating space effects into theater combat operations with space operators working day-to-day in theater air and space operations centers (AOC) and on CCDR staffs. However, the ongoing debate on the C2 of deployable space forces has hampered development of theater C2 mechanisms and associated training and exercises. Resolving this long-standing issue will improve the integration of space forces into combat operations.

Space personnel assigned to theaters, the Space Air Forces (SPACEAF or Space AOC), and other elements of the space community have worked with this C2 issue for years; yet it remains unresolved. At the heart of the issue is unity of command, a deeply engrained principle of warfare. In fact, Napoléon Bonaparte said, "Nothing is more important in war than unity of command."[1] Yet, achieving unity of command and unity of effort for space forces continues to challenge military planners, doctrine writers, and staffs. Traditionally, space forces have been thought of as global, and some argue, "Space is inherently global."[2] Newly developed capabilities and organizational constructs may shift that mind-set.

Space operations are rapidly expanding from traditional force-enhancement roles, to include on-orbit, near-space, and deployable space forces, which will be able to provide direct effects on the battlefield to achieve JFC objectives. Deployable counterspace capabilities, like the Counter Communications System (CCS or CounterComm), can deny adversary communications directly in support of the theater war fighter.[3] How will we C2 these new capabilities?

"The Operating Concept for Joint Warfighting Space (JWS)," currently in draft, attempts to provide more dedicated and re-

65

sponsive effects to theater commanders. The mission statement of JWS provides a vision of the future: "Expeditionary space forces develop, plan, and execute responsive JWS operations under JFC control to achieve desired effects of rapid theater response, space superiority and decision superiority to successfully accomplish operational and tactical missions in support of strategic objectives."[4] However, JWS only addresses on-orbit and near-space capabilities in development.[5] This does not resolve the ongoing debate over deployable space forces, such as CCS, which will undoubtedly be part of a growing OCS component of theater campaign plans.

Overview

To determine where we are going with the C2 of deployable space forces, it is important for the reader to understand where we have been. This chapter will first discuss command relationships in Operation Enduring Freedom (OEF), OIF, and recent exercises. The relationships and execution of the relationships have varied widely over time. Myths regarding space power are a key reason for disagreements on C2 of space forces.

To help resolve C2 issues, two myths regarding space power are addressed. The first myth asserts that space power is inherently global. The second myth, fueled by the first, dictates that space power must be centrally controlled globally by a space professional. This will frame our doctrinal discussion.

The chapter continues with a close examination of AFDD 2-2, *Space Operations*, and AFDD 2-2.1, *Counterspace Operations*. While current doctrine addresses the C2 of deployable space forces, the interpretation of the doctrine varies widely. The addition of counterspace capabilities adds a degree of urgency to resolving C2 issues. Counterspace capabilities will be able to provide key effects on the battlefield for the JFC. AFSPC has outlined a vision for counterspace in its *Strategic Master Plan (SMP) FY06 and Beyond*. It includes the newly acquired CCS and other counterspace capabilities.[6] Additionally, the *SMP* outlines a goal of full-theater integration of counterspace capabilities.[7] Is there a way to structure this vision into a concept to support theater JFCs?

JWS has the potential to improve integration of space effects into combat operations while improving responsiveness to the war fighter. Since the concept does not currently include deployable space forces, expanding it to do so will be examined in detail. Ironically, JWS has already incorporated many of the OEF and OIF lessons learned from deployable space forces, laying a solid foundation for expansion. The JWS expansion would normalize the presentation of all space forces dedicated to support the JFC through the transfer of OPCON to the JFC, which will likely be delegated to the COMAFFOR/CFACC.

Past Command Relationships

A variety of command relationships for deployable space forces, including OPCON, TACON, "split-TACON," and direct support, have been used in recent exercises and contingencies.[8] However, we have not achieved a "normalized" presentation of deployable space forces to the theater, despite the language in AFDD 2-2, which states, "When deployed, Air Force space forces are normally attached to an AETF [Air and Space Expeditionary Task Force] under OPCON of the COMAFFOR. When the COMAFFOR is also the JFACC, he may be given TACON of other Service space forces in excess of their organic requirements," thus limiting the scope of the discussion.[9] Although command relationships have been an issue for almost a decade, we will start our examination with OEF.

Operation Enduring Freedom

Command relationships for deployable space forces were an issue during preparations for OEF. Ultimately, command relationships were resolved with the development of a split-TACON relationship and ad hoc C2 procedures. The split-TACON relationship existed between deployable space forces and the CFACC, who had TACON for execution; and commander, Space Air Forces (COMSPACEAF), who had TACON for planning. Imagine the dilemma of a space-operations crew commander receiving conflicting direction from two different organizations with TACON. The OEF experience raises a couple of key questions for war fighters. Is unity of command possible with a "split" C2 relationship? Is space so different that it requires new command relationships not found in our joint or Air Force doctrine?

Operation Iraqi Freedom

US Central Command Air Forces (USCENTAF) and SPACEAF discussed command relationships extensively in preparation for OIF. The CFACC requested TACON while initially, only direct support was being offered. Ultimately, TACON was determined to be the command relationship.[10] However, the coordination of roles and responsibilities between the USCENTAF, Prince Sultan Air Base (PSAB) CAOC, and the SPACEAF AOC continued well into combat operations. This ad hoc coordination of procedures, roles, and responsibilities could have been avoided had the Air Force emerged from OEF with a clear vision for C2 of deployable space forces. Similarly, different organizations took dramatically different lessons from OIF regarding command relationships. Theater AOCs continued to request OPCON/TACON, while the Space AOC maintained that direct support was the correct relationship.

One key takeaway, which all members of the space community should consider, is that the lessons-learned conferences must include all of the principal players. SPACEAF, USCENTAF, and USSTRATCOM all hosted separate lessons-learned conferences following the conclusion of OIF major combat operations. However, all three conferences lacked many of the key players from the other organizations needed to effectively work through outstanding issues or address the wide variance in space "lessons learned."[11] Widely differing accounts of C2 during OIF have emerged. The following is a post-OIF account from the Fourteenth Air Force Weapons and Tactics Division:

> The CFACC often exercises TACON of Navy, Army, and Marine assets. These assets receive C2 from the Air Operations Center where missions are planned, directed, coordinated, and controlled via an Air Tasking Order (ATO). *However, in OIF the CFACC did not command and control space assets.* In fact, during OIF, the CFACC sent guidance in the form of an Air Operations Directive (AOD) to the Space AOC. The AOD provided CFACC guidance for future operations. From this AOD, the Space AOC built a Space Tasking Order [STO], which was approved by the CFACC (SCA) and directed the employment of space forces. Additionally, all combat assessment functions were also performed at the Space AOC. Per

the establishing directive between the CFACC and Space AOC, the CFACC controlled the tempo, timing and effects of space assets. The Space AOC was responsible for the planning. The CFACC did not plan the missions; this was done by the Space AOC strategy and plans divisions. The CFACC did not task assets; this was done via the STO (which was approved by the CFACC). This then raises the question: *"If the CFACC did not plan, task, or assess these assets, what command relationship existed?" This was, in fact, a Direct Support relationship, vice a delegation of TACON to the CFACC.*[12] (emphasis added)

Space personnel who worked in the PSAB CAOC during OIF have a different perspective based on their experience and the memorandum of understanding between CENTAF and SPACEAF.[13] The CFACC exercised TACON of attached space forces during OIF. The PSAB CAOC accomplished operational-level planning, direction, coordination, and control. In addition to the AOD, the CAOC sent master air attack plan (MAAP) guidance to the Space AOC directing timing, tempo, and effects for creation of the unit STOs. The deployed unit STOs, unlike ATOs, incorporate detailed tactical-mission planning. During OIF, this tactical-mission planning was done at the Space AOC in direct support to the CFACC. However, the STO sent to the deployed units was from the CFACC and approved in the PSAB CAOC. The Space AOC was invaluable in conducting tactical-mission planning; however, this should have been transparent to the deployed units since the STO was from the CFACC. Additionally, the CFACC does not conduct tactical-mission planning for Army, Navy, or Marine assets. Space personnel in the CAOC conducted operational-level planning in coordination with Army, Navy, Air Force, and Special Operations personnel for integration of space effects and incorporated them into the AOD and the MAAP. The CFACC planned, tasked, and executed attached space forces from the PSAB CAOC in coordination with joint forces requiring effects in-theater. The PSAB CAOC also conducted operational assessment.[14] Clearly, the roles and responsibilities debate did not end after OIF.

The preceding discussion illustrates the challenges faced with C2 of deployable forces. In OEF, the relationship was split-TACON. In OIF, the CFACC had TACON, and at least some at SPACEAF believed this relationship was direct support. We have clearly not yet achieved unity of command and unity of effort for deployable space forces.

In 2004 the Air Force Doctrine Center (AFDC) and Fourteenth Air Force conducted a series of meetings with theater leaders to discuss command relationships for deployable space forces. While providing a good dialogue, at its core there is a fundamental disagreement on the nature of space-power employment. Direct-support advocates argue, "Current C2 constructs for air, land, and sea might suffice if space power were not different from other forms of military power."[15] We see this kind of thought manifest itself in terms such as *split-TACON*. Space, air, land, and sea forces all have different characteristics and capabilities. However, after thorough review of Joint Publication 0-2, *Unified Action Armed Forces (UNAAF)*, a reader will not find different C2 constructs for air, land, and sea forces. In fact, the joint community treats global space forces like global mobility forces with global C2. In the same vein, a JFC has theater mobility assets assigned or attached and should have theater space assets assigned or attached as well.[16]

The debate over roles and responsibilities within command relationships continues today. Theaters continue to advocate for OPCON/TACON of deployable space forces, and Fourteenth Air Force continues to advocate direct support as the optimal relationship. Support is a command relationship; however, it is "by design, a somewhat vague but very flexible arrangement."[17] The supported commander will exercise general direction, but the supporting commander determines forces, tactics, methods, procedures, and communications.[18] The supporting commander takes actions to fulfill the needs of the supported forces "within existing capabilities, consistent with priorities and requirements of other assigned tasks."[19] Resolving disagreements is difficult when issues arise, since the common superior is the secretary of defense (SecDef).

Space Myths

Recent exercises have included TACON and direct-support relationships. The success or failure of these relationships depends on your point of view. However, the struggle to agree on roles and responsibilities continues, and the lack of a normalized presentation of forces persists. This continued debate on command relationships deflects focus from the full integration of space effects into joint war fighting. While our space doctrine outlines OPCON as the "normal relationship," there has been resistance to efforts by theaters to exercise OPCON of deployable space forces. Two myths of space-power employment play a role in this resistance.

Myth no. 1: Space Power Is Inherently Global

Most of our current space capabilities are on-orbit assets and are part of global constellations. However, we must step back from the generalization that *all* space capabilities are global. The JWS concept addresses this issue and states, "JWS will drive changes to our space doctrine and drive us to reconsider the 'all space is global' dogma."[20] Additionally, our current space doctrine recognizes that there are different types of space forces: global space forces, theater space forces, and theater organic space forces.[21]

Theater space forces, such as our deployable counterspace forces, need to become an organic part of the JTF as effects providers. For example, a JFC planning a campaign requests the CCS to disrupt adversary communications.[22] Assume that prior to planning this operation the CCS was in Colorado Springs waiting for a deployment order. Once deployed, the CCS successfully disrupts required communications as an integral part of the JFC's plan. Following the operation, the CCS returns to Colorado Springs to wait for the next theater requirement. TSgt James Logan of the 76th Space Control Squadron stated that, "it [CCS] is a mobile, no-kidding tool that will be deployed—if needed—to assist theater commanders."[23] The CCS will deploy when required to meet theater requirements and will likely support a single theater. Thus, CCS is a theater space force, not a global space force.

Myth no. 2: Space Power Must Be Centrally Controlled Globally by a Space Professional

This myth is included in Maj M. V. Smith's work, *Ten Propositions Regarding Spacepower*, as proposition no. 4.[24] A variation of this is included in Maj Samuel McNiel's work, *Proposed Tenets of Space Power*, as tenet two.[25] While most space forces are global in nature and require centralized control, not all space-power assets require this global control. We must shift our paradigm, and JWS is starting this shift: "Any assumption that JWS assets must be centrally controlled by commanders outside the supported JFC's area of responsibility (AOR) is counter to this concept. We must think outside the box."[26]

Operation Torch and the Battle of Kasserine Pass taught us valuable lessons about unity of command and the value of centralized theater C2.[27] This is exactly what theater commanders want, centralized theater C2 of space assets launched or deployed specifically to support their operations. However, global space power advocates will argue that with space power we must replace *theater* with *global* and control all space forces on a global basis to prevent inefficient space "penny packets."[28] This argument relies on myth no. 1: space power is inherently global—and is demonstrably false.

Space assets are not alone in their ability to create combat effects in multiple AORs. An F-15E Strike Eagle could strike targets in multiple AORs on a single mission. This does not affect its change of operational control (CHOP) to a JFC when required for combat in a theater. So why are we creating a different standard for space forces? We do not plan and execute air operations with global C2 because an F-15E has the capability to drop munitions in more than one theater, or was apportioned for planning in more than one operations plan (OPLAN). So why should we treat space differently? The CCS has much more in common with an F-15E than with the GPS constellation. The CCS will likely deploy to support a single theater, as compared to the GPS supporting all theaters continuously. The employment of the F-15E or CCS may cause collateral, secondary, and/or tertiary effects in other AORs. In our global information age, the ability to keep effects from crossing AOR boundaries is nearly impossible—kinetically or nonkinetically.

Another often-cited reason for centralized control is the high demand/low density of space forces.[29] Will deployable space forces, such as the CCS, be high-demand assets with combat requirements in multiple AORs at the same time? It is too early to tell, but as we field dedicated capabilities, we must ensure forces are available to support our 1-4-2-1 *NMS* with dedicated assets.[30] Not all space forces are the same, and our emerging deployable, near-space, and tactical on-orbit capabilities must not be forced into an "all space is global and must be centrally controlled" package. Can our space doctrine guide us?

Space Doctrine

AFDD 1 states, "Air and space doctrine is a statement of official sanctioned beliefs and war-fighting principles that describe and guide the proper use of air and space forces in military operations."[31] It also shapes "the manner in which the Air Force organizes, trains, equips, and sustains its force."[32] However, in our space doctrine, it is unclear what the official belief is regarding the C2 of deployable space forces. This lack of clarity impacts how the Air Force organizes, trains, equips, sustains, and employs deployable space forces.

AFDD 2-2, *Space Operations*

AFDD 2-2 is ambiguous enough that it provides commanders little help in establishing command relationships for deployable space forces. Consider this statement from AFDD 2-2: "When the effects are focused primarily on an individual theater [requirements], space forces are normally the responsibility of the theater CINC [geographic combatant commander (GCC)]. These forces can produce strategic, operational or tactical effects."[33] To a theater war fighter, this passage supports a CHOP to theater. In our evolving EBO culture, deployable systems such as CCS can generate critical effects against difficult target systems.

Counterspace systems may be used instead of, or in conjunction with, other kinetic and nonkinetic capabilities to create desired effects. Brig Gen David Deptula writes, "As technological innovation accelerates, 'nonlethal' weapons and cyberwar, enabled by information operations, will become operative means in parallel war."[34] The approval and coordination process should account for collateral, secondary, and/or tertiary effects of employment if it will affect other AORs. However, the war-fighting effects can be focused on the individual theater.

AFDD 2-2 also states,

> USCINCSPACE [Commander, USSTRATCOM (CDRUSSTRATCOM)] would retain OPCON if the deployable space force operation will have global impacts. If the space force's operation only impacts that individual theater, the NCA [President of the United States (POTUS)/SecDef] may direct USCINCSPACE [USSTRATCOM] to transfer the space forces to the geographic CINC [GCC]. *The normal relationship will be OPCON, however, a TACON or support relationship may be appropriate depending on the ability of the theater commander to conduct space operations planning.*[35] (emphasis added)

From our previous discussion on the myth that space is inherently global, we can see how this passage is used to cite why deployable space forces should not be transferred to theater. Some war fighters view any impact (including collateral, secondary, and/or tertiary effects) outside an individual theater as a global impact.

AFDD 2-2 uses the words *effects* and *impacts* somewhat interchangeably. Given our effects-based culture and focus, using *effects* is appropriate. Consider the above passage rewritten in clearer language: CDRUSSTRATCOM would retain OPCON if the space force is deployed by the POTUS/SecDef to provide required effects in multiple theaters. If deployed to provide required effects in an individual theater, the POTUS/SecDef will likely direct USSTRATCOM to transfer the space forces to the GCC. The normal relationship will be OPCON.[36] This language would provide the officially sanctioned and unambiguous belief that if we deploy space forces to provide required effects to an individual theater, they should be OPCON to the JFC they are supporting. The other theaters, which deployed space forces may affect, should be involved in the coordination process, but their involvement does not prevent the transfer of OPCON. Unfortunately, many of the ambiguities from AFDD 2-2 are expanded in our new counterspace doctrine, AFDD 2-2.1.

AFDD 2-2.1, *Counterspace Operations*

The growing importance of counterspace operations in modern warfare became clear on 2 August 2004 with the publication of AFDD 2-2.1. This document "provides operational guidance in the use of air and space power to ensure space superiority."[37] While the C2 section is ambiguous and subject to interpretation, this document addresses key planning issues, including an effects-based approach, legal considerations, course of action (COA) development, targeting, deconfliction, approval authority, rules of engagement (ROE), and assessment. There is also a chapter dedicated to C2 of counterspace forces that includes the decision tree as shown in figure 3.1.

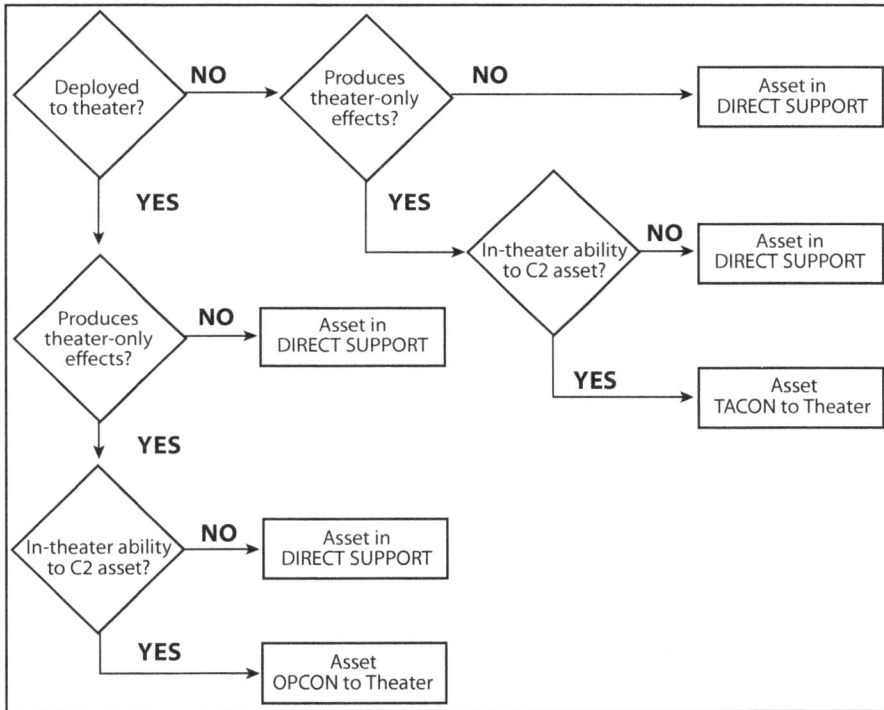

Figure 3.1. C2 decision tree for control of space assets in theater operations. (*Reprinted from* AFDD 2-2.1, *Counterspace Operations*, 2 August 2004, 16.)

The decision tree has three decision questions: (1) deployed to theater? (2) produces theater-only effects? and (3) in-theater ability to command and control assets? These questions are at the core of the debate over C2 of deployable space forces, and senior leaders in-theater and in the space community answer these questions differently based on their perspectives.

Deployed to Theater? Based on the decision tree, if the asset is not in-theater, USSTRATCOM would not transfer OPCON. For instance, if the United States Central Command (USCENTCOM) required a counterspace asset and the asset deployed to the USEUCOM AOR to support USCENTCOM, USSTRATCOM would not transfer OPCON. However, this is not consistent with Air Force doctrine. As highlighted in Doctrine Watch #3 on OPCON, "Forces bedded down in one CINC's AOR but conducting operations in support of a different CINC should be OPCON to the CINC charged with the operational mission (the supported commander)."[38] This question should be removed from the decision tree.

Produces Theater-Only Effects? What should we consider as theater-only effects? Theater commanders can interpret this as producing required effects for an individual theater. Others interpret theater-only effects as no collateral, secondary, or tertiary effects in other theaters. However, space forces are far from unique in their ability to create effects that cross AOR boundaries. Does the kinetic destruction of a phone switch in Baghdad or a Marine killing an unarmed insurgent in Fallujah, on satellite TV, create effects outside USCENTCOM? Yes. In our global information age, it is almost impossible for the United States to conduct military operations without effects spilling across AOR boundaries.

Effects across AOR boundaries are not a space issue; they are a warfare issue. The other GCCs and the Joint Staff/OSD must be involved in coordination to ensure they are aware of possible effects in other AORs. This coordination applies to all joint forces, not just space forces. A better question for the decision tree would be: Is the asset producing required effects for an individual theater?

In-Theater Ability to Command and Control Assets? OEF and OIF have demonstrated the capability to C2 space forces in-theater. During these conflicts, operational-level planning and execution was conducted in the CENTAF PSAB CAOC. Theater space-integration efforts have increased dramatically over the past five years. Permanent-party space integration in the AOCs began with W13S (Space Weapons Officers [SWO]) and has expanded to include 13S (Space Operators) and 1C6 (Enlisted Space Technicians). In 2001 the United States Air

Forces in Europe (USAFE) AOC had two W13S, one 13S, and two 1C6 personnel. In 2004 the USAFE AOC had three W13S, six 13S, and five 1C6 personnel.[39] The Air Force has also focused on getting qualified and trained personnel in the Falconer AOCs. Great strides have been made at improving the training and experience of space operators assigned or attached to Falconer AOCs.[40] Prior to OIF, Maj Gen Franklin J. "Judd" Blaisdell, HQ USAF/XOS, stated, "The Air Force has very highly qualified personnel embedded in our various Air and Space Operations Centers and Combined Air and Space Operations Centers around the world. . . . So you've got great people, a weapons school, qualified individuals that are right there with your air component and space component commanders."[41] Air Force Space Command also has an air expeditionary force (AEF) augmentation program to provide theaters with qualified 13S and 1C6 space operators to meet requirements. W13Ss across the Air Force are postured to deploy, when required, to support contingency requirements.

Traditionally, Falconer AOC space personnel have been O-4 (Major) and below. During OEF and OIF, an SSO was deployed to the CAOC to advise the CFACC. This position has evolved into the DIRSPACEFOR position, which is outlined in AFDD 2.2-1. A responsibility of this position is to "direct and monitor, on behalf of the COMAFFOR/JFACC, space forces and capabilities assigned or attached to the COMAFFOR/JFACC."[42] However, should an advisor "direct" space forces? Space personnel in the AOC are not in the chain of command of the DIRSPACEFOR, and there is certainly potential for confusion regarding the roles and responsibilities of the DIRSPACEFOR. However, in OIF, the SSO (now DIRSPACEFOR) proved invaluable to the CFACC and the space personnel in the AOC, working big-picture issues for the CFACC, such as the SCA delegation. This relieved AOC space personnel of these issues and allowed them to execute their divisional responsibilities. Space personnel are key integrated pieces of the theater AOCs, but do they have the equipment to C2 space forces?

C2 obviously requires a means to communicate. During OEF, a combination of phone, fax, and SIPRNET was used to communicate with attached forces. In OIF, InfoWorkSpace, a key initiative from Joint Expeditionary Force Experiment (JEFX)

'02, provided another means of connectivity.[43] It also provided an additional avenue for *reachback* (behind frontline support) and collaboration. While theaters still lack tactical-planning equipment for deployable space forces, additional tools are in development to further enhance equipment in theater AOCs, including the single integrated space picture (SISP). However, while enhanced equipment will improve theater C2 capabilities, it will also threaten established roles and responsibilities. Col Dwight Miller, vice commander of Fourteenth Air Force, recently stated, "Some people might be tempted to think that if they have a SISP that they can do all of this in-theater with a couple of captains. But because space remains inherently global and supporting multiple theaters simultaneously, the full space effects will still be orchestrated here in the Space AOC."[44] A new operating concept may break the back of the "all space is global" dogma and provide expeditionary space capabilities from on-orbit, near-space, and deployable space forces.

Fork in the Road

A decision on the future of space-operations integration in joint warfare is upon us, and we find ourselves at the proverbial fork in the road. Should we treat space assets supporting the requirements of a single theater just like other assets and CHOP them to theater? Or, should we centrally control all space forces with global C2 through a direct support relationship with the theater(s)? The answer should be based on what best supports the requirements of JFCs.

Doctrine can guide us, as outlined in the *UNAAF*, "C2 of joint operations begins by establishing unity of command through the designation of a JFC with the requisite authority to accomplish assigned tasks using an uncomplicated chain of command."[45] The transfer of OPCON to the JFC, likely delegated to the COMAFFOR/JFACC, will provide the unity of command and unity of effort required for the most effective integration of deployable space forces. Roles and responsibilities are clear, and there is an uncomplicated chain of command for deployed unit planning and execution. AFDD 2-2 has it right, "The normal relationship will be OPCON."[46] The AFSPC *SMP FY06 and*

Beyond presents a vision for the future of deployable counter-space forces.

The *SMP* articulates three strategic goals for counterspace mission-area planners: (1) dominant counterspace capabilities, (2) a balanced mix between space-based or terrestrial (air and surface) forces, and (3) full-theater integration. Full-theater integration would resolve most, if not all, of the outstanding issues. The theater COMAFFOR would plan for counterspace effects, synchronize counterspace effects with joint forces, task counterspace forces directly from theater operations centers, adjust operations during execution, and integrate counterspace feedback into combat/operational assessment. In short, the theater COMAFFOR would plan, synchronize, task, execute, adjust, and assess counterspace operations.[47] While it does not specifically address the command relationship, this is consistent with OPCON/TACON to the theater COMAFFOR. Additionally, Gen Lance Lord, commander of AFSPC, recently said, "We want . . . space to be employed like any other theater asset."[48] General Lord and the AFSPC *SMP* have provided the vision, but the hard work is turning the vision into reality. The expansion of JWS, to include deployable space forces, is the right concept at the right time to place a robust complement of war-fighting capabilities under JFC control.

Joint Warfighting Space

The JWS concept developed by AFSPC is a visionary work, which seeks to make space an organic part of JTFs in-theater. It seeks to do this by "optimizing existing space capabilities and developing/employing improved space and near-space systems."[49] There are six attributes outlined in the JWS concept: (1) Responsive—trained, ready, and deployable space forces; (2) Integrated—integrates with air, land, sea, and information forces; (3) Dedicated—when JWS forces CHOP to a JFC, they become dedicated theater assets; (4) Expeditionary—rapidly deployable, employable, and sustainable; (5) Interoperable and Networked—compressed kill chains through networking; and (6) Precision—high level of precision required to produce precision effects.[50]

While deployable space forces are not currently part of the JWS concept, these attributes apply to them as well.

JWS will operate an expeditionary space construct within our current AEF construct.[51] Since space is not so different, effective C2 of space forces can be conducted within existing command relationships and C2 constructs. However, because the current JWS concept fails to address deployable forces, it sets the stage for a scenario where a JFC may have OPCON of an on-orbit asset dedicated to supporting an operation but not have OPCON of a deployable asset sitting outside the command center, also dedicated to supporting operations.

JWS addresses a critical shortfall in the current space architecture by providing dedicated and responsive space forces. Currently, the JFC and JFACC compete against other theaters and national requirements for space assets. Gen John P. Jumper's white paper points out that JWS "takes operational and tactical level warfighting priorities out of competition with strategic priorities."[52] In the past, competition with strategic priorities led to some overall inefficiencies and duplication of efforts. For instance, a JFACC may request space support, which competes with other theaters or national requirements. Since the request may not have a high enough priority to guarantee support, a theater asset may also be tasked. In the future, with dedicated JWS assets, a JFC/JFACC will be able to select the optimal dedicated assets to produce the required effects. The optimal solution may be kinetic or nonkinetic; however, the JFC will have more tools at hand.

Expansion of Joint Warfighting Space

The AFSPC *SMP FY06 and Beyond* outlines a vision for counterspace, which includes full-theater integration.[53] However, given the varying interpretations of current space doctrine, it is difficult to picture how we will execute this vision. While JWS was born under a slightly different context, the overarching concept and key attributes facilitate rapid and effective incorporation of deployable space forces. This expansion would provide a JFC with a range of on-orbit, near-space, and deployable space forces that would be dedicated and responsive to theater requirements. There are clear benefits to expansion of the concept.

Unity of Command

Deployable space forces in an expanded JWS construct would CHOP to the JFC—likely delegated to the COMAFFOR/JFACC. They would be part of an AETF, in a space expeditionary wing (SEW) or space expeditionary group (SEG). For example, the SEG would be composed of a group command element and one or more squadrons. A key component of the SEG would be a mission planning cell (MPC), responsible for tactical-level mission planning based on the theater ATO/integrated tasking order (ITO). Operational- and tactical-level planning and execution would thus reside under a single chain of command, ensuring the unity of command of JWS forces under the JFC. This is a normalized presentation of forces and provides the uncomplicated chain of command outlined in the *UNAAF*.

Standardized Training and Execution of Forces

Resolving the command relationship issue and providing a normalized presentation of forces would allow long-standing training and execution issues to be resolved and standardized. Joint training is traditionally an OPCON function.[54] Prior to OIF, the CFACC conducted joint training events with attached deployable space forces to ensure they were prepared for operations. This training was beneficial and worked out many C2 procedural issues prior to combat operations. As we normalize to an OPCON presentation of forces, standardized AOC and unit training will help ensure forces are prepared for a baseline C2 architecture. An additional dividend will be ongoing training that should occur between JWS units and theater AOCs.

Out-of-cycle training exercises between JWS units and theater AOCs will be necessary to enhance unit and AOC effectiveness and readiness for combat operations. Additionally, AFSPC can effectively organize, train, and equip its forces for CHOP to theater, and provide invaluable assistance in developing training programs and leading attempts to standardize efforts between the theaters. JWS captures the importance of training. "The 'train as you fight' philosophy must be extended to routinely include JWS forces to operationalize space as core versus specialized capabilities."[55] InfoWorkSpace can facilitate training with CONUS-based units as part of quarterly AOC training events. CONUS-based space forces do not have to deploy to work through C2 scenarios, which are very important to the effective employment of space assets.

Dedicated Assets

Deployable space forces will be valuable contributors as an organic part of the JTF. When a JFACC requires the disruption of a critical military communications link, there may be several kinetic and nonkinetic options available. If the JFC/JFACC has OPCON/TACON of the various options, theater planners can find the optimal solution and have the ability to execute it directly with assigned or attached forces. In a direct support relationship, the supporting commander with TACON of counterspace assets may have other priorities and requirements within the assigned tasks, which could prevent the required support from occuring in a timely manner.[56] Thus, the JFACC may have to plan to use other kinetic or nonkinetic options to ensure the desired effects are achieved, even if a deployable counterspace system is the best solution. The proper execution of the JWS can ensure that space assets are optimally contributing to the JFC's efforts.

Trained Personnel to Augment Theater AOCs

Deployable forces, including counterspace forces, are almost certain to be critical components of future theater campaign plans. As discussed earlier, Falconer AOCs have dramatically increased the number of assigned space personnel. However, to effectively plan, task, and direct deployable forces for CHOP to the COMAFFOR/JFACC, additional trained and experienced personnel will be required. JWS can provide these qualified personnel to augment the Falconer AOCs, when required.

JWS personnel will not be liaisons; they will be working for the JFACC. One critique of the current JWS construct suggested—while it mentions permanent-party space personnel—it should address the integration of JWS personnel with permanent-party personnel. Policy should designate JWS personnel to become integral parts of the various Falconer AOC teams, where they will work with permanent-party space personnel to ensure the optimal application of space-force capabilities to create war-fighting effects. Issues with JWS expansion also exist.

Increased Footprint In-Theater

The Air Force made a concerted effort over the past several years to reduce the forward *footprint* (amount of personnel and resources physically present) of AOCs during conflicts. One could certainly argue about the effectiveness of Air Force efforts—considering the more than 1,500-person CAOC during OIF. However, of those 1,500 Airmen, less than 20 were space operators. JWS will increase the space presence in the AOC at a time when the Air Force is attempting to reduce overall numbers. The CHOP of deployable space forces will further increase JWS numbers deploying into the AOC. Perhaps this is looking at the glass half empty.

The Air Force went to great lengths to be inclusive of space operations, and AOCs are now referred to as "air *and space* operations centers." To become true air and space operations centers—a more robust space presence—to support counterspace and overall space support is a move in the right direction for the Air Force and the space community. JWS will require increased AOC space manpower within limited manpower constraints, moving the Air Force beyond the "replace 'air' with 'air and space' mentality." This not only provides graphic evidence of the force-enhancement functions of space but also recognizes the new effects space forces will create on the twenty-first-century battlefield. Additionally, experience gained while working with joint military planners and operators will help build the warrior culture desired in the space community and aid the transition from AFSPC to Space Combat Command.

Expansion of JWS Will Likely Slow JWS Approval

"The Operating Concept for JWS" is currently in draft form, and the rewriting and restaffing required will likely slow the approval of the overall concept. Since the expansion includes the C2 of deployable space forces, the coordination process inside and outside AFSPC could be lengthy. However, there is a positive to the concept still being in draft form.

The draft status of "JWS" provides the opportunity to expand the concept now and expedite resolution of this long-standing issue. Deployable space forces are more mature platforms than future JWS on-orbit and near-space capabilities and can lay a solid foundation for the C2 of future JWS forces. The concept also calls for JWS to provide immediate and near-term capabilities to support JFC needs, which deployable space forces can provide.[57]

USSTRATCOM Position Unknown

USSTRATCOM is currently undergoing a significant reorganization, to include the establishment of the joint space operations center (JSpOC). The Fourteenth Air Force commander has the lead in development of the JSpOC, and initial operational capability was targeted for 1 April 2005.[58] USSTRATCOM's position on how much control it should retain of JWS forces—in particular, deployable space forces—will have an impact on the overall viability of JWS expansion. JWS currently addresses USSTRATCOM Unified Command Plan responsibilities to provide day-to-day global support to unified commanders.[59] USSTRATCOM's position on the CHOP of forces to theater in the JWS concept is unknown.

USSTRATCOM and Components Remain Indispensable

While some on-orbit, near-space, and deployable space forces may CHOP to theater with JWS, USSTRATCOM and its components remain indispensable to the theater war fighter. Assistance with COA development, intelligence, deconfliction, and assessment will be key USSTRATCOM roles in an expanded JWS for deployable space forces. JWS does not seek to recreate the Space AOC/JSpOC in each individual theater. However, it does bring the required footprint forward to conduct operational- and tactical-level planning and execution of JWS forces. USSTRATCOM maintains its global space role and provides critical reachback support to theaters. Global centralized C2 through the JSpOC and national agencies will continue for the vast majority of space forces.

Conclusion

An expanded JWS concept has the potential to revolutionize the integration of space operations in-theater. Global space forces will remain essential to effective JTF operations, while JWS will provide a range of space capabilities dedicated and responsive to the specific requirements of the JFC. An expanded JWS will execute the AFSPC *SMP* as we move beyond the ambiguous doctrine and infinite loop of discussions on roles and responsibilities to execute a concept that recognizes the global and theater perspectives of space power employment.

This chapter examined the experiences of recent exercises and contingencies and illustrated a variety of relationships that have been used with deployable space forces. These included OPCON, TACON, split-TACON, and direct support. However, a shared belief on C2 relationships has been elusive. Unfortunately, the lessons learned have rarely been the same inside and outside the space community. All parties must work together to give future lessons-learned conferences a chance to succeed.

Two myths of space power employment were examined. The first myth asserted that space power was inherently global. While we often think of space forces as on-orbit satellites, there are also deployable space forces, which can deploy and support individual theaters. Thus, space cannot be pigeonholed with a one-size-fits-all "space is global or else" mentality. The current JWS concept is addressing this issue, and it recognizes the need to step back from the space is global dogma. The second myth, built upon the first, dictated that space power must be centrally controlled globally by a space professional. An asset deployed or launched for the specific purpose of supporting a theater JFC is not a global asset and is not being broken into inefficient penny packets. The JFACC can optimize use of dedicated space forces when the forces CHOP to the JFC.

The fork in the road is upon us, and a decision is essential that ensures space is not a different, difficult, and classified sideshow under the big tent of joint-force employment. We should not draw back into global operations centers due to the beliefs of some that "space is different" and "current C2 constructs won't work." The answer is to expand JWS to meet the needs of JFCs by providing dedicated and responsive on-orbit, near-space, and deployable space forces as an organic part of JTFs. The benefits to our war-fighting effectiveness and emerging warrior culture will be immeasurable.

Notes

1. AFDD 2-2, *Space Operations*, 27 Nov 2001, 23.

2. Lt Col Brian E. Fredriksson, "Space Power in Joint Operations: Evolving Concepts," *Air and Space Power Journal* 18, no. 2 (Summer 2004): 86.

3. John A. Tirpak, "Securing the Space Arena," *Air Force Magazine* 87, no. 7 (July 2004): 34.

4. Col Steven R. Prebeck, "Operating Concept for Joint Warfighting Space (JWS)," Draft, HQ AFSPC/XO, 10 Nov 2004, 5.

5. Gen Lance W. Lord, briefing to Gen John P. Jumper, subject: Joint Warfighting Space Update, 21 December 2004.

6. AFSPC, *Strategic Master Plan FY06 and Beyond*, 1 Oct 2003, 25.

7. Ibid., 23.

8. In OEF the CFACC had TACON for execution, and COMSPACEAF had TACON for planning. This was called split-TACON.

9. AFDD 2-2, *Space Operations*, 52.

10. Maj Mark Main, "An Examination of Space Coordinating Authority and Command Relationships for Space Forces" (unpublished paper, Fourteenth Air Force Weapons and Tactics Division, Vandenberg AFB, CA), 7.

11. The personnel at CENTCOM Forward and in the CENTAF CAOC working deployable space force C2 were not invited/did not attend the STRATCOM and AFSPC/Fourteenth Air Force lessons-learned conferences. The CENTAF conference included representation from AFSPC/Fourteenth Air Force/deployed units. However, the representatives from Fourteenth Air Force were not the primary interfaces with CENTAF during OIF. The primary interfaces were the Fourteenth Air Force Strategy Division, Combat Plans Division, and Combat Operations Division chiefs who did not attend.

12. Main, "Examination of Space," 9.

13. There was not an establishing directive between CENTAF and SPACEAF during OIF. A memorandum of understanding was coordinated.

14. This synopsis is based on discussions with personnel assigned to the PSAB CAOC during OIF and discussions at the CENTAF lessons-learned conference.

15. Fredriksson, "Space Power in Joint Operations," 3.

16. AFDD 2-6, *Air Mobility Operations*, 16.

17. JP 0-2, *Unified Action Armed Forces (UNAAF)*, 10 July 2001, III-9.

18. Ibid.

19. Ibid., III-10.

20. Prebeck, "Operating Concept for JWS," 3.

21. AFDD 2-2, *Space Operations*, 26.

22. Adam J. Hebert, "Toward Supremacy in Space," *Air Force Magazine* 88, no. 1 (January 2005): 26, http://www.afa.org/magazine/jan2005/0105space .asp.

23. Ibid.

24. Maj M. V. Smith, *Ten Propositions Regarding Spacepower*, Fairchild Paper (Maxwell AFB, AL: Air University Press, October 2002), 53.

25. Maj Samuel L. McNiel, "Proposed Tenets of Space Power: Six Enduring Truths," *Air and Space Power Journal* 18, no. 2 (Summer 2004): 76.

26. Prebeck, "Operating Concept for JWS," 4.

27. Smith, *Ten Propositions Regarding Spacepower*, 54.

28. Ibid. *Penny packets* is a term used to describe the almost worthless value of airpower when divided amongst ground units. Arthur Coningham, "Development of Tactical Air Forces," *RUSI Journal*, May 1946, 215. Within the space context, global space power advocates believe splitting space forces between theaters can cause space power to be used inefficiently.

29. Fredriksson, "Space Power in Joint Operations," 3.

30. Gen Richard B. Myers, *National Military Strategy of the United States of America, 2004*, 18. The numbers 1-4-2-1 stand for **1** defend the homeland, deter forward in and from **4** regions, conduct **2** overlapping "swift defeat" campaigns, and win **1** decisively.

31. AFDD 1, *Air Force Basic Doctrine*, 17 Nov 2003, 3.

32. Ibid.

33. AFDD 2-2, *Space Operations*, 24. The addition of requirements is based on the context of the preceding paragraph of the same section. "When the effect of employing space assets impacts national or multiple theater requirements, a centralized structure for C2, maintained by USCINCSPACE is best." (ibid.)

34. Brig Gen David A. Deptula, *Effects-Based Operations: Change in the Nature of Warfare* (Arlington, VA: Aerospace Education Foundation, 2001), 22.

35. AFDD 2-2, *Space Operations*, 28. The DOD merged USSPACECOM with USSTRATCOM on 1 October 2002.

36. Ambiguous and inconsistent language makes the coordination of command relationships more difficult rather than providing a guide that can help quickly establish the proper relationships.

37. AFDD 2-2.1, *Counterspace*, 2 Aug 2004, ii.

38. Doctrine Watch #3: *Operational Control (OPCON)*, 4 Nov 1999, https:// www.doctrine.af.mil.

39. The author was a USAFE space functional area manager.

40. *Falconer* is the designation for theater AOCs for USAFE, PACAF, CENTAF, SOUTHAF, and United States Forces in Korea. Fredriksson, "Space Power in Joint Operations," 90.

41. Scott R. Gourley, "Space Warriors," *Military Geospatial Technology* 2, no. 2 (22 Jul 2004), http://www.military-geospatial-technology.com/article .cfm?DocID=553.

42. AFDD 2-2.1, *Counterspace*, 14.

43. InfoWorkSpace is software that provides a collaborative tool. It makes available voice, chat, and file-sharing for authorized users on secure net-

works. This tool was used extensively during OIF, including with deployable space forces.

44. Gourley, "Space Warriors."

45. JP 0-2, *UNAAF*, xiii.

46. AFDD 2-2, *Space Operations*, 28.

47. AFSPC, *Strategic Master Plan*, 23.

48. MSgt Julie Briggs, "Near Space Enhances Joint Warfighting," *Air Force Print News*, 18 February 2005, https://www.af.mil/news/story.asp?storyID=123009865.

49. Prebeck, "Operating Concept for JWS," 9.

50. Ibid., 10.

51. Ibid., 9.

52. Gen John P. Jumper, "White Paper on Joint Warfighting Space," 8 January 2004, 2.

53. AFSPC, *Strategic Master Plan*, 23.

54. JP 0-2, *UNAAF*, III-8.

55. Prebeck, "Operating Concept for JWS," 14.

56. JP 0-2, *UNAAF*, III-10.

57. Prebeck, "Operating Concept for JWS," 2.

58. Gen Lance W. Lord, AFSPC/CC, to distribution, memorandum, 2 March 2005.

59. Prebeck, "Operating Concept for JWS," 4.

Chapter 4

Space Expeditionary Power

A Polemic Strategy for
Space Forces Integration

Maj Patrick A. Brown, USAF, and
Maj John F. Duda, USAF

*Tradition rests on a foundation of great deeds done to-
gether in the past. A keystone of Air Force tradition is
the Aug. 1, 1943, bombing attack on oil refineries at
Ploesti, about 30 miles north of Bucharest, Romania.
That mission stands as a monument not only to the skill
and courage of Air Force crews but also to the ability of
our combat leaders to pull together strands of a broken
plan and salvage limited success from the apparent cer-
tainty of disaster.*

—John L. Frisbee

The 328th Weapons Squadron originates from the 328th
Bombardment Squadron (Heavy), 93rd Bombardment Group,
activated 1 March 1942. Known as the *Traveling Circus*, the
93rd "took the show on the road" with three major deployments
outside of England during World War II.[1] Flying the B-24 Libe-
rator, the most notable deployment for the 93rd and 328th was
Operation Tidal Wave in 1943. Shortly after dawn on 1 August
1943, 177 US Army Air Forces (AAF) B-24s took off from bases
in Libya and headed toward the heavily defended target, deep
inside enemy territory a thousand miles away. The target was
the Ploesti oil fields in Romania, estimated to be supplying 60
percent of Germany's crude oil requirements. Overall damage
to the target was heavy; however, the cost was high. Of 177
planes and 1,726 men who took off on the mission, 54 planes
and 532 men failed to return. Today the 328th continues its
expeditionary mind-set by maintaining mobility status of all
personnel, ready for short-notice deployments.

The instructors at the 328th and the weapons school are some of the most sought-after air- and space-integration experts for major contingency and exercise deployments. The combined squadron expertise on theater combat air forces (CAF) C2, space control employment, and squadron-level operations sets it apart from most organizations. Collectively, squadron personnel have participated in dozens of operations, including OAF, OEF, and OIF; exercises Terminal Fury, Ulchi Focus Lens, Internal Look, and Austere Challenge; and numerous Blue Flags, to name but a few. Every member of the squadron is ready to deploy to a stateside or theater AOC and contribute in any combat operation, plan, or strategy division position with equal skill. The collective CAF expertise and expeditionary readiness of the 328th is the foundation of this chapter, which examines the expeditionary readiness of AFSPC forces.

AFSPC has made great strides in training personnel to fulfill expeditionary roles in command posts and AOCs around the world, and several deployable units were engaged during the most recent conflicts. Yet, AFSPC has not exhibited an expeditionary mind-set. This chapter analyzes these issues in an attempt to find a suitable framework to increase a "space expeditionary force" mind-set within AFSPC to prepare forces for the next major AEF deployment. Implementation of a space expeditionary force strengthens the bonds of AFSPC to the CAF; produces a more competent war fighter; significantly improves space force employment and support to CCDRs; and overall, resolves unity of effort and command issues plaguing the C2 of deployed space forces. Specifically, the proposed construct ensures deployable space assets continue to be led by AFSPC personnel in the deployed environment. It recommends a deputy COMAFFOR for space combining with the current DIR-SPACEFOR construct and an SEG or SEW with an MPC and space expeditionary squadrons attached to the AETF.

Onward from the Past

Some have likened the impetus for this study and attendant conference as the twenty-first-century equivalent of the Air Corps Tactical School at Maxwell Field during the interwar years, whose motto *Proficimus More Irretenti* (We make progress unhindered by custom) might well describe space weapons officers. Instead of the "bomber mafia" advocating for the future of airpower and airpower doctrine, now the "space patch mafia" does the same within the space career field. Openly warned of certain career suicide, these officers continue to push the bounds of space integration to the CAF and are quietly "infecting" AFSPC from within. While the SWO will be the first to discount the "mafia" tag and this antagonistic label, the reality is the SWO sometimes thinks and acts in many ways diametrically opposed to the current AFSPC career-officer culture. Consequently, the clash of Carl von Clausewitz's fascinating trinity: a dynamic, inherently unstable interaction of the forces of violent emotion, chance, and rational calculation, is inevitable.[2] Enmity between theater space officers and AFSPC space officers over force-employment policy has built over time. The theater space officer employs a theater model, attempting to make new ideas work, breaking AFSPC Cold War–based strategic paradigms and making enemies in the process. At what cost though? Certainly, improved space integration at the theater level is a positive result. SWOs will continue to push the limits of space integration and employment; however, they must find more inclusive strategies. Breaking down the walls between theater space officers and leadership, and placing the correct emphasis on cohesion and effects-based decision making is the answer.

Space Integration in the Recent Past

The past four years provide a wealth of data to examine space integration. Space personnel and equipment deployed for OEF, Noble Eagle, and OIF. Numerous exercises, including Blue Flag, Enable Freedom, and Terminal Fury, represent major space-integration events, each yielding further lessons observed and keys to the future AFSPC expeditionary construct. In many cases, SWOs led the way in space integration at the theater level and were a major force for change and development of C2 tactics, techniques, and procedures. While most space assets are global in nature and rightly executed from in-place AFSPC units, several units deployed in support of OEF and OIF, with weapons officers providing tactical C2 for the CFACC. Despite all this, lessons learned from these same officers unabashedly reflect an unorganized force structure and missing layers of leadership within the deployed space forces and at the CAOC. For example, an SSO was deployed to the PSAB CAOC to serve as advisor to the CFACC. Although SWOs integrated success-fully into CAOC divisions, they lacked a lieutenant colonel SWO or space officer within the divisions to interface with the SSO. The same can be said with deployable space forces. The de-ployed squadron commanders lacked a deployed wing- or group-level leader or wing/group planning element. All leader-ship functions were through reachback to AFSPC. This lack of structure posed many problems with communication and coor-dination of actions not argued in this chapter.

During OEF and OIF, direct integration between space and air operations was evident at every level in all operations. The CAOC combat operations space cell actively supported CSAR, TMD, and daily combat operations. Space personnel in combat plans and strategy ensured space was integrated into strategy at the inception and as attack plans were developed. Further, the concepts of operation and operations orders for deployable space forces were also developed in-theater. Space forces were directly supporting air and information operations throughout these conflicts. The same could be said for exercises. However, serious issues arose on how space should be integrated at the theater level. Who was the final authority? Who assumes in-herent risks? What was the SSO's role in planning and execu-tion? A space leader recently stated that the end state for sup-porting space operations "must be for planners to bring space to the fight, rather than integrate it into the fight."[3] Agreeing with this statement, SWOs have been integrating and fighting to bring space to the fight for some time. It is now time for AFSPC to resolve its issues with force presentation and com-mand relationships in order to bring the rest of AFSPC to the fight and, overall, solve unity of command and effort issues. Once resolved, development of deploying forces can receive full consideration.

Issues and Solutions to Command Relationships

Serious issues and challenges with command relationships of space forces arose during the planning for OEF. Shortly following 9/11, US Central Command Air Forces (USCENTAF) deployed to the PSAB CAOC, and space units deployed to support the contingency. When CFACC personnel presented expected command relationships, disagreement ensued over the proper structure. In the end, a split-TACON between planning and execution emerged. In after-action reports most agreed that split-TACON was doctrinally unsound and required a solution before the next engagement. During OIF planning, AFSPC argued for complete control of deployed space forces, while theater personnel argued for TACON to control the execution of units. This was an attempt to control unity of command through strict C2, with the units as the first order. Throughout 2002, debates continued until early November when senior AFSPC and USSTRATCOM leaders declared the theater air component commander would receive TACON. This decision allowed action officers to finalize plans and agreements for employment, resolving the question of who would direct employment.

Drawing on these lessons, the community must establish permanent solutions that all commanders can implement with equal vigor. The starting point in doing so should be an examination of the Air Force's AEF, followed by a discussion on how to organize space expeditionary forces, using basic joint and Air Force doctrine as a guide.

Structuring for a Space Expeditionary Force

The Culture of the . . . Air and Space Expeditionary Force is . . . everyone in the Air Force must understand that the day-to-day operation of the Air Force is absolutely set to the rhythm of the deploying AEF force packages.

—Gen John P. Jumper

As General Jumper stated in his June 2004 sight picture, "Every Airman is expeditionary, every Airman will know his/her place in the AEF system, and every Airman will be prepared to support the CCDR, whether deployed, in CONUS via reachback, or employed at home station. If you are wearing the uniform of the United States Air Force, you are a part of the AEF."[4] The AEF is the USAF methodology for organizing, training, equipping, and sustaining rapidly responsive air and space forces to meet defense-strategy requirements. Through the AEF, the Air Force supports defense-strategy requirements, using a combination of permanently assigned and rotational forces, and is the current construct for presenting AFFOR to the CCDR to meet specific theater requirements. Not only is the AEF concept a function of moving people and equipment to the right place at the right time, it also encompasses a cultural mind-set and fosters mission execution. The Air Force recognized some time ago that a shift in culture was required. Following the long tradition of expeditionary culture in other services, the Air Force embodies men and women with an "expeditionary and warrior mind-set," who understand that our mission is global and who excel in austere, volatile environments. The Air Force once held this mind-set, as evidenced by the 328th participation in the *Return to Ploesti* mission, but a cold-war, garrison mentality changed everything. Today that mentality is gone. A new culture exists that embraces the use of innovative approaches and new technologies, making the Air Force a light, lean, and lethal force anywhere in the world.

So where does AFSPC fit into the AEF concept? First and foremost, as General Jumper believes, every Airman is expeditionary ready. While AFSPC rightly does not maintain 100 percent mobility status on every person assigned to AFSPC, each wing is well versed in the training and deployment requirements of personnel. AFSPC deploys on average 600 to 1,200 personnel per AEF cycle, the majority being security forces. A limited number of operators deploy to AOCs, wing command posts, and task force headquarters, mostly in the USCENTCOM AOR, filling necessary controller, planner, combat operations, and administrative positions. During OEF and OIF, AFSPC deployed personnel within CONUS to cover manning shortfalls in critical positions and posted several squadrons overseas to support USCENTCOM. In the case of the former, these personnel fell under existing forward-deployed leadership for the duration of the deployment. However, the latter deployed as an independent squadron and did not fall under an existing or developed expeditionary group or wing. Further, the tactical-mission planning center that also provided some tactical-level planning for the space forces mission area was located stateside. USSTRATCOM maintained OPCON delegated to the AFSPC component throughout the deployment.

To further understand where AFSPC fits into the AEF, an examination of the AEF's key principles is required. The AEF's key principle is to provide capabilities, focused on effects, to accomplish the mission while balancing the commander's requirements. For our country, the AEF accomplishes **1-4-2-1** *NMS*. Homeland defense is the top priority. At the same time, a forward presence in four areas of the world must be sustainable. Further, within this construct the Air Force must be able to fight two contingencies simultaneously. In doing so the AEF construct will allow the US military to win decisively in one theater, then transition its forces to conclude operation in the second contingency. The concept is intended to instill predictability and stability during steady state and a planned and orderly transition in crisis state. Is AFSPC ready to support this construct with deployable space forces? A change in mind-set within AFSPC will advance this goal. An expeditionary culture is a way to build on this concept.

Space Expeditionary Forces Organized

In the summer of 2001, officers from the 21st Space Wing, Fourteenth Air Force, and the AFDC proposed a Space Expeditionary Concept. The concept was endorsed by the SWC commander, AFDC, AEF Center, and others, and briefed at the weapons school *reblue* that year.[5] When OEF occurred, the expeditionary concept was not employed as previously mentioned. The 21st Space Wing, which actively promoted the expeditionary concept, was told to cease discussing the topic. The space expeditionary concept proposed over four years ago was shelved.

A space expeditionary force (SEF) can work for AFSPC. Implementation would strengthen the bonds of AFSPC to the Air Force, produce a more competent war fighter, and significantly improve space-force employment and support to CCDRs. This construct is intended to provide optimal employment of space forces to achieve the supported commander's objectives. SEFs will also begin to solve the unity of command and effort issues outlined earlier. Further, an SEF structure brings AFSPC forces in-theater with requisite C2 elements for AFSPC forces, and the SEF provides for the proper leadership of space personnel and forces throughout the theater construct. When AFSPC squadrons deploy today, they deploy with no linkage to the AETF structure. The authors' opinion is they should.

Air Force doctrine now defines a DIRSPACEFOR as a senior AFSPC officer serving as the JFACC/COMAFFOR's advisor. However, as the DIRSPACEFOR is currently constructed, the position does not actually direct forces but assists the JFACC in the SCA responsibility, ensuring space access across a theater is coordinated and efficient. Therefore, the DIRSPACEFOR, if so designated, could also be dual-hatted as the deputy COMAFFOR for space when space forces are deployed. Just as the AETF wings report to the COMAFFOR, who employs the forces for the CCDR, space forces could be employed in-theater by the COMAFFOR. Reporting to the COMAFFOR would be either a space group or wing, depending on the number of forces deployed. Using the SEG as the most likely example, the SEG would deploy to a location in-theater with another expeditionary group or wing at the same base as the AOC or with the deployed space units. Embedded with the SEG is a mission planning and operations center much like one at most air expeditionary wings and groups. The current AOC structure would remain unchanged, with the exception of a lieutenant colonel SWO or space officer holding deputy positions in AOC combat operations and plans and dedicated deployed AFSPC personnel supporting embedded SWOs. Collectively, this places the responsibility of planning and directing space forces in the hands of space personnel. Furthermore, an expeditionary construct with requisite C2 in place provides the correct emphasis on war fighting and shortens the coordination lines for all parties. It also provides the foundation for future deployments of space superiority units of all kinds. This construct ensures space assets are managed by space personnel for the theater commander in the deployed environment.

Today, a theater commander's preferred C2 arrangement, deployable space forces, is from the AOC. Unfortunately, the strict employment of these forces violates the long-standing Air Force tenet of centralized control/decentralized execution. A construct that places more emphasis on units executing as tasked and less hands-on manipulation of the units' tactical employment from the AOC is desired. A team of personnel at the AOC would still be required to direct these assets during dynamic events, controlling in the same fashion as the AOC controls aircraft and redirects the fight in motion, retasking and rerolling aircraft, as appropriate. The point of departure presented here is the level of control provided to the units. A tasking order from the AOC consisting of intent, targets, and desired prioritized effects would be provided to the group for additional tactical planning. The current tasking order would become a fragmentary order of the AOC tasking order. The tactics and techniques selected would be the SEG's decision, provided they met the desired effect, previously approved options, and complied with theater constraints and restraints placed in in-theater special instructions (SPINS) and in a separate deconfliction space control order. This represents a significant change not only to how Air Force space forces are employed but also in the employment of these forces as understood by the joint community.

A further discussion on the proposed roles of the deputy COMAFFOR for Space is warranted. One principle issue to resolve with respect to deployable space forces is that of unity of command. The COMAFFOR, according to AFDD 2, "provides unity of command, one of the most widely recognized principles of war." With that said, the JFC normally delegates OPCON over all assigned and attached US Air Force forces (AFFOR), such as is possible with attached deployable space forces, to the COMAFFOR.[6] What advantages does this provide? AFDD 2 states, "The COMAFFOR has responsibility for overseeing the morale, welfare, safety, and security of assigned forces. Subordinate commanders will issue orders and direct actions in support of those responsibilities and will ensure these orders and directives are consistent with the policies and directives of the

COMAFFOR exercising administrative control (ADCON) of those forces."[7] With respect to deployable space forces, they may be attached versus assigned. Accordingly, specified ADCON is given to the commander. As a review, figure 4.1 states the AFDD 2 COMAFFOR-specified ADCON responsibilities.

---

1. Make recommendations to the JFC (or the JFACC, if the COMAFFOR is not the JFACC) on the proper employment of the forces of the US Air Force component.

2. Accomplish assigned tasks for operational missions.

3. Nominate specific units of the Air Force for assignment to theater forces.

4. Organize, train, equip, and sustain assigned and attached Air Force forces for in-theater missions.

5. Maintain reachback to the US Air Force component rear and supporting Air Force units including delineation of responsibilities between forward and rear staff elements.

6. Support operational and exercise plans as requested.

7. Inform the JFC (and the combatant commander, if affected) of planning for changes in logistics support that would significantly affect operational capability or sustainability sufficiently early in the planning process for the JFC to evaluate the proposals prior to final decision or implementation.

8. Provide lateral liaisons with Army, Navy, Marines, Special Operations Forces, and coalition partners.

9. Maintain discipline, including application of the *Uniform Code of Military Justice (UCMJ)*.

10. Establish force protection requirements.

Figure 4.1. COMAFFOR-specified ADCON responsibilities. *(Adapted from* AFDD 2, *Organization and Employment of Aerospace Forces,* 17 Feb 2000, 52–53.)

In short, this concept is a paradigm shift from current practices. By placing AFSPC personnel in key theater positions, the proper assumption of these duties takes place with the appropriate commander to maintain unity of command and effort. Further, in recognition of past arguments, while it is true that most space forces are global in nature and TACON of those forces, such as the GPS or SBIRS, would never be transferred to theater, AFDD 2 does account for deployable or transient forces in-theater. If forces deploy into a theater to conduct operations, AFDD 2 states,

> To the maximum extent possible, specific elements of ADCON should also go forward. When cross AOR operations occur, OPCON of forces should go forward to the commander executing mission, and ADCON will depend on where the forces are based. When forces are forward deployed outside the AOR with the intent of conducting sustained operations in that theater, OPCON should normally go forward to the supported JFC, and ADCON is best transferred to the COMAFFOR for the geographic region in which they are beddown.[8]

Finally, the argument that deployable space forces are global functional forces is presented. AFDD 2 states that if the forces are deployed forward in support of a regional operation and they are "totally committed to that operation and unavailable for other missions, OPCON of these [forces] may go forward to the supported JFC."[9] Assuming deployable space forces are committed to only one operation, it would then make sense to move OPCON forward. The premise of this study's recommendation is that with implementation of space forces moving forward, the necessary AFSPC leadership is also moved forward.

This structure provides the correct leadership for space forces when they need it most. Putting this construct in place will facilitate the correct emphasis on war fighting and shorten coordination lines for all parties. The inherent risk of these operations is placed in the theater on theater commanders. The Space AOC maintains a significant theater reachback role. With AFSPC taking control of assets in-theater in a way never done before, they actually regain control of assets they believed were lost when the air component commander received TACON of the assets.

The final element to this proposed structure is the SEG's MPC. The next chapter outlines the MPC roles and responsibilities and supports the overall argument of this study that planning and execution of "totally committed" deployable space forces *is* the right decision.

Mission Planning Cell Operations

The MPC's primary objectives are to determine optimum methods of accomplishing ATO tasking and then to provide this information to flight crews. MPC responsibilities begin upon receipt of unit tasking, before unit deployment or commencement of hostilities, and continue throughout the campaign.

—AFTTP 3-1.1, *General Planning and Employment Considerations*, 31 May 2004

Detailed combat mission planning in the Air Force is performed by a wing's MPC. The Air Force chooses to perform combat mission planning at this command level because it places the responsibility of how the mission will be executed with the most current tactical expert weapon systems operators. Unfortunately, wing-level or squadron-level space forces within AFSPC do not combat-mission plan. The reasons range from political sensitivities to unit capabilities to today's operational reality that space operations are not conducted through mission-type orders. Due in part to this rationale and other decisions in the past, operational and tactical planning for these units is conducted at the operational war-fighting headquarters. As mentioned earlier, this violates one of the Air Force's central tenets: centralized control/decentralized execution. Overall, this is an ill-advised way to fight wars, as it creates a single point of failure for mission accomplishment at the operational level, while ignoring the expertise to effectively employ any weapon system at the tactical level. Further, deployable space forces' TTPs are not maturing because there is no authority or responsibility placed at the tactical level, arguably the most dynamic portion of war fighting. So in order to address these observations, this section will endorse the MPC construct, including responsibilities, and illustrate how combat mission planning for deployable space forces can more effectively produce effects in support of theater objectives.

An MPC attached to the SEG in this construct is required to place an appropriate level of responsibility and authority at the lowest level of war, the tactical level. Operational planners in the theater AOC would define the boundaries based on JFC guidance and intent, as well as the JFACC's own guidance and intent, while the MPC develops a tactical combat mission plan, complying with the guidance and intent to satisfy the JFACC's air and space attack plan, developed tactical objectives, and tactical tasks. The JFACC's guidance is promulgated not only through a tasking order but also through SPINS and ROE. Political sensitivities and the potential for global effects occur with any employment of force by the United States. These possibilities are dealt with in defined constraints and restraints within the SPINS and ROE. The MPC must understand the theater SPINS and ROE to successfully combat-mission plan and avoid collateral effects much like any other MPC. Further, the MPC will be occupied by current system experts (tacticians and planners), mitigating the likelihood that collateral effects are produced due to inappropriate tasking. The MPC organization is presented in figure 4.2.

Each deployable space unit should provide at least one mission planning expert and one tactics expert to the MPC. Additionally, since space assets perform missions ranging from combat support to space superiority, the MPC gives the capability to plan a composite-force package of space capability and can easily interface with an established air-centric wing operations center's MPC. If the space MPC collaborates with a larger MPC, members will be assigned to applicable packages, such as suppression of enemy air defenses, electronic warfare, C2, and/or CSAR, to aid in tactical planning and integration.

In addition to presenting an SEG with an MPC attached, deployable space forces would need to assign mission commander or package commander responsibilities for the "space package." In designating a commander, it places authority to properly execute the mission at the tactical level with a senior operator, and, more importantly, it enables deployable space forces to execute their mission with the latitude required to be responsive to dynamic situations that typically arise within a

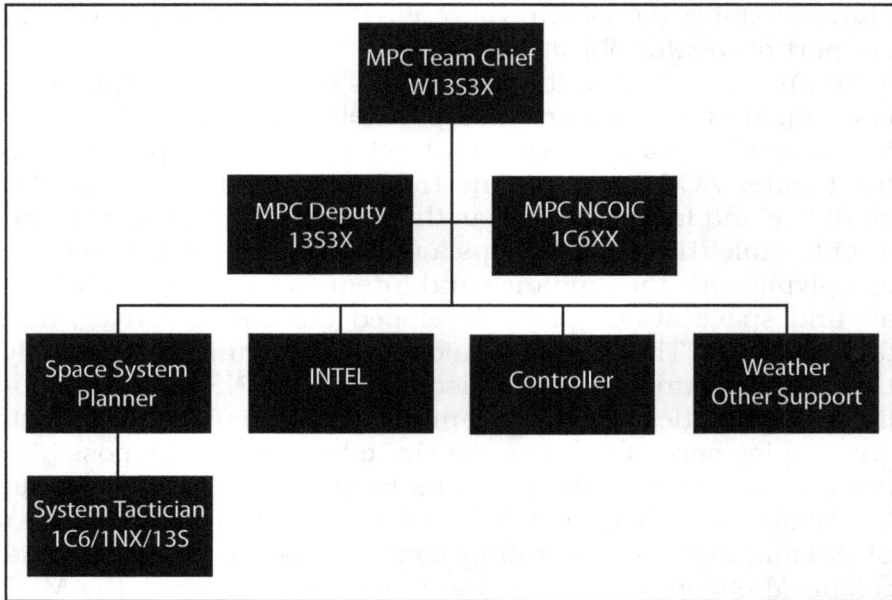

Figure 4.2. Space mission-planning cell organization. (*Created from* Major Duda's collection of published and personal data.)

given vulnerability period. These are the same concepts employed by the remainder of the CAF that enable full-spectrum combat effects. Once the MPC is employed and a mission commander is appointed, determination of MPC and MC responsibilities must be accomplished.

MPC operations are addressed in chapter 3 of AFTTP 3-1.1, *General Planning and Employment Considerations.*[10] The MPC procedures provide an excellent template from which to derive space MPC tasks. A list of major steps to be accomplished by the MPC is included in figure 4.3.

Currently, JSpOC personnel at Vandenberg AFB, California, accomplish these tasks. So why is a change required? First, the Air Force emphasizes effects-based planning, centralized control with unity of command, and decentralized execution as axioms for employing forces. In the current construct, with JSpOC doing all tasks that should be accomplished by a wing-level or group mission-planning function, there is no unity of effort or theater centralized control for deployed space forces

1. Assemble composite force planning team.

2. Perform MC/MPC chief responsibilities and assign responsibilities and deadlines for portions of combat mission plan.

3. Extract data from ATO.

4. Initiate coordination for mission particulars: who, what, when, where, why, how.

5. Compile planning materials, including: charts, imagery (if required), JMEM (space equivalent).

6. Obtain intelligence updates on specific order of battle "space package" is supporting as well as SOB. Represent on chart or map, as required.

7. Mission objective analysis.

8. Meet other package leads to formulate game plan and develop support asset objectives.

9. Identify and mitigate show stoppers.

10. Work with other MDS leads to perform simultaneous detailed mission planning.

11. Reconfirm tasking with AOC for last-minute changes.

12. MC/MPC chief finalize game plan with package lead.

13. MC/MPC chief makes sure materials are clear, concise, and usable by deployable space unit crews.

14. Assemble combat mission folders.

15. Disseminate combat-mission plan using most secure and expeditious means possible.

Figure 4.3. MPC procedures. (*Adapted from* AFTTP 3-1.1, *General Planning and Employment Considerations*, 31 May 04, tables 4-12 through 4-15. [Secret] Information extracted is unclassified.)

supporting a theater commander's plan. Furthermore, it is inappropriate for a Falconer or functional AOC to perform MPC tasks. It also removes the most qualified personnel from the decision loop on how best to achieve effects and could subsequently have negative impacts in the kill chain for space superiority, combat support, C2, and intelligence.

To reiterate, combat-mission planning for space can be performed by a wing- or group-level MPC. AFTTP 3-1.1 gives a reasonable template to follow. Allowing deployment of an SEG with an associated MPC presents space forces to the JFC in the same construct as other AFFORs. Additionally, utilizing the COMAFFOR space and populating the AOC with space personnel enable a repeatable, executable, consistent means for the JFACC to gain and maintain regional space superiority, act as the SCA, and satisfy JFC guidance and intent.

Roles and Responsibilities of Mission Partners

On the surface, this chapter tends to trivialize the complexity of this mission area. It is not done unknowingly. Numerous agencies at all levels of military and government contribute to the planning and execution of deployable space forces. The complexity of the approval process, politics at all levels, intelligence requirements, and overall immaturity in mission area equate to dozens of mission partners, each with a vital part of the puzzle. Therefore, the premise of this study is but one element on how to improve employment of space forces. The roles and responsibilities of all agencies must be categorized and assigned in great detail. It is hoped that the addition of the COMAFFOR roles and an SEG will simplify C2 channels for all agencies.

Joint Space Forces

Joint employment of space forces should also be addressed. Recently, USCENTAF took a bold step to make the DIRSPACEFOR position a joint billet. Titled the joint director of space forces (JDSF), this position calls for an Army or Air Force colonel. An opposite service deputy is also positioned. To the construct presented in this chapter, this will add additional complexity at the AOC to plan, integrate, and coordinate execution of forces. A joint MPC may also be warranted. However, the premise of this chapter still holds true. AFSPC organizes and equips forces to operate in the joint environment, with the same competent leaders deployed to theater. The other services must see the value of in-theater commanders commanding forces and a joint space director assisting all mission partners in the coordination of efforts.

Conclusion

Today in the Combined Air Operations Center you have warriors standing around the table selecting targets, and some of those warriors are space warriors. They're face to face with the kinetic warriors, and they're doing whatever it takes to make sure that we figure out how to get bombs on targets. And more and more these space warriors are taking a bigger role in our minute-to-minute activities. None of this happens without the space warriors we have in all of our services.

—Gen John P. Jumper

Just as Capt John P. Jumper, in the *USAF Fighter Weapons Review*, Winter 1976, spoke of a culture of transformation in the art of training and combat capability, today a culture of transformation in the art and employment of space forces is taking hold in AFSPC.[11] This transformation has not been easy and continues on many levels. SWOs, while small in number compared to the entire command, are leading this transformation and have become very visible on the hotly contested issues of today. During World War II, differences in doctrine and employment perspectives between Army and AAF commanders existed in sharp contrast. Yet, members of the 328th Bombardment Squadron conducted the heroic mission of *Return to Ploesti*, showing airpower's versatility, strategic importance, and expeditionary mindset. That warrior spirit exists today in space officers.

The reality for space weapons officers is that they are charged with integrating, or more aptly bringing, their capability into the CAF. Therefore, a natural conflict exists between the SWOs and AFSPC on how exactly space is employed outside of the global realm. Looking to the future, this divide must close.

Using basic doctrine and the Air Force's AEF construct, a path is ready for AFSPC to follow. AFSPC's endorsement and subsequent commitment to fulfill the obligation to position space forces in the expeditionary construct will enable the major command to best organize, train, equip, and acquire forces to fight and win the global war, while remaining postured to satisfy regional needs as directed by higher commands. This proposed construct will bring AFSPC closer to the fight with the control of deployed space forces, led by AFSPC officers working for the theater commander, and bring SWOs closer to their AFSPC roots.

Notes

1. Addison Earl Baker et al., *Ploesti: When Heroes Filled the Sky*, http://www.homeofheroes.com/wings/part2/09_ploesti.html.

2. Clausewitz speaks of a trinity in his magnum opus *On War*. Clausewitz defines the components of the trinity as (1) primordial violence, hatred, and enmity; (2) the play of chance and probability; and (3) war's element of subordination to rational policy. The trinity for this article is the interaction between the space officers, components, and Air Force/AFSPC policy, creating an adversarial relationship not unlike early airpower theorists within the US Army. Christopher Bassford, *Clausewitz and His Works* (Carlisle Barracks, PA: Army War College, 2002), http://www.clausewitz.com/CWZHOME/CWZSUMM/CWORKHOL.htm.

3. Adam J. Hebert, "Toward Supremacy in Space," *Air Force Magazine* 88, no. 1 (January 2005): 24, http://www.afa.org/magazine/jan2005/.

4. Gen John P. Jumper, "Adapting the AEF—Longer Deployment, More Forces," Chief's Sight Picture, June 2004, http://www.af.mil/library/policy/letters/pl2004_06.html.

5. *Reblue* is an active-duty term for getting back to basic roots. Tech Sgt Andrew Biscoe, "Deployed chief creates Air Force mural for dining-in," Patriot 32, no. 2 (February 2005): 6.

6. AFDD 2, *Organization and Employment of Aerospace Forces*, 17 Feb 2000, 51.

7. Ibid., 52–53.

8. Ibid., 45–46.

9. Ibid.

10. AFTTP 3-1.1, *General Planning and Employment Considerations*, 31 May 2004, chap. 4. (Secret) Information extracted is unclassified.

11. Capt John P. Jumper, "Training Toward Combat Capability (Part One)," *USAF Fighter Weapons Review* 24, no. 4 (Winter 1976): 2, https://www.mil.nellis.af.mil/usafws/wreview/winter76.pdf.

Chapter 5

Theater Space Operations in a Warfighting Headquarters

Maj John R. Thomas, USAF

As space war fighters, these are historic times. Just as the *Mercury 7* astronauts were on the forefront of developing the first manned spaceflight TTP, today's space strategists, planners, and operators are on the forefront of developing the first TTP for the air component that will execute space operations today and in the future. The events of 9/11 have driven the United States into a new combat environment, involving enemies without uniforms, who fight outside defined borders and are sponsored by weak states or nonstate actors. This new strategic environment and the global war on terror (GWOT) have transformed geographic COCOMs into standing joint force headquarters (SJFHQ). Similarly, theater air components are transforming into warfighting headquarters (WFHQ). Military forces able to conduct rapidly executable, full-spectrum operations are the focus of the defense transformation. Theater space operators, as well as those in the United States, must develop operational procedures that keep pace with this ongoing transformation. Theater space operations in this new environment must be responsive, streamlined, and flexible. They must also support full-spectrum operations and adapt to nontraditional planning and execution methods. This chapter will identify five recommendations for addressing these imperatives and improving theater space integration at the operational level.

The New Strategic Environment

Every US government agency is transforming to meet new requirements brought about by this new strategic environment. Changes in policy and strategy have occurred at every level. The *National Security Strategy, September 2002*, outlines the new focus:

> Today, [the] task has changed dramatically. Enemies in the past needed great armies and great industrial capabilities to endanger America. Now, shadowy networks of individuals can bring great chaos and suffering to our shores for less than it costs to purchase a single tank. Terrorists are organized to penetrate open societies and to turn the power of modern technologies against us. The events of September 11, 2001, taught us that weak states . . . can pose as great a danger to our national interests as strong states. Poverty does not make poor people into terrorists and murderers. Yet poverty, weak institutions, and corruption can make weak states vulnerable to terrorist networks and drug cartels within their borders.[1]

Because weak states are vulnerable to terrorist networks, the United States, using all of its instruments of power (i.e., diplomatic, information, military, and economic), must work to support nations to enable them to defend against terrorist network infiltration. The level of military support must not only have the capability to execute major combat operations but also must have the capability to execute a full range of military operations such as noncombatant evacuation operations (NEO) and foreign humanitarian assistance (FHA). These operations move the DOD towards a transformation.

Defense Transformation

The SecDef and the chairman of the Joint Chiefs of Staff (CJCS) have discussed the importance of a transformation to the defense of the United States and its interests:

> The purpose of transformation is to extend key advantages and reduce vulnerabilities. We are now in a long term struggle against persistent, adaptive adversaries, and must transform to prevail.[2]

> Sustaining and increasing the qualitative military advantages the United States enjoys today will require transformation—a transformation achieved by combining technology, intellect, and cultural changes across the joint community. The goal is Full Spectrum Dominance—the ability to control any situation or defeat any adversary across the range of military operations.[3]

The DOD is transforming to operate in this new strategic environment. Each GCC is organizing an SJFHQ, and each major command's air component is organizing a WFHQ. These organizations support a rapid transition to a full range of military operations. Planning methods, such as deliberate planning (DP) and crisis action planning (CAP), are giving way to adaptive planning, allowing strategists to develop "living" OPLANs that are continually updated and ready for execution on much shorter timelines. The draft JP 3-0, "Doctrine for Joint Operations," discusses the range of military operations to include contributions to homeland security (HS), stability operations, and major combat operations (MCO). HS involves worldwide defensive and offensive actions. Stability operations include arms control; enforcement of sanctions and maritime intercept operations (MIO); ensuring freedom of navigation and overflight; FHA; foreign internal defense (FID); NEO; peace operations (PO); strikes and raids; recovery operations; and support to insurgency and CT. MCOs typically involve a joint campaign with multiple phases.[4] The GCC, using the SJFHQ, has a primary role ranging from HS to major combat operations.

Standing Joint Force Headquarters

The SJFHQ model, developed by the United States Joint Forces Command (USJFCOM), is intended to carry the defense transformation into the GCC's AOR. Each SJFHQ includes expertise from various functional areas, such as operations, intel, logistics, and communications, and places them under a single director. USJFCOM's *Doctrinal Implications of the Standing Joint Force Headquarters* states, "The SJFHQ exploits new organizational and operational concepts and technology to enhance the command's peacetime planning efforts, accelerate the efficient formation of a JTFHQ, and facilitate crisis response by the joint force."[5] The SJFHQ is a full-time capability focused on war-fighting readiness. The organization of the SJFHQ staff enhances situational understanding of focus areas, as designated by the GCC, within the AOR. Maintaining a daily focus on these "hot spots" allows the SJFHQ to provide the core capability for a JTF and enables a more rapid transition to any kind of military operation. A significant part of the SJFHQ is the service and functional components. The air components have a plan to quickly adjust to this new construct.

Warfighting Headquarters

The air component within each SJFHQ is organizing into a WFHQ. The separation of these WFHQs from their traditional major command (MAJCOM) management staff serves the purpose of planning and preparing for contingencies within the AOR. Just like the SJFHQ, war-fighting readiness is a WFHQ's primary purpose. The mission of the WFHQ is to plan, command, control, and execute air, space, and information operations (IO) capabilities across the full range of military operations. As outlined in the AFFOR, *Command and Control Enabling Concept*, "WFHQs must be able to transition seamlessly from peacetime, day-to-day activities to major combat operations, and all levels of conflict in between."[6] Just as the SJFHQ must be ready to stand up a JTF, the WFHQ must be prepared to become the JTF. The decision to make the air component WFHQ the JTF will depend on the scope and duration of the operation. An air-centric operation, for example, most likely justifies the WFHQ as the JTF.

Theater Space Operations Imperatives

In order for theater space operations to transform in this new strategic environment, several imperatives must be addressed. First, theater space operations must be responsive, streamlined, and flexible in order to respond to compressed timeline stability operations. Unity of command is as vital to in-theater space operations as it is to in-theater air operations. The most responsive operations occur when the JFACC, as the single responsible commander, has direct access to forces conducting air and space operations in the AOR. Streamlined operations are possible when products used for planning and tasking space forces are standardized with those used for planning and tasking air operations. Maximum flexibility occurs when space strategists and planners within the JAOC work side-by-side with air and IO strategists and planners collocated in the JAOC. Effective integration and synchronization with other component operations also occur in the JAOC through the liaison elements. Also, like any other instrument of military power, theater space operations must support full-spectrum operations. Space operations strategists and planners within the WFHQ must have intimate knowledge of the AOR and the possible range of operations. In coordination with the SJFHQ, strategists and planners within the WFHQ must strive to continually analyze and understand the environment in which they operate. And, theater space operations must support nontraditional planning and execution. Military training in the pre-9/11 era focused around major combat operations lasting weeks, months, or years. Doctrine focused on conducting large-scale operations against an adversary of equal or almost equal capability. Today, most theaters are planning for and conducting operations on very compressed timelines against high-value, fleeting targets. USEUCOM, USCENTCOM, United States Special Operations Command, and USSTRATCOM have planning models that work on similarly compressed timelines. Positions, processes, and products must be in place today in order to conduct rapidly executable, full-spectrum theater space operations in today's new strategic environment.

Recommendations

Great strides have been made in recent years integrating space capabilities at the operational level of war. These five recommendations for the improvement of positions, processes, and products within a WFHQ address theater space operations imperatives and ensure these operations keep pace with the defense transformation. Each theater has implemented portions of these recommendations; however, they are not normalized and standardized across all theaters.

1. Identify standing DIRSPACEFOR per AOR.

Operations Enduring Freedom and Iraqi Freedom and many exercises since have identified the need to have a senior space presence on the COMAFFOR or JFACC personal staff. The position, once known as the SSO, has transformed into the DIRSPACEFOR. According to AFDD 2-2.1, *Counterspace Operations*, "The DIRSPACEFOR conducts coordination, integration, and staffing activities to tailor space support for the COMAFFOR/ JFACC."[7] Either wing commanders or previous operations group commanders from AFSPC currently hold the position of DIR-SPACEFOR. Oftentimes these colonels arrive in-theater at the beginning of a contingency or exercise without adequate AOR-specific training or situation awareness. The expectation is they will get "spun up" very rapidly. The uncertainty and instability of ungoverned spaces around the globe combined with com-pressed planning timelines do not allow the luxury of training the DIRSPACEFOR adequately during the rapid buildup prior to mission execution. AFDD 2-2.1 outlines several responsibilities of the DIRSPACEFOR—many of which occur during adaptive planning, sometimes long before execution. These responsibili-ties are best suited to the permanent in-theater presence of a trained DIRSPACEFOR.

To take full advantage of permanent-party DIRSPACEFORs, general roles and responsibilities as well as AOR-specific train-ing must be provided during initial training. AFSPC has done a great deal of work establishing a baseline DIRSPACEFOR initial qualification training program. The natural extension of this ini-tial training is for AFSPC to develop continuation training and for each theater to provide theater-specific mission qualification training (MQT) as well as continuation training. Theater MQT and continuation training will include frequent situational awareness about activities within the AOR. Once trained and in-theater, the DIRSPACEFOR will be equipped to provide input from adaptive planning to execution to redeployment. A DIR-SPACEFOR "living and breathing" within the theater WFHQ is the most effective use of this valuable resource.

2. Integrate space operations expertise into WFHQ operational planning teams.

As mentioned above, a WFHQ must be able to seamlessly, and sometimes rapidly, plan and execute a full range of military operations. This seamless transition from planning to execution requires close coordination across all mission areas between the AFFOR staff (A-staff) and the JAOC. Traditionally, responsi-bility for DP and CAP rested with the A-staff, which required little input from the JAOC Strategy Division. This type of relationship required the JAOC to spin-up rapidly and, in some cases, dupli-cate planning efforts to effectively meet the JFC's objectives.

Further, multiple examples identify the disconnect between A-staff (A3/5) collateral-level CAP and A-staff (A39) special technical operations-level CAP. Many times the two planning efforts occurred simultaneously without any interaction between the two planning groups. It is very difficult to develop a single-air-component strategy when the A-staff and the JAOC do not effectively coordinate across all functions. The WFHQ construct allows the A-staff and JAOC Strategy Division to work closely on DP and CAP. The C2 Enabling Concept mentions the establishment of an operations planning group or a long-range planning group, but does not include options for implementation. USAFE is developing a model that establishes operational planning teams (OPT) that mirror the USEUCOM SJFHQ OPTs. These OPTs are focused on the different ranges of military operations such as CT, NEO, and FHA. Functional area experts from the A-staff and the JAOC are assigned to each OPT. Just like the SJFHQ is tasked to analyze hot spots specified by the GCC, the WFHQ OPTs, as the air component representatives to the SJFHQ, focus their efforts on analyzing the same regions. In order to effectively plan and execute theater space operations, it is imperative that these OPTs include space operations personnel from the A-staff as well as the JAOC. This type of coordination and organization provides a seamless transition from DP and CAP within the A-staff to execution within the JAOC.

3. Normalize a space coordinating plan.

When designated as the area air defense commander, the JFACC outlines air defense operations in an area air defense plan (AADP); likewise, when tasked as the airspace control authority, the JFACC outlines airspace operations in an airspace control plan (ACP). When designated as the SCA, the JFACC should outline space operations coordination within a space coordinating plan (SCP). AFDD 2-2.1 states, "The commander with SCA is the single authority to coordinate joint theater space operations and integrate space capabilities. The SCA facilitates unity of effort within theater by coordinating joint theater space operations to support integration of space capabilities and having primary responsibility for in-theater joint space operations planning."[8] Although the JFACC's joint air and space OPLAN

113

outlines the overall conduct of air, space, and information operations, it does not go to the level of detail that is contained within an AADP or ACP. The AADP and ACP outline the method by which operations will be conducted, the units conducting operations with associated C2 details, the interaction between each unit, the communications equipment used for operations, and the battle rhythm that each unit will follow. These plans offer a "one-stop shop" for the producer of effects and the user of effects. The SCP should offer producers and users of space-derived effects a common reference to understand how effects are produced and the method by which they are requested. CENTAF has developed a model SCP, but it has not yet been normalized across the theaters.

4. Normalize an Integrated Tasking Order (ITO).

JFACCs use the ATO as the mechanism by which to task air assets under their tactical control; likewise, the mechanism used to task space assets under their tactical control is the theater STO. (Note: There are two types of STOs, one which directs global space operations and is published by the JSpOC and the other developed for theater-specific space operations). In order to effectively synchronize air and space operations—kinetic and nonkinetic effects—these assets should be tasked via an ITO. Currently, production and distribution of the ATO and STO occur independently from each other. As the JAOC becomes a weapon system, much time and money are being invested to automate the ATO process from strategy development through ATO production. Similar tools do not exist on the space operations side, relegating much of the STO process to manual procedures. Combining the ATO and STO into a single ITO, theater air and space planners could take advantage of existing, already developed tools. The ITO would then be sent to air and space MPCs, which would produce the detailed mission plans the tactical units would execute. The ITO includes information such as platform, target, timing, and effect and provides insight to mission commanders and package commanders on the assets supporting the overall mission. The ITO would be produced from a single-integrated MAAP. The MAAP briefing would contain kinetic and nonkinetic effects and present the JFACC with an overall picture of that day's air and space operations. Pacific Air Forces (PACAF) currently uses an ITO, but it has not been normalized across the theaters.

5. Normalize a Reconnaissance, Surveillance, and Target-Acquisition Annex.

The Reconnaissance, Surveillance, and Target-Acquisition (RSTA) Annex is an attachment to the daily ATO that provides detailed tasking for ISR sensors and processing, exploitation, and dissemination nodes supporting the JFACC. According to Air Force Operational Tactics, Techniques, and Procedures (AFOTTP) 2-3.2, *Air and Space Operations Center*, "This product outlines the entire JFACC ISR plan for a given ATO, possibly at multiple classification levels."[9] No standardized and normalized RSTA Annex for ISR supporting theater space operations presently exists. As mentioned above, just as theater space operations should be tasked via the ITO, ISR sensors supporting them should be tasked via the RSTA Annex as well. Personnel within the ISR Division of the JAOC produce the overall RSTA Annex. Currently, space or IO personnel develop the collection plan for theater space operations. However, ISR Division personnel should be responsible for production of the entire RSTA Annex. This will require "space-smart" intelligence personnel permanently assigned to the ISR Division. PACAF and USSTRATCOM have developed an RSTA Annex in support of exercises, but it has not been normalized across theaters.

Conclusion

The strategic environment has fundamentally changed. Consequently, the US government (specifically the DOD) is in the midst of a transformation. The DOD is transforming the geographic COCOMs and major commands to maintain day-to-day wartime readiness by continual situational awareness of activities within their AOR. This continual situational awareness and wartime readiness allows for a more rapid transition to full-spectrum operations. Theater space operations imperatives must be addressed within a WFHQ to ensure these operations effectively integrate with other operations. For theater space operations to react rapidly and provide a critical contribution to full-spectrum operations, positions such as an identified DIRSPACEFOR per AOR, processes such as space operations personnel on WFHQ OPTs, and products such as a normalized SCP, ITO, and RSTA Annex are essential.

Notes

1. Pres. George W. Bush, *National Security Strategy of the United States, September 2002* (Washington, DC: White House, 17 September 2002), 3–4.

2. Donald H. Rumsfeld, SecDef, *National Defense Strategy of the United States, March 2005* (Washington, DC: US Department of Defense, 1 March 2005), 10.

3. Gen Richard B. Myers, CJCS, *National Military Strategy of the United States, 2004* (Washington, DC: Pentagon, 2004), viii.

4. JP 3-0, "Doctrine for Joint Operations," draft, 15 September 2004.

5. USJFCOM Pamphlet 3, *Doctrinal Implications of the Standing Joint Force Headquarters (SJFHQ)*, 16 June 2003, 4.

6. AFFOR, *Command and Control Enabling Concept* (change 1), 7 March 2005, 11.

7. AFDD 2-2.1, *Counterspace Operations*, 2 August 2004, 24.

8. Ibid., 9, 23.

9. AFOTTP 2-3.2, *Air and Space Operations Center*, 13 December 2004, 6-117, par. 6.6.8.3.8.

Chapter 6

The Next Evolution for Theater Space Organizations

Specializing for Space Control

Maj Keith W. Balts, USAF

Our ongoing activities in support of the global war on terrorism highlight the fact that our space capabilities have become increasingly integrated in our national intelligence and warfighting operations.

—Peter B. Teets
Acting Secretary of the Air Force

Since Desert Storm, space power personnel and organizations at the theater operational level have been primarily focused on integrating space platform capabilities into military operations. Their contributions include educating the military on available space capabilities, transforming strategically-focused legacy systems to support theater operations, and developing space requirements geared toward the operational and tactical levels of warfare. These space power experts have significantly improved and continue to enhance space support to combat operations. In fact, this era of improved space-force enhancement has been so successful that space capabilities are now an indispensable part of any campaign plan for the United States, our allies, and even potential adversaries.

Along the way, each type of theater space organization has been an important step in the evolution of space power. Liaison officers (LNO), joint and service space support teams (SST), embedded SWOs, augmentees, Space and Information Operations Elements (SIOE), the SCA, and the newly ordained DIRSPACEFOR have had the integration of space platform capabilities at the core of their missions. They have also led theater efforts to protect these capabilities and negate the enemy's use of space platforms.

While these efforts are commendable, this question now arises: What is the next step in the evolution of the theater space-power organization? The answer depends on two differing approaches to the question. One approach focuses on continuing improvements in space-force enhancement; the other focuses on protecting these force multipliers while negating space-force enhancement strides made by future enemies. To use Air Force doctrinal terms, the first approach focuses on how various *space* platforms and forces, old and new, support multiple operational functions like strategic attack, counterair, counterland, counterspace, CSAR, weather, and others. In other words, what is the next step in the evolution of theater space-power organization *for space-force enhancement?* The second approach focuses on how multiple platforms and forces, regardless of the medium, carry out the *singular* counterspace operational function. More specifically, what is the next step in the evolution of theater space-power organization *for space control?*

This study takes the second approach by putting space control at the center of the discussion and proposing a theater space-organizational structure that is less dependent on the platforms and more focused on the specific operational function. At the theater operational level of war, operational functions, not platforms, should be the focus.[1] The author will first describe the evolution of space operations, nuances in space doctrine applicable to the discussion, and current theater space organizations. Once this groundwork has been laid, this chapter will outline a new theater space organization focused on space control and based, to some extent, on the theater personnel recovery (PR) organizational structure. Once the proposed organizational structure is defined, specific recommendations will be made to resolve doctrine, organization, training, materiel, leadership, personnel, and facilities (DOTMLPF) implications.

While this proposal concentrates on space control, it does not negate the need for theater space organizations focused on space-force enhancement. However, the US military has arrived at a point in the evolution of space power where a single theater space organizational entity cannot simultaneously support the two critical functions of space control and space-force enhancement. Continuing to put all theater operations related to space under one organizational umbrella dilutes the GCC's and JFC's ability to accomplish either of them effectively.

It is important to take a look at the evolution of space operations and to consider space transformations in the context of history. Understanding how space operations have transformed, with respect to theater operations, will provide the required justification for transformations related to theater space organizations.

Space Operations Evolution

The focus of space operations has changed since the launch of Sputnik in 1957. Subsequent decades concentrated on providing "global" space capabilities for national decision makers, but this emphasis shifted in the 1990s to distributing these capabilities to the operational and tactical levels of war.[2] Although, the Tactical Exploitation of National Capabilities (TENCAP) program has been in existence since the 1970s to drive these changes.[3] The Office of Force Transformation within the Office of the SecDef sets the milestone between these two transformational periods as Operation Desert Storm.[4] The catalyst for this change in focus can be traced to Gen Charles Horner, who took over as CINC of USSPACECOM and commander of AFSPC after serving as the CFACC in Desert Storm.[5] Using the joint doctrinal terms for space mission areas, these two transformations can be characterized as space-force enhancement at the strategic level and space-force enhancement at the lower levels of war. That is, operational and tactical as shown in figure 6.1.

The success of this emphasis shift in space-force enhancement from the strategic level to the operational and tactical levels has certainly left its mark on Air Force doctrine. Space

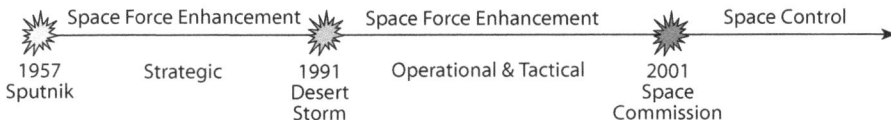

Space Force Enhancement   Space Force Enhancement   Space Control

| 1957 Sputnik | Strategic | 1991 Desert Storm | Operational & Tactical | 2001 Space Commission |

Figure 6.1. Space operations transformations. (*Adapted from* Col Jay Raymond, USAF, DOD Office of Force Transformation [address, Air War College, Maxwell Air Force Base, AL, February 2005], slide 6.)

capabilities are now a must for any combat operation. "Space assets are force multipliers across the spectrum of conflict and must be integrated into deliberate and crisis action planning, as well as operations planning, combat operations, and time-sensitive targeting to ensure timeliness of effects."[6]

However, increased reliance on space capabilities has turned our asymmetric advantage into an asymmetric vulnerability and a likely target for potential adversaries.[7] This leads to a third transformational period in the evolution of space operations, namely one focused on space superiority to protect our force-enhancement capabilities and negate any advances in space-force enhancement made by our adversaries. The Office of Force Transformation identifies the 2001 Space Commission report as the milestone for the beginning of space-superiority transformation, or, to use the joint-mission-area term, *space-control transformation*. The attempted jamming of the GPS by Iraqi forces during the initial stages of OIF provides a real-world example of military operations in this current era of space-superiority transformation.[8]

Theater Space–Control Concepts in Doctrine

All transformations should include changes to capabilities, concepts, people, and organization.[9] This chapter focuses on how theater organizations have changed or need to change to keep pace with the current space-control transformation. The discussion is also scoped to theater operations, but a similar study could be conducted for organizational changes at the national and strategic levels.

Air Force and joint doctrine have made some significant steps toward documenting specific concepts in space control. In addition to basic space doctrine, the Air Force has developed specific space-control doctrine.[10] The joint community also has plans to develop a classified appendix to JP 3-14.[11] The long-term plan for Air Force space-control doctrine is to roll the information up into the basic space volume, but this may dilute the significance space superiority plays in current and future conflicts.[12] For joint doctrine, the appendix keeps space control as a distinct doctrine, but unfortunately keeps it away from mainstream reading as a classified document. When sister-service doctrine mentions space operations, they focus almost exclusively on the space-force enhancement mission area and mention *space control* primarily to define the term. Sister-service doctrine is void of any details on how to accomplish space control for organizations assigned space-control responsibilities.[13]

Despite specific Air Force and joint doctrine focused on space control, there are some significant disconnects in doctrine related to this mission area. First, a disconnect in terminology exists on the precise term for protecting friendly and negating enemy space capabilities. Joint doctrine uses *space control* in describing the specific space mission area, while Air Force doctrine defines it as an operational function called *counterspace*, akin to *counter-air*.[14] While not a showstopper for space-superiority discussions, this may cause confusion when Air Force personnel try to articulate concepts and organizational structures in a joint community and vice versa. This chapter will primarily use space-control terminology to be more relevant in the joint community, but counterspace will be used when discussing Air Force–specific concepts.

One benefit of using the Air Force term is that counterspace also includes concise descriptions of protecting friendly capabilities and negating enemy capabilities, DCS and OCS, respectively.[15] This is something that is not as easily articulated within space control. The counterspace concept also includes SSA, a necessary component of protection and negation actions, especially with respect to complex intelligence requirements.[16]

A second doctrinal disconnect exists in describing the space-control-related duties and responsibilities for theater commanders. JP 3-14 does not explicitly list space-control duties or responsibilities for theater commanders except for force protection of space forces and coordination with USSPACECOM on campaign plans.[17] When discussing C2 of space forces, JP 3-14 states that the JFC can retain or designate the authority to coordinate and integrate space operations, but nothing specific to the space-control mission area.[18] In fact, joint doctrine primarily focuses on coordination and integration of space capabilities for space-force enhancement and has not yet transformed to meet the new era of space-control emphasis. Hopefully, JP

3-14.1 will address specific details on theater commanders' space-control responsibilities.

While not a joint document, AFDD 2-2.1 does specifically address space control, or in this case counterspace, responsibilities and authorities for theater commanders. Unfortunately, it is unclear how best to delegate these authorities within the theater chain of command. According to AFDD 2-2.1, the GCC is responsible for all space requirements and establishing command relationships necessary to meet those requirements.[19] The document does state that the JFC is responsible for space superiority in the specified AOR/JOA and recommends assigning this responsibility to the JFACC.[20] Unfortunately, the document is a bit confusing, as AFDD 2-2.1 also recommends that the JFC assign a supported commander for space operations (which presumably includes counterspace operations), a supported commander for theater counterspace operations, and the SCA.[21] SCA is mentioned here because it includes specific space-control responsibilities: facilitate space target nominations, maintain SSA, and assist JFC with theater counterspace operations.[22]

These overlapping responsibilities, titles, and authorities beg the question, What is the best way for a JFC to delegate space-control responsibilities to ensure unity of effort and unity of command by all players involved? The recommended solution is to delete generic references to space operations or space responsibilities and authorities and concentrate on specific joint mission areas. Ideally, space-control tasks should be mutually exclusive of space-force-enhancement tasks for clarity in assigning them to subordinate commanders. That is not to say the JFC could not assign both responsibilities to one commander, like the JFACC. To provide clarity in expressing space-control responsibilities, doctrine should state that the JFC may assign a supported commander for space control. A supported commander is a support-command relationship and is a much stronger designation than a coordinating authority for accomplishing space-control tasks.[23] Space control is used vice counterspace to be recognizable in the joint community. Of course, the JFC does not have to delegate any authorities, but if delegation is desired, the JFACC/COMAFFOR should be designated as the supported commander for space control. While not the focus of this study, space-force-enhancement responsibilities should be grouped under a separate SCA or equivalent and include specific wording for space-force enhancement or "information services" in the title.[24]

Despite these two disconnects in terminology and description of responsibilities, doctrine is showing significant signs of transformation to specifically address this new emphasis on space control. While the space-control concept is gaining momentum in transforming doctrine, the next section examines how theater space organizations are not necessarily meeting this level of transformation with respect to space control.

Evolution of Theater Space Organizations

Looking back on the previous transformation related to space-force enhancement, the Desert Storm milestone also triggered a transformation in theater space organizations (fig. 6.2).

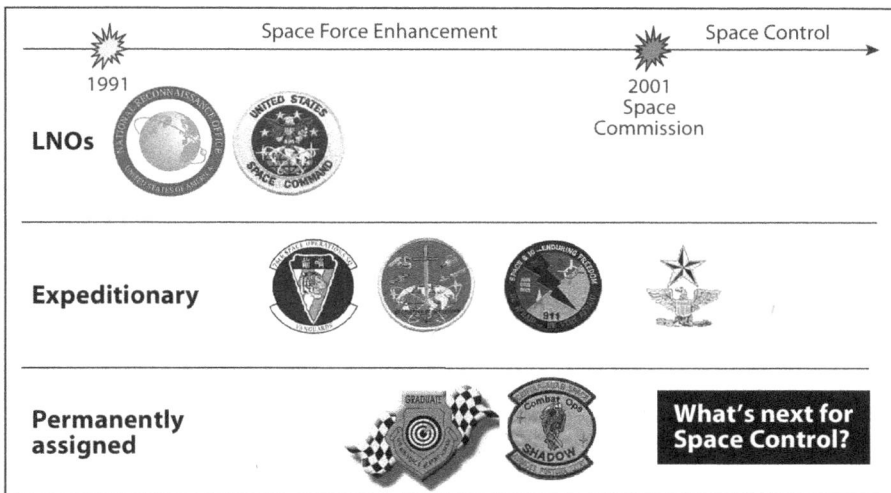

Figure 6.2. Evolution of theater space organizations. (*Adapted from* Col Jay Raymond, USAF, DOD Office of Force Transformation [address, Air War College, Maxwell Air Force Base, AL, February 2005], slides 6 and 8.)

LNOs, expeditionary organizations, and eventually permanently assigned individuals emerged to better coordinate, plan, and execute space operations in each AOR. Because of the era in which they were born, these organizations were formed with space-force enhancement as their core mission area. LNOs to the GCC from the National Reconnaissance Office (NRO), United States Space Command (USSPACECOM [now USSTRATCOM]), and other agencies provide a daily pipeline between space capability providers and theater commanders and their staffs. When the focus shifted post–Desert Storm to supporting the theaters, more personnel were required above and beyond these LNOs to meet the high demands of integration during major combat operations.

Expeditionary space organizations filled this gap and continue to provide space operations expertise to GCCs and their component commanders. USSPACECOM and its service components formed joint and service SSTs to assist theater commanders and staffs in coordinating, planning, and executing space operations in-theater. USSPACECOM went even further during OEF by sending an SIOE to USCENTCOM to further augment their deployed joint SST and LNO. USSTRATCOM now deploys a consolidated USSTRATCOM-support team to fulfill JSST and SIOE roles.[25] These expeditionary organizations proved extremely effective in jump-starting space-capability integration during major combat operations. However, since they were not permanently assigned to the theater staffs, their contributions were less effective during relative peacetime for working detailed coordination and planning efforts.

To overcome this shortfall, the Air Force deactivated the Air Force SSTs in the late 1990s after the United States Air Force Weapons School (USAFWS) began graduating SWOs for permanent assignment to air component staffs throughout the DOD. SWOs populated permanent positions with CCDR staffs as well. These were not the first space officers on theater staffs, but they represented a major transformation in how theater space officers would be trained and employed for assignment to theater headquarters. Despite this move, the Air Force did not completely eliminate the expeditionary concept. During exercises and times of major military operations, additional space officers deploy to augment the limited number of SWOs permanently assigned to theater. The Air Force also developed a senior-level expeditionary position in the years leading to OIF. The position was initially called an SSO during early development and the assistant CAOC, director for Space and Information Warfare, during the initial phases of OEF. This senior-level advisor is now documented in AFDD 2-2.1 as the DIRSPACEFOR.[26] The DIRSPACEFOR serves as the senior space advisor to the COM-AFFOR but is not permanently assigned to the CCDR's air component staff.[27]

Theater Space Organizations in Doctrine

The 2001 Space Commission's increased emphasis on space control may have transformed space-control concepts in doctrine; however, there has been no comparable transformation in theater space organizations like those triggered after Desert Storm for space-force enhancement. Instead, increased space-control responsibilities are merely added to theater space organizations' existing space-force-enhancement responsibilities. A transformation this large demands a comparable change in organization to handle the increased emphasis. To transform theater space organizations, it is important to understand the organizational shortfalls in doctrine.

Unfortunately, current organizational doctrine lacks reality and concentrates much more on liaisons and expeditionary organizations, like space support teams, instead of permanently assigned space organizations on the GCC, JFC, and component commander staffs. When discussed in doctrine, the responsibilities of the LNOs and expeditionary organizations are weighted heavily toward operational- and tactical-level space-force enhancement. This is not surprising since they were developed during the second space transformation, where emphasis was on space support to the war fighter. Space control is not totally disregarded by these organizations, but they must fulfill these responsibilities in conjunction with their space-force-enhancement responsibilities. This was not an issue in the 1990s when space-control responsibilities were not as demanding as they are during this current transformation.

A similar look at doctrine regarding permanently assigned personnel within GCC, JFC, and component commander staffs does not yield much detail. Sister-service doctrine does not address permanently assigned space expertise in-theater.[28] JP 3-14 mentions "joint space planners" in-theater and a "network of space operators" working for the GCC, but provides no significant details on how they are organized or what their responsibilities include.[29] Air Force doctrine mentions "embedded space experts" in the AOC.[30] However, only Air Force Instruction (AFI) 13-1AOC, volume 3, *Operational Procedures—Aerospace Operations Center*, lists specifics on how they are organized and their responsibilities.[31] In all cases, specific or not, organizational responsibilities are primarily focused on space-force enhancement and do not reflect the new emphasis on space control.

An increased emphasis on space control puts the current organizational structure at risk since they are expected to simultaneously meet growing space-force-enhancement and space-control responsibilities. Unfortunately, stagnant manning levels plus added breadth versus depth in training dilute theater expertise and make it less effective in both mission areas. Personnel who populate space organizations are slowly becoming "jacks-of-all-trades, masters of none" with respect to space mission areas. While there is some overlap, each mission area also interfaces with its own set of organizations. Adding more breadth instead of depth to existing theater space organizations also dilutes their ability to form effective relationships and develop combined TTP with other organizations. This includes other organizations within theater as well as those outside the theater that support or are supported by space-control operations.

The recommended solution is to increase manning, where appropriate, but also to specialize the organizing, training, and equipping of theater space personnel. This specialization ensures depth in expertise and depth in forming effective relationships for meeting the challenges associated with this space-control transformation. This transformation should not take away from space-force-enhancement responsibilities but should lead to specialized theater space organizations focused separately on each of the two main mission areas. Creating specialized theater space-control organizations will have an impact on how space-force enhancement is accomplished in-theater, but a detailed discussion of those impacts is beyond the scope of this study.

Summary

The third era of space transformation, which emphasizes the space-control mission area, is under way. This emphasis is beginning to change theater space-control concepts in doctrine but has not led to significant transformations in theater space organizations. First, GCCs and JFCs should designate their air component commander as the supported commander for space control to meet space-superiority responsibilities across the spectrum of conflict. Supported commanders need specialized space-control personnel permanently assigned to their staffs to meet increasing demands on coordinating, planning, and executing space-control operations. To do this effectively, they must be properly organized, trained, and equipped for space-control missions without the burden of theater space-force-enhancement responsibilities.

Proposed Theater Space–Control Organization

As stated earlier, a theater space-organizational structure focused on space control does not negate the need for other organizational elements concentrated on space-force enhancement. It merely elevates space control to a visible position on GCC, JFC, and subordinate commanders' staffs so space-control-specific training, exercising, coordination, planning, and execution can occur without the diversions associated with space-force-enhancement responsibilities.

By way of comparison, theater air operations could be considered one organization grouped together under the AOC construct. However, each air-related operational function has its own subordinate organizational structure to accomplish tasks in a specific mission area. Even beyond the four AOC divisions dedicated to strategy, planning, operations, mobility, and ISR, specific cells exist for weather, CSAR, counterair, TMD, and other Air Force operational functions.[32] Likewise, space power has evolved to the point where some individual functions demand

separate space-force-enhancement and space-control structures beyond generic space experts in each plan's cell or under
the Combat Operations Division (COD) space cell responsible
for all space operations.[33] The same argument can be made for
a separate theater space organization for space-force application and space support, if and when those capabilities are ready
for theater employment.

Since the JFACC should be designated the supported commander for space control, any theater space-control organization should fit within the AOC structure. Unfortunately, space
operations in the AOC are platform-centric in that they focus
on how space platforms, capabilities, and forces support other
functions in the AOC. This stems straight from the "space support to the war fighter" mind-set developed under the second
space-operations transformation. Even when the function of
counterspace is discussed in doctrine, it primarily looks to
space forces; that is, singular medium platforms, to accomplish those tasks. That said, JFACCs will always need space-
platform experts to provide support to AOC functional cells,
much like fighter, bomber, tanker, predator, and other unit
LNOs work platform issues in the AOC for other airpower functions. However, the operational level of warfare is still centered
on accomplishing functional tasks regardless of any specific
tactical platform (see fig. 6.3).

Instead of developing a theater space-control organization
from scratch, a similar function-centric organization could be
used as a model and starting point. Once again, the AOC provides many function-centric organization models to choose from.
Therefore, the right criteria must be selected to ensure applica-
bility to space control. Of the 17 air and space power functions,
many can be eliminated as potential models if they fail to meet
common space-control or counterspace characteristics.[34]

First, the model should involve joint capabilities that are not
dependent on a single medium. That is, they should not just
meet functional responsibilities by employing Air Force or air
capabilities. Most functions meet these two criteria with the exception of airlift, air refueling, and spacelift. Second, since this
is an evolutionary step, the model should be based on a relatively small theater organization. This excludes expansive orga-

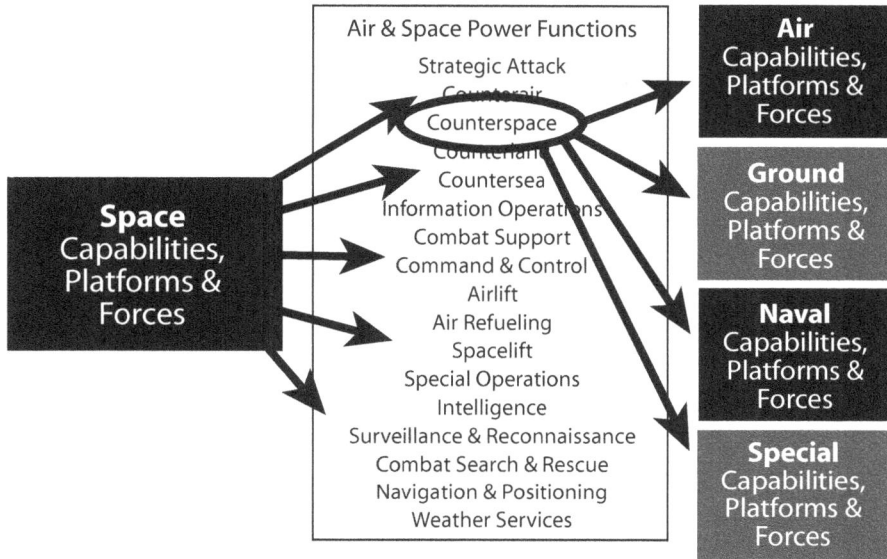

Figure 6.3. Platform-centric versus function-centric focus. (*Adapted from AFDD 1, Air Force Basic Doctrine*, 17 November 2003, 39.)

nizations like ISR with its full-up AOC division and special operations with its complete theater functional component.

Next, the functional model should be applicable to the full spectrum of conflict since SSA, DCS, and to some extent, OCS operations are not confined to major combat operations. This excludes many traditional airpower functions like strategic attack, counterland, and countersea. Also, the model should not be based on pure support functions. While counterspace operations may not be the main effort in an operation, they could be, and therefore its organizational structure should not look like a support structure. This excludes combat support, C2, PNT, and weather services. This leaves counterair, information operations, and CSAR as potential candidates.

Counterspace is often compared to counterair and to information operations, making them obvious candidates. However, IO is excluded because space control should be based on a mature and experienced organizational model. While elements of information operations have been around for almost as long as war itself, the IO concept is a fairly new one, especially with respect to specialized theater organizations. Counterspace doctrine shows many comparisons to counterair, but the final criteria were the author's personal experience and knowledge of the functional organization. Having depth in the functional area helps make for educated comparisons based on experience, not merely based on current doctrine. While the need for a specialized theater space-control organization is the key thesis of this chapter, using an IO, counterair, or some other joint operational model as a basis is definitely worth additional research. However, for the purposes of this discussion, CSAR, or the more appropriate joint term, *PR*, will serve as the functional model for developing a specialized theater space-control organization.

Using Personnel Recovery as a Model

In searching for a model, theater PR organizations provide a template for a theater space-control organization. The PR function has many characteristics in common with space control, and its structure serves as an excellent point of departure for making comparisons. More importantly, PR meets all the criteria mentioned above for selecting a comparable function.

First, PR is a joint concept supported by platforms in all mediums. PR-specific platforms do exist—the HH-60 to name one—but theater PR personnel must integrate all available platforms for effective PR operations. These include fighters, tankers, C2 and ISR platforms, and even naval, ground, and special forces, if applicable to the situation.[35]

Second, the theater PR organizational structure is relatively small compared with many other operational functions. There are no PR functional component commanders or large PR divisions at operational-level command centers. PR incidents also occur across the spectrum of conflict and are not confined to major combat operations. Theater commanders have a standing PR organizational structure to deal with these various types of incidents, from supporting a civil rescue to recovering a downed pilot in combat.[36] The same is required for space control, especially in this era of terrorism. A DCS mission may be required at any time to deal with an adversary's attempt to negate friendly space capabilities. Although this particular incident was resolved diplomatically, the jamming of Iranian Voice of America from Cuba in 2004 is a good example of a DCS event occurring in peacetime that may have required use of the military instrument of power.[37] GCCs need a standing space-control organizational structure to resolve these situations, if only to provide specialized support to their existing 24-hour joint operations center when an event occurs. Functional agencies related to space, such as USSTRATCOM and NRO, also need a 24-hour space-control point of contact in each theater to resolve incidents. If a space capability owned by USSTRATCOM, NRO, or a commercial entity with US national interests is attacked, the GCC needs a trained organization to coordinate the resolution.

Finally, PR meets the last three criteria outlined above. PR is not a support function but a necessary operational function inherent throughout the spectrum of conflict. While it is rarely the main effort, PR can be the primary mission, with other functions acting in a supporting role. Also, even though current PR organizational doctrine is under review, theater PR organizations are mature and have existed since at least World War II.[38] Finally, the author has spent seven years working with or in the joint PR community, which meets the last criteria, personal experience.

Relevant Personnel Recovery Doctrine for Space Control

Since PR was the chosen model, PR doctrine should be the starting point for developing a theater space-control organization. JP 3-50, "Joint Doctrine for Personnel Recovery," is the cornerstone of military PR doctrine. Unlike JP 3-14 and AFDD 2-2.1, JP 3-50 goes into great detail on the theater organizational structure GCCs, JFCs, and component commander's leverage to accomplish PR tasks. This PR doctrine not only lays out the detailed roles and responsibilities of the various PR-specific organizations within each theater, it also describes coordination channels these organizations have with other theater entities and external agencies.

The actual theater PR organization is outlined in JP 3-50. Key PR personnel in-theater exist on the GCC and JFC staffs, in Joint Personnel Recovery Centers (JPRC), and in personnel recovery coordination centers (PRCC) at each component. JP 3-50 provides detailed functions and responsibilities, summarized here, for each of these organizational entities. According to JP 3-50, a PR office of primary responsibility (OPR) should be identified on the GCC staff to ensure proper horizontal and vertical coordination on joint PR issues. Among its many responsibilities, this full-time individual or staff ensures a coordinated PR program exists for the AOR; maintains liaisons with PR assets, components, and host nations; develops joint-force PR SOPs, intelligence requirements, ROEs, and CONOPS; and coordinates and deconflicts PR plans, exercises, and reporting within the theater.[39]

Whether the JFC exercises command authority for PR or designates the JFACC or other component commander as the supported commander for PR, the JFC normally establishes a JPRC to plan, coordinate, monitor and/or execute, and integrate PR missions within the assigned OA. The JPRC also serves as the JFC's primary coordinator for assisting host nations or civil authorities, as authorized by the president or SecDef. Not every operation will require a fully staffed JPRC; however, one should be established when operations dictate a requirement for PR support. Doctrine even describes key personnel, materiel, and training recommendations for effective JPRC execution. The JPRC should consist of specifically trained personnel, to include a director, controllers, and intelligence personnel plus unit, multinational, and joint representation, as appropriate. In addition to personnel, the JPRC also needs a proper C2 structure and extensive exercise training. As the focal point for all PR operations within a theater, JP 3-50 lists 35 specific functions and responsibilities for the JSRC.[40] This detailed doctrine makes the JPRC an effective group of specialized, standardized, integrated, and identifiable action officers for all theater commanders and their staffs.

The last major element of theater PR organization is the establishment of a PRCC at each component. Each component commander normally establishes a PRCC to coordinate all component PR activities. If a PRCC is not established, PR activities are normally assigned to another component staff organization, like the operations section. PRCC functions and responsibilities are similar to those of the JPRC but deal specifically with the component level.[41]

JP 3-50 also includes specific details on intelligence support to PR. Like most operational functions, intelligence is a critical element for success, so "intelligence support at every level must have PR-knowledgeable personnel integrated within their staffs." Also, dedicated intelligence personnel must be assigned to the JPRC and PRCCs to ensure intelligence requirements are satisfied in a timely manner.[42]

Some key differences exist between PR and space control. An exact replica of the theater PR organization with "space-control" titles would not be appropriate for accomplishing the space-control function. First, PR is generally reactive in nature, triggered by the incident causing personnel to be isolated. While significant deliberate, crisis-action, and daily planning is required to ensure theater commanders are ready to accomplish their PR responsibilities, there are no proactive PR operations. This function is more closely related to counterland, counterair, countersea, and the combat-support function of force protection than resident in the PR community. Space control, on the other hand, has a significant OCS element which requires extensive strategy and planning. This difference is manifested in the current PR organization, where PR personnel are centered in the AOC operations division and only support strategy and planning activities as needed.

The second major difference between PR and space control is the level of support provided by functional components besides the JFACC. All functional component commanders have the responsibility to recover their own isolated personnel to the best of their abilities, but this level of effort has not been demonstrated for space control. That is not to say other components could not or should not have space-control responsibilities. Indeed they should, but the space-control transformation has not risen to that level in other components. This is evident by the lack of space-control sister-service doctrine and organizational details mentioned above. Other functional components are not excluded from space control, but their *current* level of activity with respect to space control is limited. This could and should change as the transformation filters to all the services over time.

Proposed Theater
Organization for Space Control

Despite these differences, the author's proposed theater space-control organization still has many similarities to the PR model. The GCC and JFC should designate a space-control OPR, a supported commander for space control with a joint space-control center (JSCC), and space-control OPRs at all the components. The space-control OPRs on the GCC and JFC staffs will ensure proper horizontal and vertical coordination on joint PR issues for their respective commander and liaison with USSTRATCOM, NRO, and other satellite providers, as required. While every situation is different, the JFC should normally designate the JFACC as the supported commander for space control and direct this commander to establish a JSCC. Like the JPRC description above, the JSCC would be the specialized, standardized, integrated, and identifiable group of action officers meeting the theater-functional space-control responsibilities. Figure 6.4 shows the proposed organization.

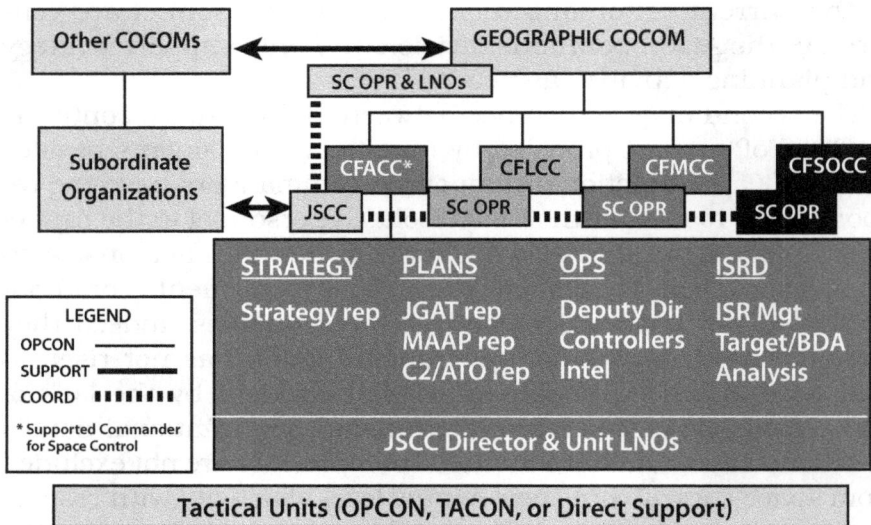

Figure 6.4. Proposed theater space-control organization

The differences between PR and space control mentioned above translate to differences between the established PR organization construct and the proposed space-control version. For instance, the current difference in how component commanders contribute to each function affects the kind of organization required at their level. Full-up PRCC equivalents, or space-control coordination centers (SCCC), are not yet needed at the component level. However, component commanders should designate a space-control OPR at the very minimum to coordinate component space-control activities. If and when the space-control transformation expands deeper across the joint community or the threat dictates their increased involvement, component commanders may need to convert the OPR into a fully staffed SCCC.

Also, the extensive planning activities required for space control mean JSCC representatives must be embedded within strategy, planning, and ISR cells. This leads to better unity of effort within the operations center hosting the JSCC, normally the CAOC, but causes problems for unity of command for the individual personnel. Do they work for their respective cell chief or the JSCC director? Who does the JSCC work for, the chief of Combat Operations, the chief of Combat Plans, the chief of the Strategy Division, or the DIRSPACEFOR?[43] The answer depends on the situation and, more importantly, on the decision of the supported commander for space control. One recommendation for doctrine is to state, "When the JFACC is designated the supported commander for space control, the JSCC should normally be assigned to the Combat Operations Division with representatives embedded in the other divisions. The JSCC director would serve as a specialty team chief within the AOC and act as the lead action officer on space-control issues for the CFACC."[44] The permanently assigned space-control OPRs and the JSCC director would also represent space-control issues in the IO cell at their respective levels within the theater.

Summary

Since the proposed theater space-control organization primarily exists at the operational level of war, the proposed structure is based on a function-centric model, not formed around the specific platforms employed for space control. This differs from current theater space-operations organizations, which grew out of the previous space transformation tied to operational- and tactical-level space-force enhancement. They are focused on how space platforms, capabilities, and forces support the war fighter.

With some accommodations for the differences between PR and space control, the proposed structure is based on the theater PR organization as outlined in the current draft of JP 3-50. Using PR as a model meets all the criteria for selecting a comparable function to space control. In short, the proposed theater-space-control organization includes OPRs on GCC, JFC, and functional component commander staffs. The JFC should designate the JFACC as the supported commander for space control and direct him or her to establish a joint space control center for accomplishing the day-to-day responsibilities for space control in-theater.

DOTMLPF Recommendations

While this proposed theater space-control construct has its focus on organizational changes, it also has implications for DOTMLPF. Fortunately, space control itself is not new to theater operations; so much of the groundwork has already been laid with respect to these categories. The impact of this proposed organization leads to recommendations in all seven DOTMLPF categories.

Organization, Personnel, and Leadership

The most obvious implication is on the personnel, leadership, and organization in-theater. These three areas are critical to ensuring unity of effort and unity of command with regard to theater space control.

Luckily some space, IO, intelligence, and other personnel already spend a considerable part of their time working space-control issues in-theater. With the space-control transformation under way, one or a small group of these individuals at the GCC and JFC levels should be identified and assigned as the space-control OPR for that commander. The most obvious choice would be an SWO already embedded on the J-3 staff and possibly already working some space-control issues. The threat level and situation in the theater would determine whether this OPR should be dedicated full-time to space control or act as the OPR in addition to other responsibilities. Component commanders should also identify their space-control OPR. Ideally, this would be a permanently assigned individual with space operations expertise or general IO expertise at a bare minimum.

Each GCC and JFC should designate a component commander as the supported commander for space control, normally the air component commander. The GCC and JFC could also retain the authority if that is more appropriate. This designation should be a separate authority other than the coordinating authority for space mentioned above. Both authorities could be delegated to the same commander, that is, JFACC, but the responsibilities should be mutually exclusive.

The supported commander for space control should then assign a JSCC director and provide the resources necessary to meet space-control responsibilities. Depending on the threat level and the situation, personnel resources should include the appropriate number of controllers, planners, intelligence representatives, and unit-level liaisons necessary to accomplish their responsibilities.

Once these individuals are identified they should begin the coordination process with other theater space organizations to deconflict responsibilities and processes already present. At a minimum, this coordination should include the individuals working space-force-enhancement issues and the DIRSPACE-FOR. While beyond the scope of this study, a comparable, specialized theater space-force-enhancement organization should be pursued to handle the ever-increasing workload associated with that transformation. Joint war-fighting space may very well be the avenue to solving this open item.[45] The JSCC and OPRs also need to deconflict with the DIRSPACEFOR, if one is present in-theater, to resolve process differences. This deconfliction may happen naturally as a product of rank, presence, and scope. DIRSPACEFOR is a senior-level advisor, whereas the JSCC director and associated personnel work at the action-officer level. As a permanent organization, the JSCC is present throughout the spectrum of conflict to handle space-control responsibilities as they present themselves, whereas the DIR-SPACEFOR may only be available during major combat operations or whenever senior-level presence is required. Finally, the scope of the DIRSPACEFOR extends beyond just space control, leaving the JSCC and OPRs to work at a more specialized level for that mission area.

The last area to consider under organization, personnel, and leadership is the effect this proposal has on organizations external to theater. Once a standardized theater space-control organization is adopted, theater OPRs and JSCCs need to work aggressively to coordinate TTPs with organizations representing space capabilities that need protecting, organizations that can provide OCS capabilities for negating adversary use of space, and agencies that provide ISR and other support capabilities for SSA. They also need to coordinate with other JSCCs for theater space-control operations that extend beyond the borders of a single AOR.

Doctrine

Specific doctrine recommendations have already been discussed but are included here as a consolidated list of recommendations for how organizational concepts should be documented. First, joint and Air Force doctrine needs to resolve discrepancies in terminology for space control. Time and experience will determine whether *space control* and *counterspace* will continue to exist in the military lexicon. Until one term goes away or a new term replaces both, discussions between Air Force and the joint community will be hampered by cumbersome translations.

Doctrine must also do more than simply document the proposed theater space-control structure outlined in this study. It must also include detailed functions and responsibilities, to include intelligence-related activities, for each element of the organization. As a model, PR doctrine does an excellent job detailing responsibilities and interaction among the various theater PR elements. In listing these responsibilities, space-control responsibilities should be removed from the coordinating authority for space, or SCA, description in joint and Air Force doctrine. GCCs and JFCs should designate a supported commander for space control to delegate specific authorities associated with this mission area.

Training

Merely changing doctrine and organization does not guarantee success for theater space-control operations. Theater space-control personnel must be trained in this new construct. Likewise, other theater personnel and external agencies and organizations that interface with theater space-control personnel also need training on the construct. This construct includes the theater space-control organization itself, its functions and responsibilities, and TTPs specific to their sphere of influence.

To accomplish this task, JSCC-specific curriculum should be added to service and joint schools. For personnel assigned to the AOC, this training should be added to the existing AOC initial qualification training (IQT) curriculum at the Air Force Command and Control Training and Innovation Group (AFC²TIG). To address the joint community, JSCC-specific curriculum should also be added to the Counterspace Planning and Integration Course and other courses at the National Security Space Institute (NSSI).[46] By comparison, the PR community has comparable courses for JSRC personnel in the AFC²TIG AOC IQT Course[47] and at the Personnel Recovery Education and Training Center (PRETC), the PR equivalent to NSSI.[48] To meet complete transformational demands, space-control intelligence concepts must also be added to intelligence school curricula. A specific course for intelligence support to space control should be developed at the NSSI similar to the PRETC's PR220, Intelligence Support to PR Course.[49] To ensure this JSCC academic training is institutionalized, theaters should conduct frequent realistic space-control exercises and include external organizations as much as possible.

Materiel and Facility

Finally, this new organizational construct needs a place to live. Fortunately it is a relatively small organization and, to some degree, is already being accomplished in theater operational-command centers. Therefore, existing C4 systems and operations centers are adequate for near-term JSCC operations. Having said that, there may be some additional space required for any significant increases in personnel associated with a fully staffed JSCC.

Once this specialized organization is formed in-theater, one of their first tasks would be to identify any additional space-control capability and ISR requirements needed to fulfill their responsibilities. This could lead to the need for fielding specialized systems or making space-control–specific modifications to existing systems.

Conclusion

The current space operations transformation emphasizing space control has significant implications for theater space organizations. First, this transformation has led to new theater space-control concepts in doctrine, but some disconnects still exist. These doctrinal disconnects include different joint and Air Force terminologies for protecting friendly and negating enemy space capabilities, *space control* and *counterspace,* respectively. The other disconnect deals with how the authority for space control is delegated within a theater. Many conflicting options are offered in doctrine, but the recommended solution is to separate force-enhancement authority from space-control authority and assign a supported commander for space control. Furthermore, GCC and JFC should assign this authority to the air component commander and JFACC/COMAFFOR, respectively.

Second, theater space organizations must transform to adapt to the emerging space-control emphasis. The current organizations grew out of the efforts from the previous space transformation. Therefore, they are platform-centric, focused on space-force enhancement, instead of function-centric, focused on space control. Theater space organizations focusing on space-force enhancement must continue, but specialized organizations focused on the space-control function are required to overcome challenges associated with diluting expertise and relationships. Several theater functional organizations could be used as a model, but PR offers a model that meets several mutual criteria between the two functions.

Modifying the PR model slightly to overcome differences between the two functions yields a specialized, standardized, scalable, integrated, and identifiable theater space-control organizational structure. GCC and JFC staffs would include a space-control OPR for horizontal and vertical coordination to support senior-level decision making. Space-control OPRs should also be identified at the functional component to assist in this coordination and support. The supported commander for space control, normally the JFACC/COMAFFOR, should establish a JSCC within the operations center and ensure representatives are integrated across the following functional areas: strategy, plans, operations, and intelligence. The JSCC should also include access to unit liaisons involved in space-control operations. This organization has implications across DOTMLPF elements. Besides the obvious organizational recommendations outlined above, changes must also be made to doctrine, personnel, leadership, training, materiel, and facilities to institutionalize this proposal and ensure it effectively meets the challenges of the space-control transformation.

Notes

1. JP 3-0, *Doctrine for Joint Operations*, 10 September 2001, II-2–3.

2. Col Jay Raymond, USAF, DOD Office of Force Transformation (address, Air War College, Maxwell Air Force Base, AL, February 2005), 6.

3. Gary Federici, *From the Sea to the Stars: A History of U.S. Navy Space and Space-Related Activities* (Washington, DC: Naval Historical Center, Department of the Navy, June 1997), 4.11.1, http://www.history.navy.mil/books/space/Chapter4.htm.

4. Raymond, address, 6.

5. Ibid., 8.

6. AFDD 2-2, *Space Operations*, 27 November 2001, vii.

7. Ibid., 6.

8. Jeremy Singer, "U.S.-Led Forces Destroy GPS Jamming Systems in Iraq," *Space News*, 25 March 2003, http://www.space.com/news/gps_iraq_030325.html.

9. Donald H. Rumsfeld, SecDef, *Transformation Planning Guidance* (Washington, DC: Department of Defense, April 2003), 3, http://library.nps.navy.mil/uhtbin/hyperion-image/TPGfinal.pdf.

10. AFDD 2-2.1, *Counterspace Operations*, 2 August 2004.

11. CJCS, *Joint Publications Status Report*, Joint Doctrine Branch, 30 December 2004, http://www.dtic.mil/doctrine/publications_status.htm.

12. Maj William Pell Thompson (Air Force Doctrine Center), interview by the author, 10 March 2005. See also *Joint Publications Status Report*, 30 December 2004.

13. FM 100-18, *Space Support to Army Operations*, 20 July 1995; and SECNAV Instruction 5400.39B, "Department of the Navy Space Policy," 26 August 1993.

14. JP 3-14, *Joint Doctrine for Space Operations*, 9 August 2002, x; and AFDD 1, *Air Force Basic Doctrine*, 17 November 2003, 42–43.

15. AFDD 1, *Air Force Basic Doctrine*, 43.

16. AFDD 2-2.1, *Counterspace Operations*, 2.

17. JP 3-14, *Joint Doctrine for Space Operations*, II-2.

18. Ibid., III-1–3.

19. AFDD 2-2.1, *Counterspace Operations*, 12.

20. Ibid.

21. Ibid.

22. Ibid., 13.

23. JP 1-02, *Department of Defense Dictionary of Military and Associated Terms*, 12 April 2001 (As amended through 31 August 2005), 124, 515.

24. Maj Tyler Evans (ACSC student), interview by the author, 10 Mar 2005.

25. Todd C. Schull, "Space-Operations Doctrine: The Way Ahead," *Air and Space Power Journal* 18, no. 2 (Summer 2004): 96–102.

26. AFDD 2-2.1, *Counterspace Operations*, 14.

27. Ibid.

28. FM 100-18, *Space Support to Army Operations*; and SECNAV Instruction 5400.39B, "Navy Space Policy."

29. JP 3-14, *Joint Doctrine for Space Operations*, I-2, II-5.

30. AFDD 2-2, *Space Operations*, 27.

31. AFI 13-1AOC, vol. 3, *Operational Procedures—Aerospace Operations Center*, 1 July 2002.

32. Ibid., 15–16.

33. Ibid.

34. Ibid.

35. JP 3-50, "Joint Doctrine for Personnel Recovery," second draft, 19 July 2004, F-1.

36. Ibid., II-1.

37. Tom Carter, "Castro Regime Jamming U.S. Broadcasts into Iran," *Washington Times*, 16 July 2003, A13, http://www.washtimes.com/world/20030715-114937-2635r.htm.

38. Lt Gen Michael W. Wooley, "America's Quiet Professionals: Specialized Airpower—Yesterday, Today and Tomorrow," *Air and Space Power Journal* 19, no. 1 (Spring 2005): 59–66.

39. JP 3-50, "Joint Doctrine for Personnel Recovery," II-1–3.

40. Ibid., II-5–11.

41. Ibid., II-13–15.

42. Ibid., II-15.

43. AFI 13-1AOC, vol. 3, *Aerospace Operations Center*, 2–3.

44. Ibid., 86.

45. Steven R. Prebeck, "Operating Concept for Joint Warfighting Space (JWS)" (working paper, Peterson AFB, CO: Air Force Space Command, 27 July 2004), 2.

46. Counterspace Planning and Integration Course (CPIC), course description, National Security Space Institute, http://www.thenssi.com/courseinfo .asp?Page=Course.

47. Air operations center initial qualification training, Personnel Recovery Course, course description, 505th Training Squadron, https://505ccw .hurlburt.af.mil/505trg/505trs/aocpr.htm.

48. Joint Personnel Recovery Agency (JPRA), Personnel Recovery Education and Training Center, course catalog, http://www.jpra.jfcom.mil/Military/ pretc.cfm.

49. Ibid.

Chapter 7

Applying Air Mobility
Lessons Learned to Space C2

Maj Stuart Pettis, USAF

For countries that can never win a war with the United States by using the method of tanks and planes, attacking the U.S. space system may be an irresistible and most tempting choice . . . the Pentagon is greatly dependent on space for its military action.

—Wang Hucheng
Beijing Xinhua Hong Kong Service

Purposeful interference with U.S. space systems will be viewed as an infringement on our sovereign rights . . . the US may take all appropriate self-defense measures, including the use of force.

—Bill Cohen
Secretary of Defense

The two statements above were chosen with care. The first indicates that at least one potential adversary has identified US reliance on space assets as a potential COG during conflict. In addition, while the threat from adversarial nation-states is troubling, nonstate actors, such as China's *Falun Gong*, have conducted actual jamming activities.[1] The second statement, taken from the DOD policy governing space, states that the US military must be prepared to defend against and overcome any attack on our space assets. However, what does this mean and how should we be organized to meet this potential threat?

While some would argue space is an extension of the air medium and that principles which apply to other terrestrial forms of military power also apply to space, there are unique attributes to space assets that must be addressed. First, depending on the orbit, satellites may have a field of view (FOV) which covers approximately one-third of the Earth's surface. The second attribute, ownership and control of space systems, is extremely fragmented between DOD, non-DOD US government, and civilian owners. Thirdly, space systems tend to function as "system-of-systems." The final unique attribute of on-orbit assets is their persistence.

These unique attributes might lead some to advocate a global command structure. However, any attempt to lump all space systems into a "global asset" bucket is inadvisable. Some space assets should fall under a more traditional C2 structure. For practical purposes, neither C2 system is wholly correct for all space systems. Rather, we must utilize positive aspects from each model to be most effective. In this regard, space C2 is analogous to the C2 structures used for air mobility forces. This study makes a comparison of this analogy. A suggested structure based on the Air Mobility Command (AMC) tanker airlift control center (TACC) and the theater airlift system for space C2 will be presented.

Sometimes Space Is Different

During a joint exercise, I had a conversation with an Army infantry officer and a Navy F-14 pilot. As we debated and discussed each of our services' idiosyncrasies, it became apparent that each of us had a different perspective on the battlespace. The infantry officer's perspective was shaped by how far he could move in a day, measured in tens of miles. What concerned him most were those enemy assets, normally artillery pieces and usually just tens of miles away, that could put his troops at risk. The regions the carrier battle group could operate within shaped the Tomcat pilot's perspective. He was also concerned with the time it took the battle group to steam there and the range of his aircraft. While substantially more than that of the infantry officer's, his perspective was still limited.

When it was my turn to speak, I gave a two-part answer on my perspective of the battlespace. First, I explained that Airmen have a global perspective, that the Air Force could employ aircraft from inside or outside a CCDR's AOR to achieve combat effects throughout the battlespace. Airmen can also employ assets from outside an AOR, to include the CONUS, to achieve those same effects within it. However, I then explained that space operators could create combat effects in multiple regions around the world simultaneously. In other words, Airmen have a limited global perspective, but space operators have a truly global perspective.

As figure 7.1 shows, the FOV for a particular geosynchronous satellite in this constellation covers approximately one-third of the Earth's surface. Anyone within this FOV can utilize the communications services provided by that satellite. Also, multiple theater commanders and their forces could simultaneously use the same particular satellite.

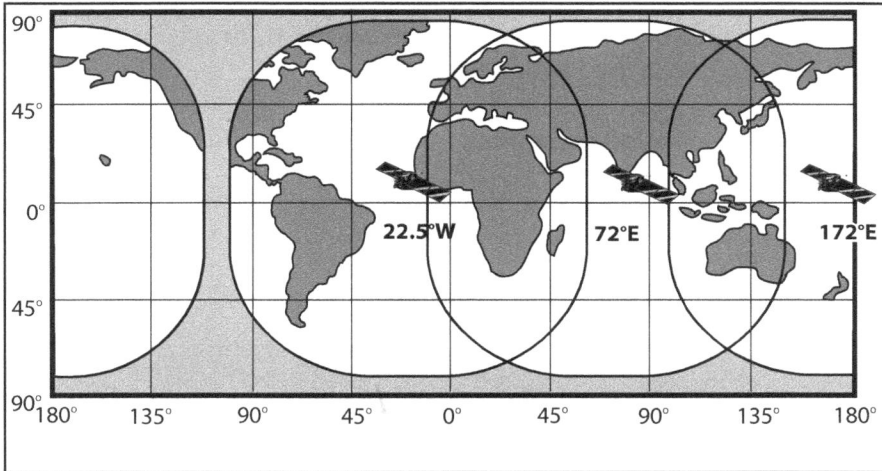

Figure 7.1. Fields of view for the Navy's UFO satellites. (*Adapted from* figure 2-5, FLTSATCOM coverage areas, Integrated Publishing, Information Technician, http://www.tpub.com/inch/17.htm.)

Not as apparent is the obverse of the discussion above: just as anyone within a given satellite's FOV could use that satellite, anyone within the same FOV could attack the satellite. Continuing the system-of-systems discussion from above, for signals going around the globe, an attack anywhere in the path of the signal could disrupt it.

This is exactly what happened in July 2003 when the Broadcasting Board of Governors, the United States federal agency which oversees nonmilitary international broadcasting, denounced the Cuban government for blocking US-based programming critical of the Iranian government. In this instance, jamming originating in a country in SOUTHCOM's AOR interfered with programming originating in the CONUS and intended for Iran within CENTCOM's AOR.[2]

The implication of the unique FOV and perspective generated by it is that on-orbit space assets provide a unique global perspective and the ability to affect multiple AORs simultaneously. The traditional way of dividing up assets by geographical means should not be used when a functional grouping of assets, such as those used for air mobility, is more appropriate.

The next unique aspect of space assets is the extremely fragmented C2 used for on-orbit space assets. A very cursory glance at the organizations operating military or military-utilized on-orbit space assets produces table 7.1.

Table 7.1. Organizations operating military or military-utilized on-orbit space assets

Organization	Assets
Air Force Space Command	MILSTAR GPS SBIRS DSCS Wide-band Gapfiller System DMSP
US Army Strategic Command	DSCS
Naval Network Warfare Command	FLTSATCOM Ultra-high frequency follow on
National Reconnaissance Office	Intelligence satellites
National Security Agency	Intelligence satellites
National Oceanographic and Atmospheric Administration	DMSP Geostationary Operational Environmental Satellite Polar-Orbiting Environmental Satellite
National Aeronautics and Space Administration	Solar and Heliospheric Observatory
Defense Information Services Agency	Allocates bandwidth on DOD communications satellites
Commercial and Consortia Satellite Owner/Operators	Provide satellite service to the DOD

The result of this fragmentation is that no one agency controls or has visibility into the operations of all on-orbit assets being utilized by the DOD. Given the mandate articulated in the DOD Space Policy to protect our on-orbit assets, this fragmentation makes protecting those satellites almost impossible. An adversary could attack any DOD space asset, and without a unified response, each agency would be forced to fight individual battles.

The third attribute that makes space systems unique is that they operate as system-of-systems. For example, while a single satellite could provide communications for a large region, two or more satellites and ground equipment are required to transmit a signal around the globe. To get an accurate position from the GPS, a user needs a minimum of four satellites, while 24 satellites are needed to achieve global coverage. Even nonorbital space assets, such as missile warning radars and space surveillance systems, require multiple sensors coupled with a command center to produce their desired effects. This attribute makes penny packeting individual space assets, especially on-orbit assets, extremely difficult.

A final unique attribute of on-orbit assets is their persistence. Once in position on-orbit satellites have mission lives measured in years, often exceeding decades. This means that they are on orbit prior to, during, and after most conflicts. This implies that they are best suited for a mature C2 structure, which is in place throughout a conflict vice a contingency C2 structure like a JTF.

Fighting and Winning a Defensive Counterspace Fight

As mentioned, nation and nonnation actors have either publicly stated or demonstrated an ability to target on-orbit assets. As military professionals, it is our responsibility to anticipate any threat and create a counter to that threat. Before examining the C2 structure required for that fight, we first need to discuss what actions are required at the tactical, operational, and strategic levels of war.

Our ability to win a future counterspace fight begins at the strategic level of war well before the fight takes place. Hopefully, several years in advance, our national decision makers will indicate who our potential adversaries may be. At the same time they would develop an appreciation for what their overall political and military objectives would be in a conflict with the United States. A component of this appreciation will be how they might attempt to target our space capabilities to help achieve those objectives. This appreciation will be used by commanders to field new space capabilities and tactics to overcome their anticipated actions.

At the same time, our intelligence professionals, along with our operations personnel, need to use that guidance to determine how an adversary would employ them during war and how these threats would affect our assets. Armed with this knowledge, our operators can build operational- and tactical-level countertactics.

Why do we need both operational-level and tactical-level tactics? Because a response to an enemy attack should consist of both actions taken to protect individual victim satellites at the tactical level and then actions at the operational level to protect the system-of-systems—all the potential victim satellites in the FOV of a threat. To take action at one level and not the other does not adequately answer the attack.

What actions would be encompassed in the operational-level counter tactics? At a broad level, the actions required to counter an attack by a ground-based threat would be:

- Prior to attack, have intelligence use indications and warnings to detect preparations for an attack.
- Once an attack occurs, regardless of the owner or operator, a command center provides an alert to other operators.
- Geolocate the source of the threat.
- Based on the geolocation, protective actions for other potential victim satellites within the FOV of the threat need to be directed.
- An appropriate response needs to be directed against the threat. If this is a kinetic response, a request for a COCOM with kinetic assets needs to be made.

How Did Air Mobility Tackle the Problem?

There are two functionally aligned communities within the United States Air Force: air mobility and special operations. Of the two, air mobility has the closest parallels to space, and there are lessons from air mobility that apply to space. Both communities have forces that function as system-of-systems and usually provide effects to COCOMs without changing OPCON of their forces. Air mobility assets can also operate, using either a functional or geographic chain of command, independent of where they are geographically situated.

Air mobility forces are divided by the SecDef's Forces for Unified Commands into forces assigned to USTRANSCOM, a functional command, and those owned by COCOMs, geographic commands. The basic division between the forces is that USTRANSCOM and its USAF service component, AMC, own strategic airlift assets such as C-5s, C-17s, C-141s, and most of the tanker fleet. COCOMs, such as United States Pacific Command and USEUCOM, are given small amounts of tactical airlift assets, such as C-130s and tankers, for use in their theaters. Control of strategic air mobility assets controlled by AMC is exercised by the TACC. Control of tactical air mobility assets is exercised either through an air mobility operations control center (AMOCC) or through the air mobility division (AMD) of an AOC. Figure 7.2 illustrates this C2 structure.

This structure was created not by design but as the result of a compromise when the TACC was created in 1992. Prior to the creation of the TACC, Military Airlift Command, the predecessor to AMC, utilized a three-tier command structure. Taskings would flow from the MAJCOM to one of two geographically organized numbered air forces (NAF) and then to a specific wing. Geography determined which NAF received the tasking. For example, cargo intended for Europe would be given to the East Coast NAF. The East Coast NAF would then parcel out the tasking to a wing, based on the overall operations tempo. Air mobility forces outside the CONUS used a smaller scale but similar arrangement, where taskings from the COCOM flowed through an AMOCC and then to an air mobility unit.

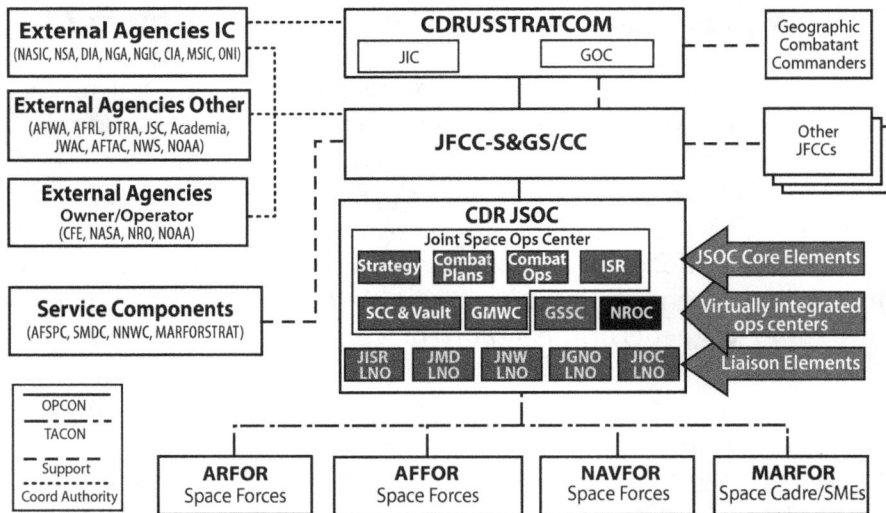

Figure 7.2. Air mobility command and control. (*Reprinted from* AFDD 2-6, *Air Mobility Operations*, Air Force Doctrine Center, 1 March 2006.)

The pitfall with this arrangement was that there was no central agency in position to optimize air mobility needs across the DOD as a whole. Instead, each wing fought its own fight. For example, there was a tasking for half a C-141 load of equipment from Fort Bragg, North Carolina, to Ramstein AB, Germany, on one day and a tasking for half a C-141 load of equipment from Fort Campbell, Kentucky, to Ramstein AB, Germany, the next day. No one was in a position to identify and optimize that cargo movement. As air mobility assets decreased and taskings increased in the post–Desert Storm era, this arrangement could not continue.[3]

As a result, in 1992 AMC created the TACC. As part of its charter, the TACC looked for efficiencies and ways to optimize cargo movements. However, the COCOMs balked at giving up total control of their air mobility assets. As a result, the SecDef brokered a compromise that allowed the COCOMs to retain control of their assets and gave them the ability to request additional airlift assets, as required. For example, during Operation Enduring Freedom, USCENTCOM was given C-17s to help with their airlift into Afghanistan.[4]

While this may seem inefficient, in practice it has worked very well. In general, TACC has championed optimizing cargo movements, while theaters are focused on ensuring responsiveness to the theater commander's needs. In addition, the forward basing of air mobility assets turned into a huge benefit. For example, the TACC commander during OEF indicated that humanitarian airdrops into Afghanistan would not have happened as quickly or when desired by CENTCOM without USAFE air mobility personnel at Rhein-Main AB and Ramstein AB, Germany, leaning forward, based on the USAFE commander's direction.[5]

Lessons for Space Command and Control

As discussed above, control of on-orbit space assets is currently fragmented. This is unfortunate because a legitimate threat exists, and to fight and win a DCS fight, we need an organization with a global perspective and the ability to direct and influence all DOD space operators. At the same time, normal geographic divisions do not apply to space assets, and space systems function as system-of-systems.

Others also share this view. USSTRATCOM issued a FRAGO that designated the AFSPC commander:

> As its Global Space Coordinating Authority (GSCA) to identify and establish a Joint Space Operations Center to provide all COCOMs with requested space support. As our GSCA, AFSPC has authority to provide direct support if necessary until the establishment of the Joint Functional Component Commander–Space & Global Strike (JFCC-S&GS), at which time, the JFCC-S&GS will issue a follow on FRAGO with further guidance. All other USSTRATCOM components will provide support to the Global Space Coordinating Authority as required.[6]

The JFCC-S&GS command center, much like the TACC, is a significant improvement because it places all of STRATCOM's space assets under a single commander with global situational awareness. The question now is What should the JSpOC consist of? What should its responsibilities be? More importantly, what are the JSpOC's operational roles and responsibilities during a DCS fight? Figure 7.3 shows a preliminary look produced by Fourteenth Air Force and its assessment of the C2 relationships. This proposed structure places all STRATCOM-assigned space

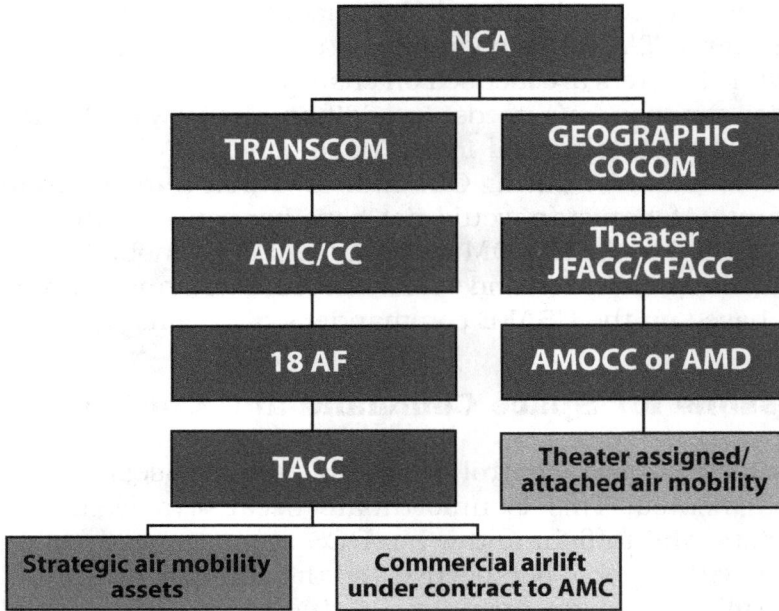

Figure 7.3. Proposed JSpOC organizational structure. (*Adapted from* Briefing, Maj Gen Michael A. Hamel, commander, Fourteenth Air Force, subject: Joint Space Operations Center, ver. 2, 1 March 2005, 8.)

forces under a single commander. It then gives the commander coordination authority with other owners and operators.

While placing all STRATCOM assets under a single commander is a positive improvement, is a coordination-only relationship with other owners/operators sufficient? In laymen's terms, a coordination relationship means that the JSpOC commander can talk directly with other owners and operators. As a part of this discussion, the JSpOC commander can advise of an actual or impending attack and discuss actions he/she is directing for the forces under STRATCOM. Other DOD owners and operators do not have to follow the advice or heed the warning of the JSpOC commander. They also are not required to notify the JSpOC commander of any attacks on their space assets.

What is missing is the ability to direct protective actions for on-orbit space assets owned and operated by others. While perhaps the best answer to this dilemma would be to place all

DOD-owned and -operated satellite systems under the JSpOC, this is probably politically impossible.

Are there any other command relationships that could satisfy the need to direct protective measures without giving STRATCOM OPCON or TACON? In the post-9/11 world, COCOMs have begun using TACON for force protection to give a single commander the ability to better posture their myriad of installations and facilities to meet the terrorist threat. This authority was authorized in a SecDef memorandum on 28 September 1998 and directs that "geographic CINCs will exercise directive authority (TACON) for the purposes of force protection, in the covered countries, over all DOD personnel."[7] Only USEUCOM enacted this as authorizing "commanders to change, modify, prescribe and enforce force protection measures for all DOD elements and personnel under the CCDR for force protection. TACON for force protection includes the authority to inspect, assess security requirements, to direct DOD activities to identify the resources required to correct deficiencies, and submit budget requests to parent organizations to fund identified corrections."[8] In practice this led to the designation of a single commander within a geographic area to hold TACON for force protection, allowing him/her to direct force protection measures over all DOD personnel and installations in that area. For example, within USEUCOM, the Third Air Force commander held TACON for force protection for the United Kingdom, allowing him/her to direct force protection for the USAF-occupied air bases in East Anglia, USN personnel in Cornwall, and USA personnel at the port of Ipswich.

Applying this concept of control to space assets would give the JSpOC commander the ability to exercise limited control over other space assets within the DOD without changing OPCON or providing complete TACON. It eliminates the pitfalls identified above by requiring other commanders to follow direction from the JSpOC commander and also to notify him/her of any attacks on JSpOC assets. In short, it would create a single space fight under a single commander rather than a collection of coordinated fights under various owners and operators.

Another key element we should take from air mobility lessons learned is the advantages in having some forces under a single functional commander while having other forces under a COCOM.

For air mobility the advantage is having one agency with a global perspective chartered to optimize cargo movements and forward-deployed forces focused on meeting the COCOM's immediate objectives.

For space forces, the advantages are similar: a global agency focused on those inherently global functions while giving theater commanders control of those assets needed to accomplish their mission. Unfortunately, in space the divisions are as clean as with air mobility assets. However, it appears that on-orbit assets should fall under the JSpOC commander. This will allow him/her to fight and win the DCS fight. As long as the combat effects delivered by those space assets continue, COCOMs should not have to worry about efforts taken by the JSpOC to ensure their delivery. At the same time, theater space personnel should be kept informed of the fight, especially if it looks like kinetic effects will be needed to counter the threat.

As for those assets which should be given to the theater, current doctrine provides a "litmus test" that uses the following criteria for CHOP of assets. The first question in the litmus test is Is the asset deployed? The second question is Does the asset produce theater-only effects? The final question is Does the theater have the ability to C2?[9]

A look at how the air mobility community CHOPs assets is useful. Because doctrine is ambiguous, the litmus test used for deciding when to CHOP an airlift asset is based on a theater's ongoing need for dedicated airlift, lack of sufficient resources, or need for additional resources. Therefore, to apply the air mobility lesson to space assets, the litmus test should be: Does the theater commander require the preponderance of the asset's capability?

Conclusion

While space assets have unique attributes, we can look toward other functionally aligned communities within the Air Force for lessons learned. The air mobility community's C2 structure holds great promise as a model for space C2. Rather than attempt to use a single C2 model, air mobility uses a global C2 structure to optimize global requirements with a complementary geographic C2 structure. This structure optimizes those assets which operate best as system-of-systems while allowing geographic commanders the ability to use organic air mobility to rapidly respond to their local needs. Applying this model to space creates the global C2 structure needed to win a DCS fight. It also allows assets to be "given" to a geographic commander when required. The final lesson learned from air mobility is the ambiguous litmus test used to CHOP assets to a theater. Rather than formally define a litmus test like space doctrine, air mobility doctrine leaves this ambiguous, providing greater flexibility.

Whatever the outcome of our debates on this C2 structure, we should never lose sight of the fact that our adversaries are looking for ways to attack us and that we must be prepared to fight and win this battle. Key to winning this fight is organizing our forces to meet and overcome any attack.

Notes

1. Peter B. DeSelding, "AsiaSat Assessing Safeguards after Four Hours of Pirated Broadcast," *Space News* 15, no. 47, 8 December 2004, http://search.space.com/spacenews/archive04/asiasatarch_120604.html.

2. "U.S. Accuses Cuba of Jamming Broadcasts to Iran," *PBS.org*, 17 July, 2003, http://www.pbs.org/newshour/media/media_watch/july-dec03/jamming_07-17.html.

3. Lt Gen Mike Wooley, commander, AFSOC, interview by the author, 2 March 2005. General Wooley was the TACC commander from January 2000 to June 2002.

4. Ibid.

5. Ibid.

6. USSTRATCOM, OPORD 05-02, FRAGO 04, 3 Feb 05, https://halfway.peterson.af.mil/2Letters/cc/AFSPC%20Policy%20page/Establishment%20of%20the%20Joint%20Space%20Operations%20Center--2Mar05.pdf. Assigned GSCA to commander, AFSPC/COMAFFOR, and directed the establishment of a JSpOC. FRAGO 04 directs the commander, Fourteenth Air Force, to develop and implement an action plan to establish the JSpOC.

7. AFDCH 10-01, *Air and Space Commander's Handbook for the JFACC*, 16 January 2003.

8. Third Air Force Instruction (3AFI) 10-245, *Air Force Antiterrorism Standards*, 16 Feb 04.

9. AFDD 2-2.1, *Counterspace*, 11 August 2004.

Chapter 8

Counterspace Command and Control

Looking to History for Advice

Lt Col Bill Liquori, USAF, and
Lt Col Chance Saltzman, USAF

Former Air Force chief of staff General Jumper declared counterspace operations "critical to success in modern warfare."[1] Inasmuch, space professionals must endeavor to improve the C2 relationships and doctrine associated with counterspace systems. In particular, the complex relationship between planners in theater AOCs and those at the Fourteenth Air Force AOC provides many challenges. The complication of a functionally focused team directly supporting theater needs creates a strained working relationship between the two entities. The C2 seam that this creates is problematic for the optimal execution of counterspace effects in-theater. A brief review of the Vietnam War, Desert Storm, and Iraqi Freedom highlights similarities in the history of C2 of joint air operations and provides insight into counterspace doctrine and improvements to critical C2 relationships.

Before reviewing historical case studies, one must understand the nature of current counterspace problems. The need for significant counterspace effects in OIF exposed a problematic seam between AFSPC's designated planning and execution authority, Fourteenth Air Force, and theater counterspace planners trying to integrate counterspace effects into the CFACC air and space operations plan. Without counterspace doctrine or mutual agreement, both sides occasionally suffered from preconceived and parochial views of appropriate C2 relationships. In addition to divergent C2 views, distrust—or at least misunderstanding between the two planning groups—created a less than optimal working relationship. A strained atmosphere surrounding C2 is not unique to the counterspace arena, and counterspace planners can learn much from the development of similar relationships surrounding joint air operations.

159

Command and Control
Disagreement in Vietnam

The Vietnam War provides a textbook case of what to avoid when cultivating a strong working relationship across the C2 seam. The US military fought this war while enduring a bitter disagreement over C2 of joint air operations. In 1966 the senior Air Force commander in South Vietnam, Lt Gen Joseph Moore, argued he should be the single manager for all aviation assets. The Air Force felt this was the most effective and efficient method of controlling operations, but other services disagreed. The Army began to use their own helicopters for missions like troop insertion, resupply, and battlefield fire support. Gen William Westmoreland, commander, United States Military Assistance Command Vietnam, captured the passions and anger surrounding this issue with a passage in his memoirs. According to General Westmoreland, Gen Curtis LeMay, chief of staff of the Air Force, chastised him for trying to infringe on Air Force turf by using helicopters and "tongue-lashed" General Moore for failing to uphold Air Force doctrine. Additionally, the Air Force's efforts to control Marine aviation caused extreme displeasure because it violated Marine combined arms doctrine.[2]

By 1968 General Westmoreland had grown tired of a situation "too ponderous, too extravagant with resources, [and] too conducive to error" and designated General Moore's replacement, Gen William Momyer, to be the single manager for air operations. Westmoreland received vociferous objections from the Army and Marine service chiefs and reported with frustration that he "was unable to accept that parochial considerations might take precedence over my command responsibilities and prudent use of assigned resources."[3] Because there was no doctrinal answer, the commander-in-chief, United States Pacific Command had to resolve the dispute by granting General Momyer "mission direction" over Marine aircraft. This ambiguous and ad hoc concept resulted in each service interpreting the term as they wanted, and the Marines never relinquished control.[4] Distrust, parochialism, and lack of clear doctrine at the service interface prevented effective C2 of joint air operations.

Beginnings of Cooperation

In the period between Vietnam and Desert Storm, several actions occurred to improve the working relationships and doctrine between the services. First, the Air Force and Army chiefs of staff, who experienced C2 frustrations firsthand in Vietnam, made a concerted effort to improve the relationship. They mandated a partnership between the Air Force's Tactical Air Command (TAC) and the Army's Training and Doctrine Command (TRADOC), which resulted in a joint office called the Directorate of Air-Land Forces Application (ALFA) and numerous improvements in air-ground operations coordination.[5] Most importantly, it established an atmosphere where both sides shared perspectives and cooperated to solve problems based on parochial interests.

Several years later, the Department of Defense Reorganization (Goldwater-Nichols) Act of 1986 expanded the mandate for interservice cooperation to all services. The act expanded the role of CINCs by giving them total responsibility for employing joint forces assigned to them. Air operations felt the impact of the Goldwater-Nichols Act directly because of the joint interface required for integrated operations.[6] These events certainly did not eliminate all problems with C2 of joint air operations, but they paved the way for improved doctrine and relationships in time for Operation Desert Storm.

Improved Command and
Control in Operation Desert Storm

Operation Desert Storm proved to be a watershed event highlighting the improvements in interservice campaign planning and operations, which greatly benefited joint air operations. First, the CFACC concept, a natural doctrinal outgrowth of the Goldwater-Nichols Act, allowed a much greater degree of coordination in air operations than possible in Vietnam. The CFACC, General Horner, benefited from the centralized decision-making process his predecessors wanted, but he recognized doctrine could not substitute for cooperation and mutual confidence.[7] This recognition inevitably resulted from his experiences in

Vietnam and rising through the ranks during the TAC-TRADOC partnership era. As a result, Horner built a strong relationship with his CINC, who trusted him fully and did not get overly involved in controlling air operations.[8]

Even though he was the recognized single manager for joint air operations, General Horner had to work some of the same issues as his predecessors, but he did so in a more conducive environment. First, there were complaints from Army commanders about insufficient coverage of their targets, to which the Air Force countered that the CFACC based all his decisions on the CINC's priorities. Even though this issue was due largely to problems with a CINC that was dual-hatted as the ground component commander, all sides found a compromise in the Joint Targeting Coordination Board (JTCB).[9] Clear doctrine also helped establish a compromise with the Marines, who placed some of their aircraft under CFACC control but kept control of aircraft supporting Marine ground forces. Horner claimed mixed results with this agreement, but today's planners should note the success that was generated by the willingness of each service to see the other's perspective and find mutually acceptable solutions.[10]

Further Improvements in Operation Iraqi Freedom

Operation Iraqi Freedom marked the continued maturation of the C2 of joint air operations based on strong working relationships. The CFACC, General Moseley, and Marine leaders displayed an unprecedented willingness to find a mutually agreeable solution regarding control of Marine aviation. They agreed to place all Marine aircraft on the ATO, but allowed Marines to retain tactical control of organic Marine air assets through a direct air support center. To further improve the relationship, General Moseley requested and received a senior Marine aviator to serve on his AOC staff. This relationship helped establish an innovative kill box deconfliction system within the fire support coordination line that achieved great success in Iraq. In fact, both sides have trumpeted the success of the relationship in securing devastating ground support for Marine forces and in allowing the CFACC to shape the deep battlespace with extra aircraft. This success would not have been possible without the "development of personal relationships, from the Generals on down. Parochial views gave way to dialogue."[11] Since Army–Air Force coordination was not as effective, the Marine successes show how much cooperation can contribute to a successful solution. Whatever the future holds for C2 interfaces, it must be remembered that success will depend on a strong working relationship based on trust and cooperation.

Counterspace Command and Control Issues

As these improvements in joint air operations were developed, the debate regarding the C2 of counterspace systems has also grappled with its own C2 seams, relationships, and doctrine. In the counterspace arena, the main seam exists between the theater AOC and the Fourteenth Air Force AOC. During initial planning for OEF, a disagreement developed between the two sides. Without guiding counterspace C2 doctrine, each developed its own strategies. Theater AOC planners, citing the JFACC as the single manager for air and space forces, requested OPCON of counterspace systems to provide the JFACC the greatest possible flexibility. Fourteenth Air Force planners preferred a direct support relationship for two reasons. The supporting relationship provided greater flexibility for AFSPC's global taskings, and it facilitated the accomplishment of nontransferable mission-planning tasks.

In addition to lack of doctrinal clarity, the lack of effective working relationships also caused problems. Theater planners did not argue the unique planning tasks, but they disagreed with the control required to perform that planning. Theater planners believed that in-theater space planners were in the best position to integrate effects into the overall campaign.[12] To help resolve these issues, AFSPC sponsored several working groups. Attendees routinely left these meetings perpetuating the C2 relationship they believed was appropriate prior to the meeting. The prewar planning devolved into acrimonious debate and diminishing trust in intentions and ability on both sides of the interface. This atmosphere created a stalemate of rigid adherence to organizational preferences, with each side willing to wait until combat situations mandated a final decision.

Prior to OIF, the relationships and doctrine had not been substantially improved; thus, the same counterspace C2 issues resurfaced. Ultimately, the disagreement forced a compromise with Fourteenth Air Force, in direct support of CENTCOM, who exercised TACON. During this conflict, the creation of senior space coordinators at the CINC headquarters and on the CFACC staff further complicated the C2 debate. With split coordination and guidance efforts in-theater and disagreement over the appropriate level of control required for effective planning, counterspace planning proceeded with the idea that combat conditions would resolve the issues. When combat conditions finally occurred, routine and preplanned operations were handled well, but the need to adjust dynamically to changing threat conditions showed that the C2 seams were problematic.

The aftermath of OIF showed promise for a reengaged discussion. The Air Force published its first counterspace doctrine, AFDD 2-2.1, which codified terms, concepts, and roles. The document does not mandate a standard C2 structure. It provides situational suggestions, but leaves the solution to counterspace planners on both sides of the C2 seam.[13] With regards to C2 doctrine, historical air operations again may provide some key insights and considerations.

Director of Space Forces and Director of Mobility Forces: One in the Same?

In 2004 the Air Force's Counterspace Operations doctrine was published, outlining the function of the DIRSPACEFOR.[14] In short, the DIRSPACEFOR will work routine senior-level coordination issues between components and represent the CFACC to organizations outside the joint force. Similarly, the director of mobility forces (DIRMOBFOR) is the "designated coordination authority for air mobility with all commands and agencies both internal and external to the joint force."[15] Because the titles and duties are so similar, space planners must be clear about the appropriateness of using the air mobility model in assessing counterspace C2 relationships.

The DIRSPACEFOR and DIRMOBFOR positions have similarities and differences that must be understood to avoid making incorrect assumptions about C2 responsibilities. Similarly, senior officers with expertise and theater familiarity should fill both positions. Also, both positions are attached to the COMAFFOR and located in-theater to ensure close coordination with the overall theater air effort. Lastly, both positions are tasked with performing similar functions, including integrating, coordinating, deconflicting, prioritizing, and directing their particular areas of expertise. However, within these functions there are significant differences which change the roles of each position.

There are two key differences between the two positions that space personnel must assess in order to avoid C2 problems. First, the overarching task assigned to the DIRMOBFOR is to be "responsible for integrating the total air mobility effort for the JFACC."[16] In contrast, the DIRSPACEFOR merely conducts "coordination, integration, and staffing activities to tailor space support for the JFACC."[17] Although this may seem like only a semantic separation of responsibilities, it becomes significant as C2 responsibilities are executed. For example, in the Gulf War the JFACC, General Horner, told his senior airlifter, "I don't know anything about airlift. You take your airlift, and if you need anything from me, you let me know. I'm too busy fighting the air war."[18] For mobility operations, this type of relationship creates problems because although command responsibility of mobility forces is given to the JFACC, responsibility minus command is delegated to the DIRMOBFOR. As a result, mobility planners have concluded that the JFACC needs an expert mobility advisor but also an expert with C2 authority (OPCON/TACON) delegated directly from AMC to control theater air mobility operations.[19]

In OIF, USSTRATCOM was in a direct-support relationship with USCENTCOM to provide space capability. As a result, the JFACC did not have complete command responsibility of space capabilities. While he still needed an expert space advisor, that expert did not require C2 authority to integrate theater space effects. From this it seems that the position of director is more appropriate for space than air mobility because unlike the DIRMOBFOR, the DIRSPACEFOR must focus on coordinating, integrating, and staffing space support rather than on controlling space capabilities in-theater. This difference leads to the second key distinction between the two positions.

The second major difference between the two directors is that the DIRMOBFOR conducts his/her responsibilities by directing the AOC's AMD, while the DIRSPACEFOR has no such division in the AOC.[20] The AMD plans, coordinates, tasks, and executes the air mobility mission but because space integration duties are spread throughout the AOC, the DIRSPACEFOR must facilitate and coordinate space activities across multiple AOC divisions.[21] The presence of an AOC division dedicated to mobility operations is indicative of the fact that unlike space capabilities in-theater, mobility operations require C2 well beyond the effects they achieve in-theater. Space effects in-theater cut across multiple mission areas in a way that demands an integrator and coordinator rather than a commander. Furthermore, the DIRMOBFOR is in a position to control *intratheater* airlift with little regard to impacts outside the AOR. However, all space effects must be considered for their impacts outside the theater and therefore require an in-theater director focused on the extensive coordination with agencies outside the AOR. In summary, it must be recognized that the position of DIRSPACEFOR is different from that of DIRMOBFOR, and understanding his/her role as an integrator and advisor rather than a controller of space capabilities will improve doctrinal understanding of counterspace C2.

A Way Ahead

Before the still smoldering relationship ignites again, personnel on both sides of the interface should look to joint air operations history for advice. The Vietnam and Iraq case studies show the key to improved control for joint air operations was developing a relationship based on trust, cooperation, and a willingness to put aside parochial positions. James Winnefeld and Dana Johnson offer two appropriate suggestions. First, both sides "should be mindful of service and joint doctrine [and organizational preferences], but not be bound by [them] when [they do] not support the mission at hand." Next, the theater and space AOC planners should "establish a close personal rapport

. . . [and] create an atmosphere [where] each sees cooperation and coordination as a necessary preliminary step in defeating the enemy." [22]

To help create this atmosphere, this study proposes several suggestions. As demonstrated by the TAC-TRADOC partnership and the two conflicts in Iraq, successful change occurs when commanders above the "iron majors" understand the needs of others and place priority on cooperation. Air Force AOC directors, including the Fourteenth Air Force AOC, should initiate discussions to exchange perspectives and formalize a partnership for improving the counterspace C2 interface, much like ALFA accomplished for the joint air operations interface in the 1970s. This step would place a priority on cooperation and innovative solutions and would discourage parochial rigidity.

A second lesson is the importance of understanding the perspective and concerns of the other side of the C2 seam. A great place to start increasing perspective is the training ground for many future counterspace planners—the 328th Weapons Squadron (WPS) at the USAF Weapons School. The squadron is currently sending students to the Fourteenth Air Force AOC for an orientation.[23] The 328th WPS should ensure this trip exposes the students to the complexity of counterspace C2 by having AOC personnel share their procedures, perspectives, and recent counterspace experiences with theater AOCs. Additionally, the 328th WPS should schedule a seminar session where students discuss relevant issues, including counterspace C2, with an experienced DIRSPACEFOR. These discussions would open a cooperative dialogue between Fourteenth Air Force and future theater space personnel, as well as provide the perspective of a DIRSPACEFOR, who coordinates with both sides of the interface. Finally, this group must fully understand and promote the Air Force's counterspace doctrine. By exercising the doctrine, learning its strengths and weaknesses, and improving it, counterspace C2 will be far better in future wars.

Another group that can contribute to sharing perspectives across both sides of the counterspace seam is the AFSPC Weapons and Tactics Branch. In managing AEF assignments for space forces, they should provide augmentees exposure to multiple perspectives by scheduling them to participate in exercises from each side of the C2 interface. This would provide the added benefit of allowing the augmentee to work with the DIR-SPACEFOR from both sides of the seam. Furthermore, in managing the billet structure for SWOs, the weapons and tactics branch should research the feasibility of switching AOC planning positions to a tier-two, second-assignment billet. The benefit would be a more experienced weapons officer with a seasoned perspective of the issues on both sides of the C2 seam.

While many challenges could threaten successful counterspace operations in the future, a crucial enabler is improving the relationship between theater AOC personnel and Fourteenth Air Force AOC personnel. Additionally, exercising and improving the Air Force's counterspace doctrine and avoiding ad hoc C2 relationships will help overcome feelings of distrust. The long history of joint air operations highlights the importance of working with solid doctrine and establishing a working relationship based on trust, cooperation, and shared perspectives. Space personnel on both sides of the C2 interface must heed the lessons of history to build an improved counterspace relationship and appropriate doctrine as a springboard to future success by employing these critical elements of modern warfare.

Notes

1. AFDD 2-2.1, *Counterspace Operations*, 2 August 2004, Foreword.

2. James A. Winnefeld and Dana A. Johnson, *Joint Air Operations: Pursuit of Unity in Command and Control, 1942–1991* (Annapolis, MD: Naval Institute Press, 1993), 68–71.

3. Gen William D. Westmoreland, *A Soldier Reports* (Garden City, NJ: Doubleday, 1976), 342–44.

4. Winnefeld and Johnson, *Joint Air Operations*, 73–74.

5. Dr. Harold R. Winton, "An Ambivalent Partnership: US Army and Air Force Perspectives on Air-Ground Operations, 1973–1990," in *The Paths of Heaven: The Evolution of Airpower Theory*, ed. Col Phillip S. Meilinger (Maxwell AFB, AL: Air University Press, 1997), 411.

6. Winnefeld and Johnson, *Joint Air Operations*, 100–101.

7. Ibid., 133.

8. John Andreas Olsen, *Strategic Air Power in Desert Storm* (Portland, OR: Frank Cass Publishers, 2003), 132.

9. Winnefeld and Johnson, *Joint Air Operations*, 125.

10. Rebecca Grant, "Marine Air in the Mainstream," *Air Force Magazine* 87, no. 6 (June 2004): 60–64.

11. Ibid., 62.

12. Maj Keith Balts (counterspace planner, CENTAF), interview by author, 14 December 2004.

13. AFDD 2-2.1, *Counterspace Operations*, iii, v.

14. Ibid., 14.

15. AFDD 2-6, *Air Mobility Operations*, 25 June 1999, 20.

16. Ibid.

17. AFDD 2-2.1, *Counterspace Operations*, 14.

18. Ted E. Carter, Jr., "Theater Air Mobility: Historical Analysis, Doctrine and Leadership," *Air Force Journal of Logistics* 24, no. 3 (Fall 2000): 27–35.

19. Ibid., 31.

20. AFDD 2-6, *Air Mobility Operations*, 21.

21. Ibid.

22. Winnefeld and Johnson, *Joint Air Operations*, 147.

23. Maj Robert Sheehan (328th WPS, operations director), interview by author, 14 December 2004.

Chapter 9

Bridging the Gap

Five Observations on
Air and Space Integration

Lt Col J. Christopher Moss, USAF

In 1998 General Jumper, then commander of Air Combat Command, declared that the Air Force would know air and space were truly integrated "when people stop talking about it."[1] If the intensity and scope of the talk at the recent SWO conference are any indication, it appears the Air Force may have more to do in its efforts to integrate air and space.

The conference, held 17 March 2005 at Maxwell AFB, was cosponsored by AETC and AFSPC to solicit ideas on how to enhance the integration of air and space capabilities at the operational level of war. SWOs from across the Air Force delivered a wide range of presentations—from employment concepts for the SCA to methods of normalizing counterspace force presentation to the JFC—all articulating ways to further the Air Force's air- and space-integration efforts.

This section summarizes the author's conference presentation, which recounted five observations for improving air and space integration drawn from personal experiences working air and space integration in two tactical fighter wings, a MAJCOM, and multiple CAOCs in both PACAF and USAFE from 1998 to 2003. To be certain, neither the presentation nor this summary attempts to articulate *the* single testable answer on how to integrate air and space. Rather, each merely seeks to describe the recurring trends that space professionals experience while working in the air side of the Air Force.

Background

The Air Force began to focus on air and space integration in the aftermath of Desert Storm.[2] Touted as the first space war, the conflict showed the true potential of space systems to support modern combat operations. In particular, airpower would be best able to realize revolutionary advances by aggressively incorporating information provided by space systems. As a result, the Air Force initiated a broad campaign to integrate its air and space systems more effectively. Throughout the 1990s, these efforts focused largely on how to exploit space products and information to support air operations.[3] The author describes this type of air and space integration as *force-enhancement integration.*

The Air Force implemented significant changes in pursuit of force-enhancement integration. For example, in 1992, it established the Space Warfare Center to develop new space-integration capabilities. A year later, the Air Force established the Fourteenth Air Force to serve as the war-fighting component to USSPACECOM and to ensure war fighters were supported by the best space capabilities available.[4] Shortly afterward, the Fourteenth Air Force created the space operations center to serve as "one-stop shopping" for DOD units requiring space support for the Air Force. Eventually, in AFDD 2-2, *Space Operations*, the Air Force codified its views on space and space integration.

In the early 2000s, however, the Air Force was compelled to broaden its approach to air and space integration. In 2001, the Commission to Assess United States National Security Space Management and Organization highlighted the importance of space as an independent medium. The commission's report concluded:

> We know from history that every medium—air, land, and sea—has seen conflict. Reality indicates that space will be no different. Given this virtual certainty, the U.S. must develop the means both to deter and to defend against hostile acts in and from space. This will require superior space capabilities. Thus far, the broad outline of U.S. national space policy is sound, but the U.S. has not yet taken the steps necessary to develop the needed capabilities and to maintain and ensure continuing superiority.[5]

In response to the commission's findings, SecDef Donald Rumsfeld directed the Air Force to, among other things, assume responsibilities as executive agent for space and to prepare for the prompt and sustained conduct of offensive and defensive space operations.[6] In effect, Secretary Rumsfeld and the space commission expanded the concept of air and space integration so that, in addition to exploiting space systems to enhance air operations, air and space integration would entail ensuring unity of effort among independent air and space operations in support of a task force commander's objectives. The author refers to this type of air and space integration as *space-control integration.*[7]

The Air Force responded to the new aspect of air and space integration by establishing the 76th Space Control Squadron (76th SPCS) to conduct OCS and DCS operations.[8] In 2004, it equipped the squadron with the CCS to disrupt enemy satellite communications.[9] Shortly afterward, it created the 25th Space Control Tactics Squadron (25th SCTS) to develop TTP for space-control operations.[10] The Air Force complemented those efforts by revising its space doctrine. AFDD 2-2 was updated to articulate C2 relationships for independent space operations. The Air Force also published its first doctrine on counterspace operations, AFDD 2-2.1.

The two doctrine documents represent the evolution of air and space integration. Today, the Air Force is working to advance both forms of integration: force enhancement and space control. Yet, these concepts of integration are not always compatible, and differing interpretations over how best to pursue and deconflict the two have created tension in the Air Force. In fact, if the presentations given at the SWO conference are any indication, most of the issues facing air and space integration stem from differences between the two concepts of integration.

Observations

The observations and recommendations in the author's briefings are generally applicable to both facets of air and space integration—although some are more relevant to one than the other. In all cases, however, they reflect one SWO's interpretation of air and space integration from a theater (i.e., non-AFSPC) perspective.

Observation 1. The integration of air and space requires knowledge of both air and space operations.

To successfully integrate air and space requires knowledge of both air and space operations. In force-enhancement integration, integrators must understand how space information is used by air systems. In counterspace integration, integrators must comprehend operational-level air execution to ensure synchronization and unity of effort among air and space operations.

To date, the Air Force's approach to air and space integration has focused on giving broad space education to the air side of the Air Force and giving specific air training to a relatively small group of specially selected and experienced space operators. However, the broader space segment of the Air Force has been largely excluded from similar training. This reality hinders the complete integration of air and space. As space professionals conduct their operations, they must do so with an understanding of how those operations fit into the larger operations of the Air Force. For example, AFSPC has worked hard to develop systems capable of pushing near-real-time information to the cockpit of tactical aircraft. However, less work has been put into understanding *when* and *how* that information should be pushed to the cockpit. The space operators' lack of understanding about the nature of fighter operations has led them to produce user interfaces that are less than ideal. In other words, just because we *can* push data to the cockpit, doesn't mean we always *should*. Knowing when we should requires an understanding of air operations. Similarly, it is one thing for our GPS operators to know what a PDOP (position dilution of precision) of 50 means in technical terms. It is quite another to know how that value impacts the accuracy of a JDAM (joint direct attack munitions), PLGR (precision lightweight GPS receiver), or a Have Quick radio. As a general statement, however, space operators are not taught this type of information during their space systems training. Simply put, the lack of training on how air systems use space information hinders the integration of air and space.

The effects of space operators' incomplete training are compounded by a lack of firsthand experience in how space systems support air operations. By limiting the number of space operators assigned to theater commands to conduct air and space integration, the Air Force impedes integration. In my experience, there is no substitute for being at the place where the integration occurs. During my tour in PACAF, I often said that more space integration happens over a beer at the squadron bar than will ever happen in a classroom or on an operations floor. That's because the personal relationships that develop from common experiences facilitate in-depth exchanges on what exactly space can and cannot do for air operations; or how space operations can and cannot be used to support overall campaign objectives.

To overcome these obstacles requires three things. First, AFSPC and AETC should expand space training so that *all* courses on space have in-depth modules covering how a given space system's products or services fit into the joint fight. AFSPC has made great progress in this area with the AS200 and the Advanced System Training courses. However, AFSPC can provide that training to a broader audience and conduct more tailored training if it makes sure that all initial and unit qualification training as well as continuation training have robust modules on how space data is used in air operations. DSCS III operators in the 3d Space Operations Squadron should expect to learn how ground-mobile forces use DSCS communications, why DSCS III channel 1 is important, who uses it, with what equipment, and with what operating concepts. Such training, combined with the continued push to teach air operators about space, is an important first step to bridging the air-space gap.

However, academics are not enough. Therefore, the second step is to provide space operators firsthand exposure to air operations to complement their academics. Today, there are a significant number of space personnel in billets outside of AFSPC. For example, when the author served as the functional area manager for space personnel in USAFE, over 50 core space personnel were assigned to the command. Unfortunately, all but nine were in career-broadening assignments. In other words, they were not in positions that provided them an opportunity to see how space data and products are exploited during air operations. Maximizing the integration of air and space requires increased assignment opportunities for space personnel to billets where they can obtain firsthand experience integrating air and space. Maj John "Stitch" Thomas's excellent presentation on space integration in a WFHQ may provide such opportunities.[11] Major Thomas advocates placing space professionals on OPTs in every theater command. As OPT members, these space professionals would be charged with preparing the plans and procedures necessary to integrate air and space components in-theater.

The last step necessary to enhance air and space integration leverages the gains made by the first two. To complete the cycle of training and assignments to improve integrating air and space, AFSPC must exploit the air experience gained by those space professionals who have been assigned to theater-integration billets. The AFSPC developmental teams could be used to ensure that space professionals who go to space-integration positions outside AFSPC return to positions within AFSPC to leverage that experience.

Consider the potential benefit of a DSCS III operator from AFSPC who receives an assignment to a combat communications squadron to work an LST-5 or initial communication package in direct support of air operations. Certainly, having seen satellite communications from a systems and user perspective, that operator would have a much deeper understanding of satellite communications *writ large*. Now consider if that same operator were assigned to be a MILSTAR flight commander after his or her tour in combat communications. Air and space integration would surely benefit from a space professional whose experience is based on multiple satellite communications systems, end-user employment, and issues associated with direct support to air operations. Perhaps that same individual could then move to the 76th SPCS to work with the CCS. Who better to develop TTP for a CCS system than an operator with this level of experience? Similar arguments could be made for missile-warning operators to progress from the 12th Space Warning Squadron to the SBIRS to an AOC TMD cell or for a GPS operator to progress from 2d Space Operations Squadron to the 422d Test Squadron or 17th Test Squadron and then to the 25th SCTS.

But today such deliberate progressions are extremely rare. More typically, the Air Force relies on a relatively small number of well-trained generalists as the primary means of conducting air and space integration. These integrators come almost exclusively from the USAFWS. Established in 1996, the space division of the USAFWS evolved from the AFSPC STS, which was originally founded specifically to provide a select group of space professionals with sufficient space experience to conduct air and space integration. By 1996, however, it became clear that air and space integration required a deeper understanding of air operations. As a result, AFSPC and ACC agreed to establish a space division at the USAFWS. From its first class, the USAFWS Space Weapons Instructor Course curriculum differed from the STS in that it included robust training on air systems and their employment. Space operators were completely integrated with air operators during nearly all air academics to ensure a common education. That air training was followed by an exhaustive space-systems training and, more importantly, instruction in how they would support air operations and how this could be leveraged to enhance the joint fight.

To date the space division of the USAFWS, recently redesignated the 328th WPS, has graduated nearly 150 SWOs. However, less than half of those are currently working space-integration jobs. Others have completed their five-year obligation to serve in SWO billets, are attending professional military education, or have been moved to non-SWO billets (e.g., MAJCOM staffs, executive officers, members of commanders' action groups, etc.).[12] This leaves a relatively small number of space officers with sufficient training and experience to conduct air and space integration. This reality is at the heart of my second observation.

Observation 2. Current air and space integration efforts are fragile.

As the Air Force has come to rely on SWOs to perform the bulk of air and space integration—both force enhancement and space control—they have become high-demand, limited assets. In the process, the Air Force's overall air and space integration efforts have become fragile. The Air Force made a conscious decision to concentrate on the operational level of war as the focus of its integration efforts. As a result, the baseline manning for space personnel in the Falconer AOCs is fairly robust. So much so, that when filled, these positions consume nearly one-third of current SWO manning.[13]

However, bridging the gap of air and space requires integration efforts outside the AOC as well as inside. Properly trained integrators are needed at MAJCOMs to incorporate space into organize, train, and equip decisions as well as to develop policy and guidance for theater space-integration efforts. Furthermore, to integrate air and space fully requires efforts in such places as the Air Force Doctrine Center, the Air Staff at NAFs, the NRO, and the full range of organizations within AFSPC. One could argue that tactical fighter and mobility wings, joint unified commands, and schools across the Air Force also require space personnel to help realize full integration.

However, filling such positions adequately is a challenge. Typically, space integrators in these non-AOC billets are one-deep; as is the case at the 35 FW, HQ USAFE, Third Air Force, Seventh Air Force, the Air Force Doctrine Center, and many others. Such one-deep manning creates difficulties for integration. First, the success or failure of a unit's space-integration effort can rest on the training, motivation, and expertise of a single individual. This has the potential to create very uneven integration efforts across the Air Force. Further, when a single space integrator is on leave, supporting an exercise, deployed, or TDY, the unit is deprived of *all* of its manning; that is, it has *no* space-integration personnel on hand to support the unit's mission.

The continuing decrease in the numbers of graduates from the USAFWS compounds that problem by creating gaps in the manning of non-AOC units. When the number of graduates lags the number of open billets for a given year, non-AOC units go without backfills for space integrators. For example, when Weapons Instructor Course class 00B produced insufficient graduates to replace departing SWOs, some units, such as the 51 FW, were left with no space-integration manning. This left PACAF and the 51 FW with few options. Either it could let the 51 FW go without a SWO for six months until the next class graduated from the USAFWS or it could send other SWOs TDY to help cover the 51 FW until the next WIC class could produce a replacement. PACAF chose the latter option. Unfortunately, the SWOs sent to fill in at the 51 FW also came from one-deep positions in their home units. Therefore, while these SWOs were deployed to the 51 FW, their home units were left without space-integration manning.

Such problems are further exacerbated by the fact that non-AOC space programs are largely autonomous. In other words, they are not typically governed by any higher headquarters (HHQ) regulations or accountable to HHQ inspections.[14] This virtually ensures the programs are not institutionalized. As a result, space integration efforts in PACAF often bear little resemblance to those in USAFE or CENTAF. Even within the same command and unit, the lack of institutionalized programs leads to significant changes as SWOs PCS (permanent change of station) and are replaced by SWOs with different perspectives.

To overcome these problems, the Air Force must find ways to increase the robustness and redundancy of its space-integration programs. In terms of manning, the Air Force must continue to fill theater-integration billets with trained and motivated space personnel. Further, it must work to increase the presence of space personnel in-theater. Obviously, it is not possible to provide AOC-level space manning to every unit where integration occurs, but AFSPC must strive to overcome the problems of one-deep manning. Once again, Maj Thomas's essay on space integration in a WFHQ may provide the answer on how to increase robustness to provide a pool of trained space personnel for a given HQ. This action would also have the added benefit of increasing space personnel exposure to air operations as recommended in my first observation.

Next, to reverse the trend in weapons school applications, AFSPC should develop a campaign plan for increasing interest in, and applications for, the USAFWS. In addition to continued support from AFSPC's senior leadership, that plan should focus on AFSPC wings to emphasize the importance and value of the USAFWS to the Air Force, AFSPC, and the individual.

Finally, the Air Force should establish air- and space-integration standards to help institutionalize space-integration programs. Specifically, AFSPC should work with the theater commands to define minimum training, equipment, and performance standards for personnel conducting space integration. Further, the commands should make their space-integration programs accountable by developing space-integration evaluation criteria for HHQ inspections. Such efforts will make existing space-integration programs more standard and more routine throughout the Air Force.

Taken collectively, these actions will make air and space integration more reliable and more redundant. While this is an important advance in air and space integration, their benefits can be undermined by the inefficiencies associated with competition over the development and fielding of dedicated space-integration tools.

Observation 3. Air and space integration requires specialized tools.

Both force enhancement and space control integrating air and space require specialized tools such as:

- computer applications—the Space Battle Manager Core System (SBMCS);
- reference material—Air Force Tactics, Techniques, and Procedures (AFTTP) 3-1, vol. 28, *Tactical Employment, Space*, 2002; and
- unique hardware—the Air Defense System Integrator.

To date, many of the tools used to support integration have also been designed to support nonintegration space operations. In several instances, the integration and nonintegration requirements competed for funding and priority during development of the tools. That competition and the need to serve multiple customers have worked to dilute the ability of the tools to support integration efforts.

For example, AFTTP 3-1, volume 28, is structured for three distinct purposes: (1) to serve as a tactical reference manual for space operators within AFSPC, (2) to serve as a space-familiarization guide for nonspace personnel across the Air Force, and (3) to be used as a reference source for space integrators working in the theater commands. The competing demands of the volume's three audiences necessitated trade-offs and compromises during its 2002 rewrite. These, in turn, diluted the volume's value as a space-integration reference manual.[15] Similarly, during the spiral development of the SBMCS, AFSPC was continually forced to make priority trade-offs between the software modules that were meant to support AFSPC mission requirements and those that were meant to support theater space-integration requirements. Although most modules were eventually fielded for SMBCS, competition between its various customers led to delays in fielding several integration modules.

To overcome these types of inefficiencies, AFSPC should work with theater commands to identify space-integration needs and to develop systems that expressly meet those needs. Until such tools are fielded, however, integrating air and space is likely to require extensive training in both air and space systems. This limits the number of personnel qualified to conduct integration and contributes to the fragility described in observation two. The bulk of integration today is conducted by SWOs, which highlights the fourth observation.

Observation 4. The USAFWS is critical to air and space integration.

Currently, the primary source of training for personnel conducting air and space integration is the 328th WPS at the USAFWS. Although true for both types of integration, this is particularly true for space-control integration. The 328th WPS provides training on air and space systems and employment that is unique for its breadth and depth. That training is combined with an unparalleled environment for practical application during the USAFWS graduation exercise, mission employment, and Red Flag exercises. The 328th WPS produces, perhaps, the only personnel in the Air Force who can talk with equal fluency about air and space.

The future viability of the program is in jeopardy due to the decreasing numbers of applications. For example, for the fall class of 2004 there were 19 applications for 10 class slots. However, the spring 2005 class only received 11 applicants for eight slots. Of these, only eight met the minimum qualifications. For the fall 2005 class eight applicants applied for eight slots; six were selected.[16] These numbers are even more alarming when compared to numbers from the author's class in 1999, where over 100 candidates applied for 12 slots. There are several reasons why AFSPC is experiencing this trend. One reason relates to the company grade officers (CGO) in AFSPC, another involves the leadership in AFSPC, while yet another concerns the SWOs themselves.

Although space has been a part of the USAFWS for nearly 10 years, the typical CGO in AFSPC still knows very little about the school. On the flying side of the Air Force, by contrast, CGOs are fully aware of the USAFWS and the role it plays in airpower. Most flying squadrons have a dedicated weapons officer, and many of the squadron, group, and wing leadership personnel are weapons officers. This gives CGOs ample opportunity to learn about the school. On the space side of the Air Force, however, this is not the case. There are relatively few weapons officers in space wings and still fewer in senior leadership positions within AFSPC, leaving AFSPC CGOs somewhat uninformed about the USAFWS.

What AFSPC CGOs do know of the USAFWS is that it is an extremely challenging program. Unlike many other Air Force programs, students can, and do, routinely "wash out" of the USAFWS. This can be discouraging and intimidating to potential applicants—especially in a culture such as AFSPC that demands near perfection in training and evaluation. Many CGOs see the potential to wash out of the course as a strong incentive to look elsewhere for opportunities, such as serving as an executive officer or competing for the Air Force intern program. These realities combine to decrease applications to the USAFWS.

Generally speaking, there is very little push from the group and squadron leadership in AFSPC to counter that decrease. This is understandable, given the current concept for using 328th WPS graduates. In effect, group and squadron leaders are encouraging some of their best CGOs to leave their units to attend a school and then will likely assign them outside of AFSPC for three to six years. In other words, the units wind up giving up an asset, with no tangible return on their investment.

Finally, CGO applications to the USAFWS are decreasing because of SWO arrogance—both perceived and real. The perception of arrogance stems from a cultural divide between what SWOs are taught at the USAFWS and the predominant culture in AFSPC. In the USAFWS, as in much of the flying side of the Air Force, dialogue about operational issues is often blunt and critical. To those unaccustomed to it, such dialogue can appear pretentious and condescending. Yet, the USAFWS teaches that such frankness is essential to identifying, correcting, and thus preventing operational errors.

At the same time, there have been occasions when the direct-ness of the USAFWS has been overdone and was inappropriate to the situation in which it was used. In these cases, SWO ar-rogance is not only perceived, but also real. That arrogance has been cited as a reason some AFSPC CGOs have decided not to apply to the USAFWS.[17] To the degree that this is true, the few instances where CGOs have the opportunity to interact with SWOs may have worked to discourage USAFWS applications.

Reversing this trend requires a change in culture in AFSPC. As part of the campaign to promote the USAFWS described ear-lier, AFSPC should embrace the frank and direct style of opera-tional evaluation that is employed on the flying side of the Air Force. Second, space operators' attendance at the USAFWS must be seen as an investment in the Air Force's ability to inte-grate air and space. In other words, rather than viewing a space officer's attendance at USAFWS as a loss for the unit and the command, AFSPC leadership should regard it as fulfilling the command's responsibility to provide space personnel to the USAFWS as part of the Air Force's overall integration effort.

As AFSPC promotes the importance of the USAFWS, it must remember that the school is much more challenging than most other Air Force training programs. As such, it is fairly common for students to wash out of the program. Traditionally, in AFSPC, failure to complete a training program is seen as a significant black mark on an operator's record. If the command wishes to increase applicants to the school, however, it should view the USAFWS differently. Given the demanding nature of the course, applicants should be assured that students who do not com-plete the course will not be viewed with prejudice.

Finally, AFSPC should remember that the USAFWS is a pro-gram that serves the larger Air Force. For over 50 years, the school has been one of the genuine successes of US combat training. Today, that success is due, in large measure, to the extraordinary fidelity and comprehensiveness of the training the school provides. In other words, the school focuses its train-ing on all the systems required to wage the modern fight. Main-taining that success requires all squadrons at the USAFWS to dedicate a significant portion of their training time to under-standing other weapons systems, not just their own. That is why space students attend the same academies on air-to-air missiles as do the Viper and Eagle students. Likewise, students from the flying squadrons attend space academies as a standard part of their curriculum. To ensure that each squadron supports the broader learning at the school, ACC serves as the executive agent for each squadron's training curriculum.

Recently, however, AFSPC has made several requests to change the curriculum at the weapons school to sacrifice blocks of air training to allow more time to focus on expanded space training. Such a change potentially undermines the value that comes from an integrated training program. To ensure that all courses remain integrated and properly balanced between air and space, ACC should remain the approval authority for the space-training curriculum at the USAFWS.

Disputes such as these, along with differences in culture and perspectives, have led to tension between those inside and outside the command over the "best" way to integrate air and space. Among those outside the command, tensions have led to the perception that AFSPC and those inside the space community tend to view space parochially.

Observation 5. The space community is perceived as parochial in space matters.

Regardless of whether these perceptions are true, perception is reality. The author experienced enough of it during his time at the wing, in AOCs, and at a MAJCOM to be convinced that it is not a matter of particular individuals nor confined to specific issues. For example, despite experience in spacelift operations, his comments submitted on the Operationally Responsive Spacelift Mission Needs Statement were rejected simply because they were submitted from his position as chief of Space Weapons and Tactics in USAFE (i.e., outside the command). Similarly, theater representatives were intentionally excluded from the recent AFOTTP 2-3.4, "Air Force Operational Tactics, Techniques, and Procedures," drafting conference. When they asked why, they were told they could provide their input when the document was released for comments. The recurring disagreement between the theater space integrators and those in AFSPC over the best C2 arrangement for deployable space assets is yet another example.

While none of these issues is beyond compromise, collectively, they represent a recurring difference of opinion between personnel inside and outside of the command on how best to integrate air and space. Moving beyond these disagreements requires AFSPC and the theater commanders to work together on integration. Specifically, AFSPC should require space personnel outside the command to help shape integration efforts. This means actively soliciting participation during the development of integration procedures and working to find common ground when resolving differences. Similarly, theater integrators must contribute meaningfully to AFSPC integration efforts. AFSPC should support the theater's indigenous space operations and valid initiatives that originate outside the command. Maj Keith "Weed" Balts and Maj Mark "Leno" Schuler presented such ideas during the conference. One would hope AFSPC and theaters will work together to evaluate their presentations to determine if they represent an improvement in air and space integration.[18] In this regard, the SWO conference represents an excellent first step.

Conclusion

To date, the Air Force has been tremendously successful at force-enhancement integration. Recently, it has made impressive strides in space-control integration. However, that does not mean there isn't room for improvement. My conference presentation was an attempt to highlight some ways the Air Force can make such improvements.

The five observations presented herein are just one SWO's opinion on some of the issues confronting air and space integration. Those opinions are the result of seven years of air- and space-integration experience *outside* AFSPC. It is quite certain that the same issues may appear in an entirely different light when viewed from *inside* the command. Given this possibility, it would appear that the more space integrators inside and outside the command can discuss the issues involved in air and space integration, the more likely we are to identify ways to improve it.

Conferences like this one are an excellent way to generate such discussion. However, more frequent discussions between AFSPC and the theater commands would be even better. Perhaps, a series of roundtables could be scheduled to rotate through the commands to continually discuss the issues facing integration. Those discussions should continue until all integrators agree that there is nothing left to discuss. Only then, as General Jumper observed, will we know that air and space are fully integrated.

Notes

1. Gen John P. Jumper, USAF, commander, Air Combat Command, Langley AFB, VA, to all staff, e-mail, February 2000.

2. Benjamin Lambeth, "The Synergy of Air and Space," *Aerospace Power Journal* 12, no. 2 (Summer 1998): 11.

3. Ibid., 14.

4. Vandenberg Air Force Base, "14th Air Force History," http://www .vandenberg.af.mil/~associates/14af/14af_history/fact.html.

5. Donald H. Rumsfeld, *Report of the Commission to Assess United States National Security Space Management and Organization* (Washington, DC: Government Printing Office, 11 January 2001), x, http://www.defenselink.mil/ pubs/space20010111.html.

6. SecDef Donald H. Rumsfeld to the Honorable John Warner, chairman of the Committee on Armed Services, memorandum, 8 May 2001.

7. For an excellent yet concise description of the evolution of the two forms of integration, see Major Balts, "Organization for Worldwide Space Control Operations: Establishing Theater Space Control Coordination Centers as the Next Step in Organizing Space Power at the Operational Level" (paper presented at the SWO Conference, Maxwell AFB, AL, 17 March 2005).

8. The 21st Space Wing, 76th Space Control Squadron, "Fact sheet," http://www.peterson.af.mil/21sw/library/fact_sheets/76spcs.htm.

9. John A. Tirpak, "Securing the Space Arena," *Air Force Magazine* 87, no. 7 (July 2004): 33.

10. Lt Col Don Ridolfi (commander, 25th SCTS), interview by author, 10 May 2005.

11. Maj John R. Thomas, "Theater Space Control in a Warfighting Headquarters" (paper presented at the SWO Conference, Maxwell AFB, AL, 17 March 2005).

12. Air Force SWO functional manager (ACC/XOTW), interview by author, 14 March 2005.

13. Calculated from the list of SWOs maintained in AFSPC's Space Personnel AEF Tracking System as of 10 May 2005, https://halfway.peterson.af.mil/ dotw/Documents/ww%20billet%20slide%20-%20August%2004.PPT#510,1, CurrentW13SBillets-Worldwide.

14. Headquarters PACAF has made the most progress in this area. The first generation of SWOs created space-integration CONOPs that were approved by the respective wings and NAFs. In 2001 Maj Dean "Deanis" Helmick, the Fifth Air Force SWO, conducted the Air Force's first staff assistance visit on a space-integration program when he inspected the program at the 35 FW. He conducted a similar inspection for the 18 FW and led the effort to have unit space-integration program inspections conducted by Headquarters PACAF. Unfortunately, this huge step forward has not been replicated in other commands.

15. The author participated in the 2002 Air Force Space Command Weapons and Tactics Conference, which included a session to lay the groundwork for the 2002 AFTTP 3-1, volume 28 rewrite session. During that session, the participants were required to modify inputs to the volume to ensure it would meet each of its three purposes.

16. Air Force SWO functional manager, interview by author, 14 March 2005.

17. SWO arrogance was commonly cited as a reason for not applying to the USAFWS during informal discussion between the author and AFSPC CGOs from 1999 to 2005.

18. See Balts, "Organization for Worldwide Space Control Operations"; and Maj Mark Schuler, "It Isn't Space, It's Warfare! Joint Warfighting Space and the C2 of Deployable Space Forces" (paper presented at the SWO Conference, Maxwell AFB, AL, 17 March 2005).

Abbreviations

1-4-2-1	*National Military Strategy*
9/11	11 September 2001
25th SCTS	25th Space Control Tactics Squadron
76th SPCS	76th Space Control Squadron
328th WPS	328th Weapons Squadron
AADP	area air defense plan
AAF	Army Air Forces
ACC	Air Combat Command
ACE	Advanced Composition Explorer
ACP	airspace control plan
ADCON	administrative control
AEF	air expeditionary forces
AETC	Air Education and Training Command
AETF	air and space expeditionary task force
AFC²TIG	Air Force Command and Control Training and Innovation Group
AFDC	Air Force Doctrine Center
AFDD	Air Force doctrine document
AFFOR	Air Force forces
AFI	Air Force instruction
AFPC	Air Force Personnel Center
AFSOC	Air Force Special Operations Command
AFSPC	Air Force Space Command
AFTTP	Air Force tactics, techniques, and procedures
ALFA	Air-Land Forces Application
AMC	Air Mobility Command
AMD	air mobility division
AMOCC	air mobility operations control center
AO	area of operations
AOC	air and space operations centers
AOG	air operations group
AOR	area of responsibility
ARS	advanced reconnaissance system
AST	advanced system training
A-staff	AFFOR staff
ATO	air tasking order

189

C2	command and control
CAF	combat air forces
CAOC	combined air operations center
CAP	crisis action planning
CAS	complex adaptive systems
CCDR	combatant commander
CCS	countercommunications system
CDRUSSTRATCOM	commander, United States Strategic Command
CENTAF	Central Command Air Forces
CENTCOM	US Central Command
CFACC	combined force air component commander
CGO	company grade officer
CHOP	change of operational control
CJCS	chairman of the Joint Chiefs of Staff
COA	course of action
COCOM	combatant command
COG	center of gravity
COMAFFOR	commander, Air Force forces
COMSPACEAF	commander, Space Air Forces
CONUS	continental United States
CSAR	combat search and rescue
CT	counterterrorism
DCS	defensive counterspace
DIRMOBFOR	director of mobility forces
DIRSPACEFOR	director of space forces
DMSP	Defense Meteorological Satellite Program
DOD	Department of Defense
DOTMLPF	doctrine, organization, training, materiel, leadership and education, personnel, and facilities
DP	deliberate planning
DSB	Defense Science Board
DSCS	Defense Satellite Communications System
DSCS III	Defense Satellite Communications System III
DSP	Defense Support Program
DT	developmental teams
EBO	effects-based operations

F2T2EA	find, fix, track, target, engage, and assess
FAM	functional area manager
FHA	foreign humanitarian assistance
FID	foreign internal defense
FOV	field of view
FRAGO	fragmentary order
FSST	forward space support teams
GBS	global broadcast service
GCC	geographic combatant commander
GMF	ground mobile forces
GPS	global positioning system
GSCA	global space coordinating authority
GWOT	global war on terror
HHQ	higher headquarters
HQ	headquarters
HS	homeland security
IMINT	imagery intelligence
IO	information operations
IQT	initial qualification training
ISR	intelligence, surveillance, and reconnaissance
ITO	integrated tasking order
JAOC	joint air operations center
JDSF	joint director of space forces
JFACC	joint force air component commander
JFC	joint force commander
JFCC–S&GS	joint functional component commander–space & global strike
JOA	joint operations area
JP	joint publication
JPRC	Joint Personnel Recovery Center
JSCA	joint space coordinating authority
JSCC	joint space control center
JSpOC	joint space operations center
JTCB	joint targeting coordination board
JTF	joint task force
JWS	Joint Warfighting Space
LNO	liaison officer

MAAP	master air attack plan
MAJCOM	major command
MASINT	measurement and signature intelligence
MCO	major combat operations
MILSTAR	military strategic and tactical relay system
MIO	maritime intercept operations
MPC	mission planning center
MQT	mission qualification training
NAF	numbered air force
NEO	noncombatant evacuation operations
NMS	*National Military Strategy*
NRO	National Reconnaissance Office
NSSI	National Security Space Institute
OA	operational area
OAF	Operation Allied Force
OCS	offensive counterspace
OEF	Operation Enduring Freedom
OIF	Operation Iraqi Freedom
OODA	observe, orient, decide, and act
OPCON	operational control
OPLAN	operations plan
OPR	office of primary responsibility
OPT	operational planning teams
PACAF	Pacific Air Forces
PNT	positioning, navigation, and timing
PO	peace operations
POTUS	president of the United States
PR	personnel recovery
PRCC	personnel recovery coordination cell
PRETC	Personnel Recovery Education and Training Center
PSAB	Prince Sultan Air Base
RSTA	reconnaissance, surveillance, and target acquisition
RTIC	real-time information to the cockpit
SAMS	surface-to-air missile sites
SATCOM	satellite communications
SBIRS	space-based infrared system

SBMCS	Space Battle Management Core System
SCA	space coordinating authority
SCCC	space control coordination center
SCP	space coordinating plan
SD	Strategic Command Directive
SecDef	secretary of defense
SEF	space expeditionary force
SEG	space expeditionary group
SEW	space expeditionary wing
SIGINT	signals intelligence
SIOE	Space and Information Operations Element
SISP	single integrated space picture
SJFHQ	standing joint force headquarters
SMP	strategic master plan
SOCEUR	Special Operations Component, United States European Command
SOCPAC	Special Operations Component, United States Pacific Command
SPACEAF	space air forces
SPINS	special instructions
SSA	space situation awareness
SSO	senior space officer
SST	space support teams
STO	space tasking order
STS	Space Tactics School
SWC	Space Warfare Center
SWO	space weapons officer
TAC	Tactical Air Command
TACC	tanker airlift control center
TACON	tactical control
TAF	tactical air force
TENCAP	tactical exploitation of national capabilities program
TMD	theater missile defense
TO	theater of operations
TRADOC	Training and Doctrine Command
TTP	tactics, techniques, and procedures
UCP	Unified Command Plan
UFO	ultrahigh frequency follow-on

UN	United Nations
UNAAF	Unified Action Armed Forces
USAFE	United States Air Forces in Europe
USAFWS	United States Air Force Weapons School
USCENTAF	United States Central Command Air Forces
USCENTCOM	United States Central Command
USCINCSPACE	commander-in-chief, US Space Command
USEUCOM	United States European Command
USJFCOM	United States Joint Forces Command
USSOCOM	United States Special Operations Command
USSPACECOM	United States Space Command
USSTRATCOM	United States Strategic Command
USTRANSCOM	United States Transportation Command
VOA	Voice of America
WFHQ	warfighting headquarters
WS	weapon systems

Glossary

al-Qaeda	Sunni Islamist terrorist organization
Falconer	theater AOCs
Falun Gong	banned religious group in China
InfoWorkSpace	software for secure nets
Internet Café	terrorist C2 center
kill chain	(see F2T2EA)
penny packets	splitting space forces between theaters
Ploesti	oil fields in Rumania
Reblue	getting back to basic roots
space control	(joint community)
system-of-systems	satellite group
Traveling Circus	93rd Bombardment Group

Bibliography

21st Space Wing, 76th Space Control Squadron. "Fact sheet." http://www.peterson.af.mil/21sw/library/fact_sheets/76spcs.htm.

505th Training Squadron. "Personnel Recovery Course." Course description. https://505ccw.hurlburt.af.mil/505trg/505trs/aocpr.htm.

Air Force Doctrine Center (AFDC). *Doctrine Watch #3: Operational Control (OPCON)*, 4 Nov 1999. https://www.doctrine.af.mil/DoctrineWatch/.

Air Force Doctrine Center Handbook (AFDCH) 10-01. *Air and Space Commander's Handbook for the JFACC*, 16 January 2003.

Air Force Doctrine Document (AFDD) 1. *Air Force Basic Doctrine*, 17 November 2003.

AFDD 2. *Organization and Employment of Aerospace Forces*, 17 February 2000.

AFDD 2-2. *Space Operations*, 27 November 2001.

AFDD 2-2.1. *Counterspace Operations*, 2 August 2004.

Air Force Instruction (AFI) 13-1AOCV3. *Operational Procedures—Aerospace Operations Center*, 1 July 2002.

Air Force Space Command (AFSPC). *Strategic Master Plan FY06 and Beyond*, 1 October 2003.

Anderegg, C. R. *Sierra Hotel: Flying Air Force Fighters in the Decade after Vietnam*. Washington, DC: Air Force History and Museums Program, 2001.

Arquilla, John, and David Ronfeldt. "The Advent of Netwar (Revisited)." In *Networks and Netwars: The Future of Terror, Crime, and Militancy*, edited by John Arquilla and David Ronfeldt. Santa Monica, CA: RAND, 2001.

———. "Information, Power, and Grand Strategy: In Athena's Camp—Section 1." In *In Athena's Camp: Preparing for Conflict in the Information Age*, edited by John Arquilla and David Ronfeldt. Santa Monica, CA: RAND, 1997.

Arquilla, John, David Ronfeldt, and Michele Zanini. "Networks, Netwar, and Information Age Terrorism." In *Strategic Appraisal: The Changing Role of Information in Warfare*, edited by Zalmay Khalilzad, John P. White, and Andrew W. Marshall. Santa Monica, CA: RAND,1999.

Baker, Addison Earl, Lloyd Herbert Hughes, John Louis Jerstad, Leon William Johnson, and John Riley Kane. *Ploesti: When Heroes Filled the Sky*. Pueblo, CO: Home of Heroes. http://www.homeofheroes.com/wings/part2/09_ploesti.html.

Balts, Maj Keith. "Organization for Worldwide Space Control Operations: Establishing Theater Space Control Coordination Centers as the Next Step in Organizing Space Power at the Operational Level." Paper presented at the Space Weapons Officer Conference. Maxwell AFB, AL, 17 March 2005.

Barnett, Thomas P. M. *The Pentagon's New Map: War and Peace in the Twenty-First Century*. New York: G. P. Putnam's Sons, 2004.

Bassford, Christopher. *Clausewitz and His Works*. Carlisle Barracks, PA: Army War College, 2002.

Billman, Lt Col Gregory M. "The 'Space' of Aerospace Power: Why and How." Master's thesis, University of Pittsburgh, May 2000.

Biscoe, TSgt Andrew. "Deployed Chief creates Air Force mural for dining-in." *Patriot* 32, no. 2 (February 2005): 6.

Black, J. Cofer, ambassador-at-large, coordinator for counterterrorism, Department of State. *Testimony before the House International Relations Committee, Subcommittee on International Terrorism*. Washington, DC: US Department of State, 1 April 2004. http://www.state.gov/s/ct/rls/rm/2004/31018.htm.

Boyd, John R. "A Discourse on Winning and Losing." Photocopies of briefing slides. Maxwell AFB, AL: Air University Library, August 1987.

Briefing. Maj Gen Michael A. Hamel, commander, Fourteenth Air Force. Subject: Joint Space Operations Center, ver. 2, 1 March 2005.

Briggs, MSgt Julie. "Near Space Enhances Joint Warfighting." *Air Force Print News*, 18 February 2005. https://www.af.mil/news/story.asp?storyID=123009865.

Bush, Pres. George W. *National Strategy for Combating Terrorism, February 2003*. Washington, DC: White House, 14 February 2003.

Carter, Ted E., Jr. "Theater Air Mobility: Historical Analysis, Doctrine and Leadership." *Air Force Journal of Logistics* 24, no. 3 (Fall 2000): 27–35.

Carter, Tom. "Castro Regime Jamming U.S. Broadcasts into Iran." *Washington Times*, 16 July 2003.

Chairman of the Joint Chiefs of Staff (CJCS). *Joint Publications Status Report.* Joint Doctrine Branch, 30 December 2004. http://www.dtic.mil/doctrine/publications_status.htm.

Chairman, Joint Chiefs of Staff Instruction (CJCSI) 6130.01C. *CJCS Master Positioning, Navigation, and Timing Plan*, 31 March 2003.

Christol, Carl Q. *The Modern International Law of Outer Space.* Elmsford, NY: Pergamon Press, 1982.

Coningham, Arthur. "Development of Tactical Air Forces." *Journal of the Royal United Services Institution*, May 1946.

Coram, Robert. *Boyd: The Fighter Pilot Who Changed the Art of War.* New York: Back Bay Books, 2002.

Department of Defense (DOD). *Report of the Defense Science Board Task Force on Training Superiority and Training Surprise.* Washington, DC: Office of the Undersecretary of Defense for Acquisition, Technology, and Logistics, January 2001.

Deptula, Brig Gen David A. *Effects-Based Operations: Change in the Nature of Warfare.* Arlington, VA: Aerospace Education Foundation, 2001.

DeSelding, Peter B. "AsiaSat Assessing Safeguards after Four Hours of Pirated Broadcast." *Space News* 15, no. 47 (8 December 2004). http://www.space.com/spacenews/archive04/asiasatarch_120604.html.

DiBella, Anthony J., and Edwin C. News. *How Organizations Learn: An Integrated Strategy for Building Learning Capability.* San Francisco, CA: Jossey-Bass Publishers, 1998.

DOD Directive (DODD) 3100.10. *Space Policy*, 9 July 1999.

Drew, Lt Col Dennis M. "Of Trees and Leaves: A New View of Doctrine." *Air University Review* 33, no. 2 (January–February 1982): 40–48.

Federici, Gary. *From the Sea to the Stars: A History of U.S. Navy Space and Space-Related Activities.* Washington, DC: Naval Historical Center, Department of the Navy, June 1997.

Field Manual (FM) 100-18. *Space Support to Army Operations*, 20 July 1995.

Fredriksson, Lt Col Brian E. "Space Power in Joint Operations: Evolving Concepts." *Air and Space Power Journal* 18, no. 2 (Summer 2004): 85–95.

Glenn, Maj Kevin B. "The Challenge of Assessing Effects-Based Operations in Air Warfare." *Air and Space Power Chronicles*, 24 April 2002. http://www.airpower.maxwell.af.mil/airchronicles/bookrev/glenn.html.

Gourley, Scott R. "Space Warriors." *Military Geospatial Technology* 2, no. 2 (22 Jul 2004).

Grant, Rebecca. "Marine Air in the Mainstream." *Air Force Magazine* 87, no. 6 (June 2004): 60–64.

Hammond, Grant T. *The Mind of War: John Boyd and American Security*. Washington, DC: Smithsonian Books, 2001.

Headquarters Fourteenth Air Force, History Office. "14th Air Force History." *United States Air Force Fact Sheet*. http://www.vandenberg.af.mil/~associates/14af/14af_history/fact.html.

Hughes, Dr. Thomas. "The Cult of the Quick." *Aerospace Power Journal* 15, no. 4 (Winter 2001): 57–68.

Joint Personnel Recovery Agency (JPRA). Personnel Recovery Education and Training Center (PRETC). Course catalog. http://www.jpra.jfcom.mil/Military/pretc.cfm.

Joint Publication (JP) 0-2. *Unified Action Armed Forces* (*UNAAF*), 10 July 2001.

JP 1-02. *Department of Defense Dictionary of Military and Associated Terms* (As amended through 14 April 2006), 12 April 2001.

JP 3-0. *Doctrine for Joint Operations*, 10 September 2001.

JP 3-14. *Joint Doctrine for Space Operations*, 9 August 2002.

JP 3-50. "Joint Doctrine for Personnel Recovery." Second draft, 19 July 2004.

Jost, Jurgen. *External and Internal Complexity of Complex Adaptive Systems*. Sante Fe, NM: Sante Fe Institute, 16 December 2003. http://www.santafe.edu/research/publications/workingpapers/03-12-070.pdf.

Jumper, Capt John P. "Training Toward Combat Capability (Part One)." *USAF Fighter Weapons Review* 24, no. 4 (Winter 1976).

Jumper, Gen John P. "Adapting the AEF—Longer Deployment, More Forces." *Chief's Sight Picture*, June 2004. http://www.af.mil/library/policy/letters/pl2004_06.html.

———. "Joint Warfighting Space." White Paper, 8 January 2004.

Keidel, Robert W. *Seeing Organizational Patterns: A New Theory and Language of Organizational Design.* San Francisco, CA: Berrett-Kockler Publishing, 1995.

Lambeth, Benjamin S. *Mastering the Ultimate High Ground: Next Steps in the Military Use of Space.* RAND Report MR-1649-AF. Santa Monica, CA: RAND, 2003.

———. "The Synergy of Air and Space." *Aerospace Power Journal* 12, no. 2 (Summer 1998): 5–14.

Lord, Gen Lance W. AFSPC/CC. To distribution. Memorandum, 2 March 2005.

———. Briefing to Gen John P. Jumper. Subj.: Joint Warfighting Space Update, 21 December 2004.

Mahan, A. T. *The Influence of Sea Power Upon History, 1660–1783.* Boston, MA: Little, Brown and Co., 1918.

Main, Maj Mark. "An Examination of Space Coordinating Authority and Command Relationships for Space Forces." Working paper, Fourteenth Air Force Weapons and Tactics Division, Vandenberg AFB, CA.

Mann, Edward C., III, Gary Endersby, and Thomas R. Searle. *Thinking Effects: Effects-Based Methodology for Joint Operations.* Maxwell AFB, AL: Air University Press, 2002.

McNiel, Maj Samuel L. "Proposed Tenets of Space Power: Six Enduring Truths." *Air and Space Power Journal* 18, no. 2 (Summer 2004): 71–83.

Meyers, Gen Richard B. *National Military Strategy of the United States of America.* Washington, DC: Department of Defense, May 2004.

National Security Space Institute. Counterspace Planning and Integration Course (CPIC). Course description. https://www.peterson.af.mil/nssi/(qms1jlq1ykpcgqrinf1on245)/index.aspx.

Olsen, John Andreas. *Strategic Air Power in Desert Storm.* Portland, OR: Frank Cass Publishers, 2003.

Post, Jerrold M., M.D. "Killing in the Name of God: Osama bin Laden and Al Qaeda." *Future Warfare Studies*, no. 18. Maxwell Air Force Base, AL: USAF Counterproliferation Center, November 2002.

Prebeck, Col Steven R. "Operating Concept for Joint Warfighting Space (JWS)." Working paper, Air Force Space Command, Peterson AFB, CO, 27 July 2004.

———. "Operating Concept for Joint Warfighting Space (JWS)." Draft. HQ AFSPC/XO, 10 November 2004.

Project RAND. *Preliminary Design of an Experimental World-Circling Spaceship.* RAND Report SM-11827. Santa Monica, CA: Douglas Aircraft Company, Inc., 2 May 1946.

Raymond, Col Jay. DOD Office of Force Transformation. Address. Air War College, Maxwell Air Force Base, AL, February 2005.

Reynolds, Glenn A., and Robert P. Merges. *Outer Space: Problems of Law and Policy.* Boulder, CO: Westview Press, 1989.

Rumsfeld, Donald H., SecDef. *Report of the Commission to Assess United States National Security Space Management and Organization.* Washington, DC: Government Printing Office, 11 January 2001.

———. *Transformation Planning Guidance.* Washington, DC: Department of Defense, April 2003. http://library.nps .navy.mil/uhtbin/hyperion-image/TPGfinal.pdf.

———. To the Honorable John Warner, chairman of the Committee on Armed Services. Memorandum, 8 May 2001.

Schuler, Maj Mark. "It Isn't Space, It's Warfare! Joint Warfighting Space and the C2 of Deployable Space Forces." Paper presented at the Space Weapons Officer Conference. Maxwell AFB, AL, 17 March 2005.

Schull, Todd C. "Space-Operations Doctrine: The Way Ahead." *Air and Space Power Journal* 18, no. 2 (Summer 2004): 96–102.

Schwartz, Peter. *The Art of the Long View.* New York: Doubleday Currency, 1991.

Secretary of the Navy (SECNAV) Instruction 5400.39B. *Department of the Navy Space Policy,* 26 August 1993.

Shalizi, Cosma Rohilla. *Methods and Techniques of Complex Systems Science: An Overview.* Ann Arbor, MI: Center for the Study of Complex Systems, University of Michigan, 9 July 2003.

Singer, Jeremy. "U.S.-Led Forces Destroy GPS Jamming Systems in Iraq." *Space News*, 25 March 2003.

Slife, Lt Col James C. *Creech Blue: General Bill Creech and the Reformation of the Tactical Air Forces, 1978–1984*. Maxwell AFB, AL: Air University Press, 2004.

Sloan, Stephen. *Beating International Terrorism: An Action Strategy for Preemption and Punishment*. Maxwell AFB, AL: Air University Press, April 2000.

Smith, Maj M. V. *Ten Propositions Regarding Spacepower*. Fairchild Paper. Maxwell AFB, AL: Air University Press, October 2002.

Sole, Ricard V., and Sergei Valverde. *Information Theory of Complex Networks: On Evolution and Architectural Constraints*. Santa Fe, NM: Santa Fe Institute.

Spires, David N. *Beyond Horizons: A Half Century of Air Force Space Leadership*. Maxwell AFB, AL: Air University Press, 1998.

Strategic Command Directive (SD) 404-3. *Space Support to Joint Force Commander or Designated Space Coordinating Authority*, 6 February 2004.

Third Air Force Instruction (3AFI) 10-245. *Air Force Antiterrorism Standards*, 16 Feb 04.

Thomas, Maj John R. "Theater Space Control in a Warfighting Headquarters." Paper presented at the Space Weapons Officer Conference. Maxwell AFB, AL, 17 March 2005.

Tirpak, John A. "Securing the Space Arena." *Air Force Magazine* 87, no. 7 (July 2004): 30–34.

"U.S. Accuses Cuba of Jamming Broadcasts to Iran." *PBS.org*, 17 July 2003. http://www.pbs.org/newshour/media/media_watch/july-dec03/jamming_07-17.html.

US Department of State. *Chronology of Significant International Terrorist Incidents, 2003* (Revised 6/22/04), Appendix A, 1. http://www.state.gov/documents/organization/33890.pdf.

US Joint Forces Command Pamphlet 3. *Doctrinal Implications of the Standing Joint Force Headquarters (SJFHQ)*, 16 June 2003.

US Strategic Command. *OPORD 05-02, FRAGO 04*, 3 February 05.

Waller, J. Michael. "Iran and Cuba Zap U.S. Satellites." *Insight on the News* 19, no. 18 (19 August–1 September 2003): 35.

Watts, Barry D. *Clausewitzian Friction and Future War.* Washington, DC: Institute for National Strategic Studies, National Defense University, 2004.

Westmoreland, Gen William D. *A Soldier Reports.* Garden City, NJ: Doubleday, 1976.

Winnefeld, James A., and Dana A. Johnson. *Joint Air Operations: Pursuit of Unity in Command and Control, 1942–1991.* Annapolis, MD: Naval Institute Press, 1993.

Winton, Dr. Harold R. "An Ambivalent Partnership: US Army and Air Force Perspectives on Air-Ground Operations, 1973–1990." In *The Paths of Heaven: The Evolution of Airpower Theory,* edited by Col Phillip S. Meilinger. Maxwell AFB, AL: Air University Press, 1997.

Wooley, Lt Gen Michael W. "America's Quiet Professionals: Specialized Airpower—Yesterday, Today and Tomorrow." *Air and Space Power Journal* 19, no. 1 (Spring 2005): 59–66.

Zanini, Michele, and Sean J. A. Edwards. "The Networking of Terror in the Information Age." In *Networks and Netwars: The Future of Terror, Crime, and Militancy,* edited by John Arquilla and David Ronfeldt. Santa Monica, CA: RAND, 2001.

Contributors

Maj Keith W. "Weed" Balts (BS, University of Wisconsin; ME, University of Colorado) is currently the Advanced Programs Command Lead for Air Force Space Command, Peterson AFB, Colorado. Previous assignments include chief of space operations for Central Command Air Forces Headquarters; combat deployments for Operation Southern Watch and Operation Enduring Freedom; and chief of the tactics division at the National Reconnaissance Office. Major Balts is a graduate of the USAF Weapons School, Squadron Officer School, and Air Command and Staff College.

Maj Patrick A. "Buster" Brown (BBA, Midwestern State University; MSA, Central Michigan University) is assistant director of operations at the 328th Weapons Squadron, USAF Fighter Weapons School, Nellis AFB, Nevada. Previous assignments include chief, space plans and special technical operations for USCENTAF/Ninth Air Force; and space team lead Strategy Division and STO cell during OIF. Major Brown is a graduate of the USAF Weapons School and Squadron Officer School.

Maj John "Zip" Duda (BSME, University of Pittsburgh; MBA, Embry-Riddle Aeronautical University) is the operations officer at the 328th Weapons Squadron, USAF Fighter Weapons School, Nellis AFB, Nevada. Previous assignments include wing SWO and later, chief, Space Control Plans, 21st Space Wing, Peterson AFB, Colorado; and chief of training, Bravo Flight commander, 4th Space Surveillance Squadron, Holloman AFB, New Mexico. Major Duda is a graduate of the USAF Weapons School, Squadron Officer School, and Air Command and Staff College.

Maj Tyler "Razor" Evans (BSEE, Purdue University) is operations officer, Ground Operations, Aerospace Data Facility, Buckley AFB, Colorado. Previous assignments include space weapons and tactics officer for Joint Task Force, Southwest Asia, supporting Operation Southern Watch; instructor at the 328th Weapons Squadron, USAF Fighter Weapons School, Nellis AFB, Nevada; and deputy chief of weapons and tactics, Headquarters AFSPC. Major Evans is a graduate of the USAF Weapons School, Squadron Officer School, and Air Command and Staff College.

Lt Col William J. "Bill" Liquori, Jr. (BA, Boston University; MA, Webster University) is currently a student assigned to the School of Advanced Air and Space Studies at Maxwell AFB, Alabama. Previous assignments include chief, Ultrahigh Frequency Follow-on Procedures Section; chief, Launch Readiness Division, Onizuka AFS, California; and instructor and later, assistant operations officer at the 328th Weapons Squadron, USAF Fighter Weapons School, Nellis AFB, Nevada. Colonel Liquori is a graduate of the USAF Weapons School and a distinguished graduate of Air Command and Staff College.

Lt Col Michael J. "Lips" Lutton (BA, Kent State University; MS, Lesley College; Master of Military Operational Art and Science [MMOAS], Air Command and Staff College) is a member of the Secretary of the Air Force and Chief of Staff of the Air Force Executive Action Group, Headquarters, USAF, The Pentagon, Washington, DC. Previous assignments include chief, Congressional Activities Branch, headquarters USAF, Directorate of Air and Space Operations; executive officer, headquarters USAFE/ADO; and deputy chief, USAFE Special Technical Operations (STO), 32nd Air Operations Group. Colonel Lutton is a graduate of the USAF Weapons School and a distinguished graduate of Air Command and Staff College.

Lt Col J. Christopher "Elroy" Moss (BA, Purdue University; MA, Webster University; MA, Naval Postgraduate School, and Master of Airpower Art and Science [MAAS], School of Advanced Air and Space Studies) is the Operations Officer at the 4th Space Operations Squadron, Schriever AFB, Colorado. Prior assignments include chief, space weapons and tactics for headquarters USAFE; and SWO for the 35th Fighter Wing, Misawa AB, Japan. Colonel Moss is a graduate of the USAF Weapons School and the School of Advanced Air and Space Studies.

Maj Stuart A. "Millhouse" Pettis (BS, Florida State University; MS, University of North Dakota) is an Intermediate Developmental Education student at the Air Force Institute of Technology. He previously served as the chief of tactics for the Air Force Space Command's only Tactics Squadron and as chief of space and information operations plans for Headquarters, Third Air Force at Royal Air Force Mildenhall, United Kingdom. Major Pettis is a graduate of the USAF Weapons School, Squadron Officers School, and Air Command and Staff College.

Lt Col B. Chance "Salty" Saltzman (BA, Boston University; MAAS, School of Advanced Air and Space Studies) is the chief of combat plans, Joint Space Operations Center, Vandenberg AFB, California. Previous assignments include National Reconnaissance Office, Operating Division Four; instructor, academics flight commander, and assistant director of operations at the 328th Weapons Squadron, USAF Fighter Weapons School, Nellis AFB, Nevada; and chief of operational assessment, Strategy Division, Fourteenth Air Force, Vandenberg AFB, California. Colonel Saltzman is a graduate of the USAF Weapons School, Air Command and Staff College, and the School of Advanced Air and Space Studies.

Maj Mark A. "Leno" Schuler (BSCS, University of Kansas; MBA, Colorado State University; MMOAS, Air Command and Staff College) is a student at the School of Advanced Air and Space Studies, Maxwell AFB, Alabama. Previous assignments include 32d Air Operations Squadron (USAFE AOC), 5th Space Surveillance Squadron, Royal Air Force Feltwell, United Kingdom; CAOC, Prince Sultan Air Base, Saudi Arabia, during Operation Iraqi Freedom; and chief, Space Weapons and Tactics, Headquarters USAFE. Major Schuler is a graduate of the USAF Weapons School, Squadron Officer School, and Air Command and Staff College.

Maj John R. "Stitch" Thomas (BSET, Texas Tech University; ME, University of Colorado) is chief, strategy guidance, 32d Air Operations Squadron (32 AOS), Ramstein AB, Germany. Previous assignments include exercise planner in USEUCOM/USAFE/USAREUR/NATO at the Warrior Preparation Center, Einsiedlerhof Air Station, Germany; chief, space operations, 32 AOS; and chief, Space and Theater Missile Defense cell, Combined Air Forces–Northern Operations Center, Incirlik AB, Turkey. Major Thomas is a graduate of the USAF Weapons School and Squadron Officer School.

Index

Space Power Integration
Perspectives from Space Weapons Officers

Air University Press Team

Chief Editor
Philip S. Adkins

Copy Editor
Sherry Terrell

Cover Art, Book Design, and Illustrations
L. Susan Fair

*Composition and
Prepress Production*
Vivian D. O'Neal

Quality Review
Mary J. Moore

Print Preparation
Joan Hickey

Distribution
Diane Clark

www.ingramcontent.com/pod-product-compliance
Lightning Source LLC
Chambersburg PA
CBHW081358270326
41930CB00015B/3346